Paradigm Shift in Economics and Finance— The Role of Technology and Innovation

Paradigm Shift in Economics and Finance—The Role of Technology and Innovation

Editors

Dr. B.B. Tiwari

Dr. S. Ranjith Kumar

Dr. Rajeena Syed

ALLIED PUBLISHERS PVT. LTD.

Noida • Mumbai • Kolkata • Chennai • Bangalore

ALLIED PUBLISHERS PRIVATE LIMITED

D-5, Sector-2, **Noida**–201 301
Ph. Nos.: 0120-4320295/2542557/4352866 • E-mail: delhi.books@alliedpublishers.com

17 Chittaranjan Avenue, **Kolkata**–700072
Ph.: 033-22129618 • E-mail: cal.books@alliedpublishers.com

15 J.N. Heredia Marg, Ballard Estate, **Mumbai**–400001
Ph.: 022-42126969 • E-mail: mumbai.books@alliedpublishers.com

No. 25/10, Commander-in-Chief Road, Ethiraj Lane (Next to Post Office)
Egmore, **Chennai**–600008
Ph.: 044-28223938 • E-mail: chennai.books@alliedpublishers.com

P.B. No. 9932, No. 15, 3rd Floor (Next to Vijaya Bank), 5th Cross, Gandhinagar,
Karnataka, **Bangalore**–560009, Ph.: 080-41530285 / 22386239
E-mail: bngl.books@alliedpublishers.com

Website: www.alliedpublishers.com

ISBN: 978-93-89934-62-5

Published by Sunil Sachdev and printed by Ravi Sachdev at Allied Publishers Pvt. Ltd.,
D-5, Sector-2, Noida–201 301

Contents

Foreword

It is a great pleasure and honor for me to write this foreword for the book on "**Paradigm Shift in Economics and Finance—The Role of Technology and Innovation**", edited by the School of Economics and Commerce (SOEC) of CMR University, Bengaluru.

The contemporary world is witnessing a profound transformation driven by rapid technological advancements, reshaping the very foundations of finance, economics, and management. This book, Paradigm Shift in Economics and Finance—The Role of Technology and Innovation, provides an insightful exploration of these transformative trends. It delves into the multifaceted impact of technology, offering a nuanced understanding of its implications for financial systems, economic policies, and management practices. Through a diverse array of perspectives and analyses, this book bridges the gap between theoretical frameworks and practical applications, making it an invaluable resource for academics, professionals, and policymakers.

The chapters in this book collectively illuminate how technology fosters innovation, enhances sustainability, and addresses complex global challenges. From redefining traditional business models to promoting inclusive economic growth, the contributions underscore the critical role of technology in shaping a resilient and equitable future.

As we navigate this dynamic era, this book serves as a beacon of knowledge, inspiring thought leadership and informed action. It is with great enthusiasm that I present this compendium to the readers, confident that it will spark intellectual curiosity and meaningful dialogue.

This book, I am sure, will serve as a vibrant platform for the exchange of ideas and insights. It brings together the works of leading academicians, scholars, and practitioners who have shared their research outcomes, offering valuable perspectives to fellow readers and researchers. The discussions and analyses presented in this book provide a comprehensive glimpse of recent advances in the fields of Economics, Finance, Management, and Technology, aimed at fostering a robust environment for achieving the goals of "Amrit Kaal."

My best wishes are with the authors and editorial team for the resounding success of this book. May it inspire and guide readers in their pursuit of knowledge and innovation.

Dr. H.B. Raghavendra
Vice Chancellor
CMR University Bangalore

Chairman Message

I am truly exultant that CMR University has consistently been dedicated to fostering excellence in education, research, and innovation, believing in nurturing a dynamic learning environment that empowers our students and researchers to become leaders and change-makers in their respective fields.

The School of Economics and Commerce (SOEC) of CMR University has brought together a collection of invaluable insights in the book "Paradigm Shift in Economics and Finance—The Role of Technology and Innovation", which addresses topics that are currently capturing the attention of academicians, researchers, and industries on a global scale. The book emphasizes the latest trends in Economics, Finance, Management, and Technology, exploring all dimensions of these fields with a focus on achieving the Sustainable Development Goals (SDG) set by the UNDP.

I extend my warm greetings and felicitations to the authors and contributors of this book. I wish the book great success and hope it inspires readers to engage deeply with its content, advancing knowledge and innovation in the fields it covers.

Chancellor's Message

Dear Faculty Members, Students, and Esteemed Guests,

I am delighted that CMR University's School of Economics and Commerce (SOEC) is presenting this insightful book on 'Paradigm Shift in Economics and Finance—The Role of Technology and Innovation'. We live in an era where rapid changes in these fields are reshaping economies, businesses, and societies. In such a dynamic landscape, it is crucial for academic institutions like CMR University to nurture interactions with experts, instil a spirit of research in young minds, and create platforms that inspire research-oriented learning.

This book is a testimony to our combined pursuit of knowledge and innovation—key drivers in addressing complex economic challenges faced by nations across the globe. By exploring emerging trends and concepts, it serves as a treasured resource for students, researchers, and professionals, providing fresh perspectives which can influence both classrooms and workplaces.

I am confident that the ideas and discussions summarized in these pages will spark meaningful discourse and contribute to a deeper understanding of the evolving landscape of finance, economics, and management.

I extend my best wishes for the grand success of this book and hope it inspires ceaseless exploration and innovation in these critical spheres.

Dr. Sabitha Ramamurthy
Chancellor
CMR University

Pro-Chancellor Message

As the Pro-Chancellor of this esteemed CMR University, I am thrilled to witness the convergence of brilliant minds from across the globe, coming together to engage in intellectual discourse, exchange innovative ideas, and foster collaborative efforts towards advancing the frontiers of knowledge in the fields of Economics, Finance, Management, and Technology.

I extend a warm welcome to all the readers of this insightful book compiled by the School of Economics and Commerce (SOEC). The themes underscore the fact that areas like economics, finance, and technology are undergoing rapid and transformative changes. I am confident that the high-quality research and perspectives presented in this book will provide valuable insights for policymakers, contributing to the accelerated economic growth of the country. This book will undoubtedly serve as a significant milestone in the nation's journey toward achieving the $5 trillion economy target.

I congratulate the editorial team for curating such a remarkable collection. I wish all the readers a deeply enriching experience and success in their future endeavors.

Provost Message

It is with great pride that I acknowledge the publication of this academic volume, which brings together fresh perspectives and scholarly contributions in the fields of economics, finance, management, and technology. This compilation stands as a testament to the intellectual curiosity, research rigor, and collaborative spirit that define our academic community.

In an era defined by rapid technological evolution and shifting economic paradigms, the role of research in shaping inclusive and adaptive financial systems has never been more critical. This compilation of selected papers captures both the urgency and opportunity of our times—bringing together insights that can inform policy, transform practice, and inspire innovation.

My heartfelt congratulations to all the contributors, faculty, and organizers who made this endeavour possible. May this volume serve as a valuable reference for scholars, practitioners, and students alike, and continue to advance the collective pursuit of knowledge for the public good.

Dr. Tristha Ramamurthy
Provost
CMR University

Presidential Address
(Inaugural Session)

Dear Faculty Members, Students, and Esteemed Guests,

It is an absolute pleasure to stand before you today and address this gathering of bright minds and passionate learners. This conference brings together distinguished professors and experts who share their invaluable insights on Economics, Management, Technology, and various other fields that shape the world we live in. These discussions serve as more than just academic discourses; they provide us with the opportunity to reflect on our roles and responsibilities in an ever-evolving global landscape.

As students, you are driven by curiosity, ambition, and the desire to excel in your chosen fields. However, true education extends far beyond textbooks and classroom instruction. It lies in the ability to stay updated with the world around you, to engage in interdisciplinary conversations, and to participate in conferences & discussions that broaden your perspective. A law student, for example, can benefit greatly from understanding economic policies, just as a management student can gain significant insights from advancements in technology. The ability to connect different domains of knowledge will be your greatest asset in a complex, interconnected world.

In alignment with the National Education Policy (NEP), our university has introduced a range of courses designed to provide a holistic and well-rounded education. These programs offer you the opportunity to explore diverse fields, identify your strengths, and to be well-informed decisions about your future. Whether you choose to pursue postgraduate studies, engage in internships, or step into the professional world, self-awareness and adaptability will play a crucial role in your success. The future belongs to those who are not only knowledgeable but also flexible in their thinking and approach.

Beyond academic excellence, it is necessary to reflect on your values, ethics, and responsibilities toward society. Ask yourself: *What impact do I wish to create? How can I contribute meaningfully to my community, my nation, and the world?* In the past, career choices were often limited to conventional fields such as engineering, medicine, banking, or teaching. Today, the landscape has evolved, presenting countless opportunities that integrate business, research, and innovation into various industries. The challenge now is not the lack of opportunities but the ability to identify where your true potential lies and how best to harness it.

Rather than merely criticizing institutions and industries, I encourage you to take time and understand them—how they function, the challenges they face, and the role you can play in shaping them for the better. Developing this mindset will allow you to grow not only as professionals but also as individuals capable of driving meaningful change in society.

As India continues to rise as a global leader in various sectors, it is imperative for us to take pride in our achievements while also recognizing our responsibilities. Even as students, you have the power to make a difference. Service-learning programs, internships or active community engagement, reflect on what you have contributed each month. Cultivating this habit of giving back will shape you into responsible and compassionate leaders who contribute positively to society.

The COVID-19 pandemic brought along many challenges, particularly for students who were unable to experience social interactions and real-world exposure. However, it also reinforced the importance of resilience, adaptability, and community engagement. As you move forward, I urge you to embrace a mindset of continuous learning. Take advantage of the wealth of knowledge available through AI, digital platforms, and research tools. Delve deep into subjects that spark your curiosity, and never stop seeking knowledge.

Most importantly, amidst your ambitions and aspirations, do not forget the significance of inner peace. Self-reflection and mindfulness are essential in guiding you towards clarity and satisfaction. Just as we explore external knowledge, we must also explore ourselves. Once you embark on this journey of self-discovery, you will find your path, your purpose, and ultimately, happiness.

Wishing you all success in your pursuit of knowledge, and personal growth.

Thank you

Dr. Sabitha Ramamurthy
Chancellor
CMR University

Inaugural Address (Prof. Prem Vrat)

Dr. Sabitha Ramamurthy, Chancellor, CMR University, Dr. KC Ramamurthy, Prof. Prahlad Kumar, Prof. MM Goel, Shri Jayadpeep K.R. Reddy, Dr. Trisha Ramamurthy, Prof. HB Raghvendra, Dr. Praveen R., Dr. B.B. Tiwari; delegates to the conference; faculty, students, ladies and gentlemen.

I greet you all in this inaugural session of the International conference at CMR University and thank Prof. HB Raghvendra, Vice-Chancellor for inviting me to the conference as the Chief Guest at the inaugural session. The theme of the conference though looks all-encompassing yet is very relevant to focus on integrated systems approach in problem solving in a highly interconnected world where there is interplay of various aspects in influencing system behavior.

It is an honor for me to address on the theme that resonates profoundly with the very essence of our contemporary world: Economics, Finance, Management, and Technology in 2024. These four pillars not only define the landscape of our societies but also hold the key to unlocking the potential for a future of unprecedented progress and prosperity. Every system has these four aspects as well as the situational context in which it operates. The current business environment is called as VUCA (Volatile, Uncertain, Complex and Ambiguous) and in line with systems thinking and contingency theory of management; as decision makers we need to consider the interplay of economics; finance, technology and management and the situation to determine right policy options to achieve our organizational objectives. Since each of these four pillars of knowledge society are evolving; the recent advances in each of these will enable us to find the right solution to our problems using the latest knowledge on the subject.

As we gather here, we find ourselves at a pivotal juncture in history, where the convergence of these disciplines is reshaping the fabric of our existence. In every corner of the globe, technological innovation is driving economic growth, revolutionizing financial systems, transforming management practices, and fundamentally altering the way we live, work, and interact with one another.

In the realm of economics, we are witnessing a profound shift towards a knowledge-based economy driven by innovation and digitalization. Traditional industries are being disrupted, and new paradigms are emerging, presenting both challenges and opportunities. As economies navigate this transition, it is imperative that we foster environments that nurture creativity, entrepreneurship, and inclusive growth. Behavioural economics is addressing issues concerning rationalist theoretical economics.

Similarly, the domain of finance is undergoing a seismic transformation fueled by advancements in technology. From the proliferation of fintech solutions to the rise of decentralized finance (DeFi) and digital currencies, the financial landscape is evolving at an unprecedented pace. As stewards of financial systems, we must embrace innovation while ensuring stability, security, and equitable access to financial services for all. Blockchain technology is impacting supply chains to ensure safe financial transactions.

Furthermore, effective management practices are more critical than ever in navigating the complexities of our interconnected world. As organizations grapple with rapid change, leaders must possess not only technical expertise but also the ability to inspire, adapt, and drive meaningful change. Strategic management frameworks that prioritize agility, sustainability, and ethical decision-making are essential for navigating the uncertainties of the 21st century.

At the heart of this transformation lies technology, the catalyst that is driving progress across all fronts. From artificial intelligence and machine learning to blockchain and the Internet of Things, technological innovation is reshaping industries, redefining business models, and revolutionizing the way we approach challenges. However, with great power comes great responsibility, and it is incumbent upon us to ensure that technology is harnessed for the greater good, fostering innovation that is ethical, inclusive, and sustainable. It is the coordinated efforts in integrating people, process and technology for the good of human kind that is real challenge in management. Industry 4.0 concepts of managing cyber-physical systems can be a game changer if we can address concerns of cyber security.

As we contemplate the interplay of these disciplines, let us not forget the human dimension that underpins all our endeavors. Ultimately, the success of our collective efforts will be measured not only by economic metrics but also by the extent to which we improve the lives of people around the world.

In closing, I am filled with optimism for the future that lies ahead. By harnessing the transformative power of Economic, Finance, Management, and Technology in 2024 and beyond, we have the opportunity to build a world that is more prosperous, more equitable, and more sustainable for generations to come.

Thank you!

Prof. Prem Vrat

Pro-Chancellor, the NorthCap University, Gurugram

Chairman, BoG, IIT (ISM) Dhanbad

Inaugural Address: Guest of Honour (Prof. Prahlad Kumar)

"Aa no bhadrah krutvoh yantu vishwatah"

Rigveda sanhita, Mandal 1, suktam 89

"May noble thoughts come to us from every side."

In the present era of globalization where countries are fighting or are engaged in fighting with each other either on territorial issues, political ideology, supremacy of their religion or race or to show off their military and economic power, the guiding Indian philosophy for development is:

"Vasudheve kutumbkam"

i.e., the whole earth is our family.

This Sanskrit verse has its roots in *Maha Upanishad* and this was aptly adopted in, the 18th G-20 Summit held in September 2023 in New Delhi. It was translated into English as, "**One Earth, One Family, and One Future**." This translation captures the essence of global togetherness and shared aspirations. It highlights that actions in one part of the world have far reaching effects globally. It also necessitates a commitment to environmental conservation, and encourages sustainable practices and the protection of bio-diversity.

The presence of eminent personalities, academic administrators, educationists, technocrats, policy makers and game changers in the Conference and their thought-provoking ideas would definitely ignite the young minds to shape the destiny of "Vikasit Bharat" by 2047. The New Education Policy 2020 emphasizes on developing the hidden talent and potential in children and youth by incorporating and inculcating the ideas of self-esteem, confidence, constructiveness, innovation and entrepreneurship. The education system should produce such youths who are not job-seekers but are job-providers. We are aware that our country, Bharat has the largest reservoir of *'demographic dividend.'* The demographic dividend shows the potential for economic gains when the share of working-age population (15–64 years) is higher than the non-working age population (14 and younger, and 65 and older). According to the Economic Survey 2018–19, India's demographic dividend would peak around 2041, when the share of working age i.e. 20–59 years (lesser band), population is expected to hit 59 percent. It means, with more in the labour force and fewer children to support, India will have a window of opportunity for achieving higher economic growth. It is interesting to note that India had one of the youngest populations in an aging world. It was estimated that the median age in India in 2020 was around 28 years while it was 37 years in China and US, 45 years in Western Europe, and 49 years in Japan. By 2030, India's working age population is expected to be 1.04 billion i.e. 104 crore with a dependency ratio at 31.2 percent. This would be the lowest in its history. Since 2018, this bulge in the working age population is going to last till 2055 or 37 years from its beginning in 2018. It would be of interest to know the findings of a study on demographic dividend in India by United Nations Population Fund (UNFPA) which mentions:

- The window of demographic dividend opportunity in India is available for five decades from 2005–06 to 2055–56, longer than any other country in the world.
- This demographic dividend is available at different times in different states because of differential behavior of the population parameters.

The question arises why demographic dividend has become so important for the rapid economic growth of the countries. Historically, it was found that demographic dividend has contributed up to 15 percent of the overall growth in advanced countries. Japan was among the first major economies to experience rapid growth because of changing population structure. Its period of demographic dividend was 1964–2004. The changing age structure resulting in higher working age population & lower dependent population during this period enhances labour productivity, raises the women's workforce accompanied by a decline in fertility, diverts resources from spending on children to investing in physical and human infra-structure, increases the savings rate besides there is a massive shift towards middle class society, that is, the rise of aspiration class. Naturally, this situation simultaneously poses challenges before the economy. The asymmetric demographic situation in a large country like India concentrates this dividend in poorest states; they have lack of skills, are low in human development parameters, the nature of the economy being mostly informal and are likely to have jobless growth.

It is pertinent to throw more light on employment aspect. Less than half of urban workers have full time jobs while far too much of India's employment is in under-productive informal sectors. **Education, skill-building, and health care are grossly inadequate**. As per NSSO Periodic Labour Force Survey 2017–18, India's labour force participation rate for the age-group 15–59 years was around 53 percent, that is, around half of the working age population was jobless. In another Report by the NCAER (2018), out of more than 5 lakh final year bachelor's students aged 18–29 years (who were surveyed), around 54 percent were found to be "unemployable". The India Skills Report, 2023 found only half of young Indians are employable. More so, according to World Bank Report (June, 2022), female labour participation rate has been in a steady decline, having dropped from 32 percent in 2005 to 19 percent in 2021. To overcome this problem, cultural and organizational changes are needed to create on-ramps for women in the work-force and retain them. We know that The NEP 2020 addresses this issue of employment in the organized/unorganised sector – of the male/female employment. In a latest Report, it was disclosed that 36 percent fresher students of IIT, Mumbai this year, could not be placed till date. The figure for IIT, Delhi was 40 percent and IIT, Kanpur 31 percent. These students are struggling to be placed in the job market. What has emerged from the employers is that they require specific degrees rather than generic degrees. Here comes the role of the Government, private investors, institutions/ universities and the industry. The Government and other parties are required to invest in the training for emerging jobs and skills. Similar was the case with MBA degrees that till January 2024, 55 percent of degree holders could not be placed appropriately. To deal with such a problem, the need is to build human capital by:

(i) Identifying the emerging skills, and
(ii) Creating institutions for them.

The emerging skills for example may be related to:

1. Sustainability skills,
2. Data analytics,
3. Machine learning and AI modeling,
4. Synthetic Biology and Bioengineering,
5. Cyber security: protecting systems and data etc.

The United Arab Emirates (UAE) has taken a lead and established first

Artificial Intelligence College, than why India cann't emulates this? The above description clearly emphasizes on the fact that the theoretical knowledge of the subjects such as Economics, Commerce, Management and Technology is not sufficient to achieve the goal of Vikasit Bharat @ 2047 unless we address to the

Above issues seriously and create an environment of optimism, and invest in training in emerging skills and create suitable institutions. We Bhartiya have that zeal, and can transform the economy into a Vikasit Bharat by 2047, or even earlier.

Yada bhawam, tad bhawati |

i.e., you become as you think. It means that your inner thoughts create your reality.

I take an example of Artificial Intelligence (AI) and how it may affect business operations. AI powered automation and optimization algorithms have streamlined production processes, supply chain management, and resource allocation. Businesses can now operate more efficiently, reduce costs, and increase productivity, resulting in boosting economic output. Secondly, AI, in fact, create new job opportunities and transforms existing ones. Ai has created a demand for skilled professionals who can develop, implement, and maintain AI systems. Moreover, AI augments human capabilities, allowing workers to focus on more creative and high value tasks while AI handles repetitive and mundane work.

Innovations in healthcare, finance and manufacturing have led to the creation of entirely new job categories. For example, AI has driven the growth of Tele- health industry, creating opportunities for remote medical professionals and AI specialists. The financial sector also benefits from AI powered trading algorithms, leading to the rise of quant analysis and AI engineers. AI is also assisting the Government in policy-formulation, implementation, and evaluation.

In the foregoing discussion, I have restricted myself to two issues only and highlighted the importance of population dividend for our country but this advantage has poised challenges on building human capital i.e. investing in people through quality education, skill development, healthcare and jobs. A minimum of 10 million jobs per year are to be generated in the economy to reap the benefits of demographic dividend. The NEP 2020 along with the readiness of the economy to accept, adapt and adopt the emerging technological changes will convert these challenges into an opportunity to become a *Vikasit Bharat.* The education system should be flexible and should respond to the emerging areas in scientific and technological fields. The 21st century is the century for knowledge, innovation and research, and these should be utilized for sustainable steady growth of Bharat. Our aim is to move from *Amrit Kaal* to *Kartavya Kaal i.e.* to make *"India a developed nation by 2047."*

In the end, I would like to thank the organizers, especially Prof. B.B. Tiwari and his entire team along with the Registrar, Finance Officer & other officials of the University for organizing such an excellent event on the recent advances in Economics, Commerce, Management & Technology. These areas are very crucial for Bharat to become a developed country by 2047. Our period of **Kartavya Kaal** is extremely critical and important for all the Bhartiya.

Prof. Prahlad Kumar
Ex-Dean,
Faculty of Commerce,
University of Allahabad

Keynote Address: Valedictory Session (Prof. S. Indrakant)

THE JOURNEY OF THE ECONOMISTS

The path travelled by the Economists is characterised by many ups and downs coupled by sharp turnings in response to the changes in World Economy. Interestingly different Groups of Economists took different routes based on their perception of the Economy which resulted in the evolution of different Schools of Thought.

Physiocrats, who were popular in France perceived that land and land alone has the capacity to produce Surplus as it gives more output than what it consumes. In due course of time, Mercantlists dominated the scene and argued that the Trade was the Engine of the Growth. A country having larger exports and lower imports is bound to grow faster.

Adam Smith, who is considered as Father of Economics by the Continental Economists, taking more comprehensive view of the Economy made an inquiry into the nature and causes of Wealth of Nation. David Ricardo examined the dynamic Laws of Distribution of output among different factors of production namely workers, capitalists and rentiers. He argued that due to the increase in population, the cultivation of food grains is extended to less fertile land and the rent on the intra-marginal land will increase. As a result rentier class benefits while entrepreneurs suffer due to decline in land productivity. Wage rate cannot be reduced below the subsistence level. With passage of time, the rate of profit will tend to zero and there will be decline in investment. He concluded that due to scarcity of fertile land, the economy will reach Stationary State. The Technical Progress at the best will postpone the attainment of Stationary State. That is why Economics was referred as Dismal Science. T.R. Malthus, comparing the growth rate of food grains with that of population arrived at similar conclusion. He believed that food grains will grow in arithmetic progression while population grows in geomagnetic progression. In literature, these Economists are generally referred to as Classical Economists.

Thanks to the fruits of Technical Progress, no serious economic crisis were encountered by the advanced countries. So the Mainstream Economists shifted their attention from the working of the whole economy to the rational behaviour of individual economic agents like consumers, producers, workers and interaction among them. Implicit belief was that interaction among the economic agents will lead to a equilibrium situation which is optimal and beneficial to all the stake-holders. Jevons, Menger and Walras made important contribution in this Area. Marshall tried to syntheses the differences which existed among the Mainstream Economists.

However, a good number of Economists had a different view about the dynamics of the World Economy. Marx visualised that the Economy is composed of Classes having conflicting interest in which one Class (Capitalist) benefits at the expense of another Class (Workers). In other words, the Economy is composed of Classes having conflicting interest. Structralists argued that countries at the core developed at the cost of countries at the periphery. Others focused on institutional factors in the process of Development. At the same time, some Economists like Lewis, Nurkse, Rostow, and Hirschman took interest in issues relating to Growth and Development.

The honeymoon period of the Mainstream Economists came to an end in 1929 when the World Economy encountered Great Depression. Keynes looking from macro perspective diagonised that a lack of Effective Demand was the cause for the Depression and advocated for Government Intervention to boost effective demand and the capability of markets was questioned.

In due course of time the focus shifted to examination of the determinants of Long-run and Steady Growth. The works of Harrod, Domar, Kaldor, Solow and Von Neumann are worth-noting.. Building big macro-level, multi-sectoral and long-run plan models became the order of the day on account of availability of Computer Facilities. In this regard, the contributions of Leontief, Timberland, Mahalanobis, Gautam Mathur and Chakravarty were some of the important works. However, in the Era of Liberalisation, Privatisation and Globalisation, the role of these models seems to have reduced.

In the recent years, a new branch of Economics called Behavioural Economics has emerged. It is argued that people make decision based on perceived gains and losses, often valuing losses more than gains. In this respect, the contribution of Psychologists is substantial. In fact, Kahneman, a Psychologist, was awarded Nobel Prize in Economics in 2002 for his work in the field of Behavioural Economics.

Interestingly money as a medium of exchange was introduced into the Economy to overcome the difficulties like double-coincidence of Wants faced under Barter System, a system in which goods were exchanged for goods. Under Barter System, if a farmer wants to sell Milk to buy fodder for his cattle then he has to look for a person who is willing to buy milk and sell fodder. It is very difficult task. Money as a medium of exchange has simplified the operation. The farmer first sells the milk to a person Interested in buying milk for cash and with that cash buys fodder from a person selling fodder. This has smoothened the process of transaction. However, cash transaction becomes risky when the volume of transaction is large and the number of transaction is large. So on-line payment are becoming popular. Further, financial inclusion of so far unreached segments of the population is taking place at a rapid pace. Economy is getting digitalised. No doubt, it is not an unmixed blessings. Innocent persons are becoming victims of cyber crimes. In addition, old institutions like Planning Commission are being replaced by new institutions like NITI Aayog. Simultaneously financial and Fiscal Reforms having far reaching implications have been introduced. All these items have entered into agenda of Economists.

Not only the areas of Research changed with time, even the tools of analysis have undergone a radical change. The use of Mathematical and Statistical tools has become very common. Sophisticated Econometric Techniques are being used to estimate the parameters of Policy- oriented models. Availability of packages and computer facilities has enabled the the Economists to carry out a large number of simulation exercises. Articles appearing in some journals are highly mathematical in nature. In such articles, there are more equations and symbols than the number of sentences without symbols. It makes one to wonder whether it is a article in Economics or in Mathematics. Without the knowledge of quantitative techniques, it is difficult to understand the content of such articles. Long time back Walras had predicted that people without the knowledge of Mathematics have no role in Economics. It appears we are fast reaching that stage.

It is not out of place to make a few observations on Technology. In fact Technical Progress is a double-edged sword. It must be encouraged so long as it is environment-friendly but Technical Progress which adversely affects the environment should be avoided.

Release of waste water and used chemical detergent from the conventional washing machine pollutes our water bodies. A startup company in Chandigarh has come up with a new washing machine which uses less chemical detergents and water and kills bacteria by using radio frequency based microwaves.

The immense capacity of technology can be grasped by the fact Netherland with land equivalent to 2% of that of India produces 3 times the foodgrains production of India by using drone, robots, mobiles, greenhouse cultivation etc. India can also explore the possibility of a) enhancing the production of fish and other marine products by deep sea fishing, b) increasing the milk production by providing better quality of fodder at subsidised rate and thereby making livestock breeding more economical.

Perseverance and sustained interest is essential to enjoy the fruits of innovation. A factual information brings clarity on this issue. Kothilwa village near Gaya in Bihar State, is inhabitated by 700 persons and there is only one well which provides drinking water to the villagers. Farmers cultivate jowar solely depending on the scanty rainfall as the tank in the village usually gets dried up. People in the working age-group migrate to Gaya for labour work. In contrast, Loungi Bhuiyan, a farmer daily early in the morning goes to the top of the near-by hill and starts digging Canal. He pleaded with fellow villagers to join their hands in his work. Instead of helping him, they laughed at him. Even his wife and children drove him out of house accusing him as mad person and left for Gaya. Unmindful of all these things, he continued with his daily routine of going to the top of the hill early in the morning and start digging Canal single-handedly. Once the work was completed, the rain water from the hill started filling up the tank. Farmers started cultivating their land. Loungi Bhuiyan completed the work not for money or any award but only for his villagers. In recognition of his achievement, Chief Minister of Bihar, Prime Minister of India, other political leaders and Press Reporters visited the village to appreciate his work. He is called Inspiration Man of Bihar. The people who ridiculed him once as mad man have erected his statue. The country which is blessed with persons like Loungi Bhuiyan will definitely become a super power by 2047.

Dear participants perseverance and sustained interest are essential to do good Research. The conference has provided good food both to mind and body. You should be ready with your Research findings in the next Conference.

With best wishes

S. Indrakant

Visiting Professor,

Centre for Economics and Social Studies,

Begumpet, Hyderabad-500016

Needonomics for Management of Fintech with Needo-use of Artificial Intelligence (AI)

KEYNOTE ADDRESS
(Prof. M.M. Goel)

Professor Madan Mohan Goel*

Needonomics (economics of needs) and essentially refers to the study or understanding of human needs and how they drive economic behavior. In the context of the management of fintech (financial technology), understanding needonomics is crucial for developing products and services that cater to the genuine needs of consumers. India has seen significant growth in its fintech sector in recent years, with numerous companies emerging to offer a wide range of financial services leveraging technology. Some prominent fintech companies offering digital payment solutions, e-commerce services and Unified Payments Interface (UPI) ecosystem in India includes Paytm, PhonePe, MobiKwik, CRED etc. Razorpay provides payment gateway solutions, payment processing services, and business banking services for businesses of all sizes. It offers a range of products including payment links, subscription billing, and online store payments. Policybazaar is India's largest online insurance aggregator, allowing users to compare and purchase various insurance products including health insurance, life insurance, and car insurance. It provides a platform for users to research, compare, and buy insurance policies online. Zerodha is a fintech company that operates as a discount brokerage firm offering online trading services in stocks, commodities, and mutual funds. It is known for its low-cost trading model and innovative trading platforms. Lendingkart is a fintech platform that provides working capital loans and business loans to small and medium enterprises (SMEs) in India. It uses technology and data analytics to assess the creditworthiness of borrowers and streamline the lending process. CRED is a members-only platform that rewards users for paying their credit card bills on time. It offers various benefits such as cashback, discounts, and access to exclusive rewards and experiences. These are just a few examples of the many fintech companies operating in India, showcasing the diversity and innovation within the fintech ecosystem of Bharat to be Viksit by 2047.

Needonomics applies to fintech as under:

- **Understanding Consumer Needs:** Fintech companies must deeply understand the financial needs and pain points of consumers. This involves studying their spending habits, saving patterns, investment goals, and overall financial well-being.

- **Personalization and Customization**: Fintech solutions should be tailored to individual needs as much as possible. This might involve personalized budgeting tools; investment advice based on individual risk profiles and customized savings plans.
- **Accessibility and Inclusion**: Needonomics in fintech also emphasizes making financial services accessible to all, including those who are traditionally underserved or marginalized. This might involve developing solutions for people with lower incomes, limited access to traditional banking services, or those with disabilities.
- **Affordability**: Fintech solutions should be affordable for users across different socio-economic backgrounds. This means considering pricing models that are transparent and fair, with minimal fees that don't disproportionately impact those with lower incomes.
- **Financial Education:** Educating consumers about financial literacy and empowering them to make informed decisions is a key aspect of needonomics in fintech. This might involve providing resources, tools, and educational content to help users improve their financial knowledge and skills.
- **Security and Trust**: Building trust is essential in fintech, particularly when handling sensitive financial information. Fintech companies must prioritize security measures to protect user data and transactions, thereby fulfilling the need for safety and trust among consumers.
- **Innovation with Purpose**: Fintech innovation should be driven by a genuine desire to address real consumer needs rather than simply chasing technological trends. By focusing on solving actual problems faced by consumers, fintech companies can create more meaningful and impactful solutions.

To incorporate needonomics into fintech involves a human-centered approach that prioritizes understanding and addressing the genuine needs of consumers, thereby creating more inclusive, accessible, and beneficial financial services and products.

NEEDO-USE OF ARTIFICIAL INTELLIGENCE (AI)

AI plays a significant role in revolutionizing the fintech industry, offering innovative solutions to various challenges and enhancing efficiency, accuracy, and customer experience. Some key uses of AI in Fintech include:

- **Risk Assessment and Fraud Detection:** AI algorithms analyze large volumes of data to assess credit risk, detect fraudulent activities, and identify potential security breaches. Machine learning models can detect anomalies in transactions, flagging suspicious activities in real-time to prevent financial losses.

- **Customer Service and Chatbots**: AI-powered chatbots and virtual assistants provide personalized customer support, answer queries, and guide users through various financial processes. Natural Language Processing (NLP) enables chatbots to understand and respond to customer inquiries effectively, improving user experience and reducing wait times.
- **Credit Scoring and Underwriting:** AI algorithms analyze diverse data sources, including transaction history, social media behavior, and alternative data, to assess creditworthiness and streamline the underwriting process. This enables lenders to make more accurate lending decisions and offer tailored financial products to customers.
- **Algorithmic Trading and Investment Management**: AI-driven trading algorithms execute trades autonomously, leveraging vast datasets and complex models to identify market trends, predict price movements, and optimize investment strategies. AI-powered robo-advisors offer automated portfolio management services, providing personalized investment advice based on individual risk profiles and financial goals.
- **Personalized Financial Recommendations:** AI analyzes user data, including spending habits, income levels, and financial goals, to offer personalized financial recommendations and insights. This could include budgeting advice, investment suggestions, or customized insurance plans, enhancing financial literacy and helping users make informed decisions.
- **Fraud Prevention and Anti-Money Laundering (AML)**: AI algorithms analyze transaction patterns and behavior to detect suspicious activities indicative of money laundering or fraudulent behavior. By monitoring transactions in real-time and flagging potential risks, AI helps financial institutions comply with regulatory requirements and mitigate financial crime.

Predictive Analytics and Market Insights: AI algorithms analyze historical data and market trends to generate predictive insights, forecast market conditions, and identify investment opportunities. This enables investors and financial institutions to make data-driven decisions and stay ahead of market fluctuations.

Regulatory Compliance and Risk Management: AI automates compliance processes, helping financial institutions navigate complex regulatory frameworks and ensure adherence to legal requirements. By monitoring regulatory changes and analyzing compliance data, AI helps mitigate compliance risks and avoid costly penalties.

AI technologies continue to drive innovation and transformation across the fintech industry, offering powerful tools to improve decision-making, enhance operational efficiency, and deliver superior customer experiences.

Management of the contemporary world calls for the stakeholders to become street SMART (simple, moral, action-oriented, responsive and transparent) in understanding and using Gita-based needonomics. To achieve success in the endeavors, the stakeholders (C,P,D,T) must convert monkey mind (misuse of AI) to monk mind (use of SI).

CONCLUSION

To address the entire domain of the issues in economics, finance, management & technology in present times, we must understand and adopt needonomics as ethical and environmental friendly approach. Needo-adopt Gita-based Needonomics for the solutions of the contemporary problems caused by Greedonomics. Like a honey bee collecting just enough to sustain but not too much to destroy, economic practices should align with the principles of managing society responsibly. To fetch the fortunes in present times of global competition, we need to create business environment for Intellectual Property Rights (IPR) with its understanding and implications for converting into business proposition. The stakeholders must think out – of-the-box solutions on different aspects of the economy including needo-consumption, needo-saving, needo-production, needo-investment, needo-distribution, needo-altruism, needo-trade for ensuring needo-wealth, needo-health and needo-happiness of the people. To achieve success in all the endeavors of contemporary world, the stakeholders must convert monkey mind (misuse of AI) to monk mind (use of SI). We must become street SMART (simple, moral, action-oriented, responsive & transparent) with needonomics as a common sense approach.

***The writer Prof M.M. Goel is three-time Vice-Chancellor known as Propounder Needonomics School of Thought superannuated Professor of Economics from Kurukshetra University, Kurukshetra.**

E-mail: mmgoel2001@yahoo.co.in

A Study on Impact of Emotional Intelligence Factors on Job Satisfaction of College Principals and Utilizations of Emotions as a Mediating Factor

Prakash B. Kundaragi[1] and Mustak I. Mulla[2]

[1]Asst. Professor, SDVS Sangh's Annapoorna Institute of Management Research, Sankeshwar, Belagavi, Karnataka, India

[2]Research Scholar, CMR, University, Bangalore, India

E-mail: [1]drprakashaimr3@gmail.com; [2]mustak.mulla44@gmail.com

ABSTRACT

Purpose: *The research on assessing the emotional intelligence and its association with job satisfaction are becomes an emergent higher education principal. This research has conducted to evaluate the principals' emotional intelligence and their job satisfaction. This study is also aimed at to assessing the impact of factors of emotional indigence on job satisfaction of principals and utilization of emotions as a mediating factor.*

Design and Methodology: *Two hundred principals of college were involved in this research, and simple random sampling method was used to select the samples. The systematic and structured questionnaire The Schutte Self Report Emotional Intelligence Test was used to gather the primary data. Articles, Journals, websites etc were comprised for the gathering of the secondary evidence.*

Analysis Tools: *To evaluate impact of independent variables emotional intelligence factors on dependent variable satisfaction, PLS-SEM is utilized.*

Findings: *This Research has produced the result that Perception emotions have relationship with managing emotions, managing others' emotions has effect on utilizations of the emotions and utilization of emotions has significant effect on the job satisfaction. UE has played mediating role between managing others' emotions and Satisfaction the principals.*

Keywords: Job Satisfaction, Managing Own Emotions & Other Emotions, Perception, Utilization of Emotion.

1. INTRODUCTION

The present rapidly changing world completion, recognition etc significantly understand the value of the human resource through which an organization can achieve its desired goals. Managing human resource is crucial in managing biggest asset of the organization i.e. employees is one part but managing their own emotions to manage things is become challenge. EI can be opined as shaping a person's or a man's fortune and through which one can understand the way he/she perceives life (Jordan, P.J. and Troth, A.; 2011). Employees' job satisfaction also plays a vital role to manage productivity, performance, wellbeing etc. The way one can handle factors of emotional intelligence that effect on the job satisfaction in the same proportion.

George, J.M. (2000) defined EI as emotions as 'high intensity feelings that are triggered by a stimuli (internal or external to the individual). Emotional intelligence (EI) can be defined as the ability to recognize, understand, and managing both our own emotions and the others' emotions in effective manner. It includes a set of skills that empower individuals to direct social interactions, communicate effectively, empathize with others, and how to overcome from challenges in a productive manner.

Emotional intelligence and satisfaction:

In the present and modern work environment, Emotional intelligence and job satisfaction are become a vital elements having high interest, they help as a competitive advantage not only in personal life but also in organizational life (Soto-Rubio, A., *et al.,* 2020). Emotional intelligence can help professionals in variety if the circumstances and it application plays a vital in the professional workplace (Khan Karishma. *et al.,* 2022). Emotional intelligence (EI) has much attracted among the community of managers, researchers and educators (Daus & Ashkanasy, 2005), based on this opinion need to analyze does EI improves satisfaction or not. Durra Ibrahim (2023) has found that there is positive and significant relation between EI and job satisfaction, higher the level of emotional intelligence you experience effects greater job satisfaction. Farazmehr, Z. and Tabatabaei, S. (2015) found that an individual employee having high degree of emotional intelligence experience favourable job satisfaction. Hü lya Gü ndü zs Çekmecelioğlu *et al.* (2012) also have found that there is significant and positive relationship between emotional intelligence and internal satisfaction. Emotional recognition has higher level of relationship with job satisfaction.

EI helps empower the leaders in the educational institutions (Tench, 2016). EI always plays a vital role in effective teaching, enhancing students' performance, and transformative learning (Nelson *et al.*, 2005). To manage class and students' performance, principal being leader need to look after teacher retention tactics (Nelson *et al.*, 2005). Valente *et al.*, (2019) fond that to manage discipline in classes, regarding gender, qualification and service time, teachers' EI influences crucially.

Objectives

- To assess the effect of Emotional Intelligence factors on satisfaction.
- To assess the Utilization of emotion as a mediating factor among emotional intelligence and job satisfaction.

Conceptual Framework

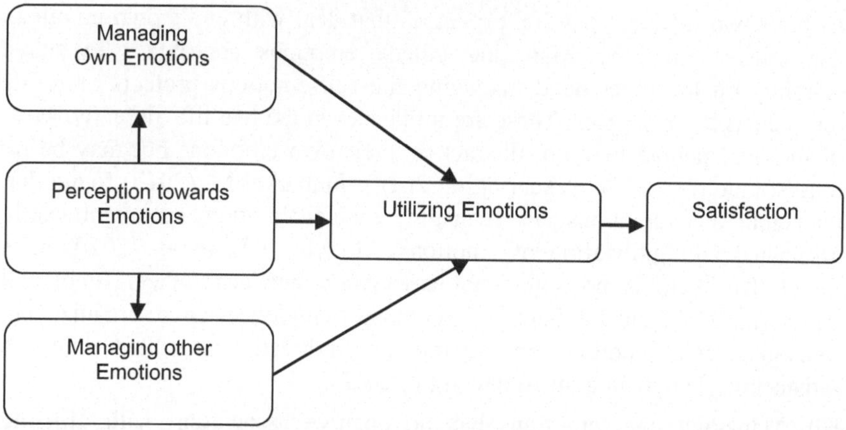

2. LITERATURE AND HYPOTHESIS

Perception of emotions with Managing own, others' emotions and Utilization of emotions:

Gong Mengting & Archer Lester A. C. (2021) have found in their work "Emotional intelligence in educational leadership doctoral students: Examining association based on gender and age, that women had greater scores for Perception of Emotion and Utilization of Emotion, and men had greater mean scores for Managing own and others' emotions. Further they found that there is no differences present between males and females. Kaur J. and Junnarkar M. (2017) have found in their research "Emotional Intelligence and Intimacy in Relationships" that perception of emotion is positively correlated with managing own emotions and managing others emotions also. Further they found that perception of emotions, managing own emotions and managing others' emotions are significantly associated with utilization of emotions. The emotion that is engaged regularly by the employees and their action at the work was positively associated with job satisfaction of the employees (Fisk G.M. and Friesen J.P.; 2012).

$H0_1$: Perception towards emotions has no positive association with managing own emotions.

$H0_2$: Perception towards emotions has no positive association with managing others' emotions.

$H0_3$: Perception towards emotions has no positive association with utilizing emotions.

$H0_9$: Managing others' emotions has no effect on the job satisfaction through Utilization of emotions.

2.1 Managing Own and Managing Others' Emotions with Utilizing Emotions

EI have two different parallel processes that deal with one's own emotions and others' emotions: Managing others' emotions contributes to active learning; on the other hand managing the self-emotions protects or refills one's energetic resources. These are influences in the real life mutually. Most of the time people may not distract by their own emotions but may be by others' emotions (K.A. Pekaar *et al.*, 2018). Junnarkar M. (2017) found that managing own emotions and managing others' emotions are significantly associated with utilization of emotions. Munyug T.E. *et al.* (2020) have found that there is no significant association between Others Emotional Appraisal (SEA) and Job Satisfaction amongst employees in the organization. Managing own emotions are directly are indirectly associated with job satisfaction (Psilopanagioti A. and *et al.*, 2012).

$H0_4$: Managing own emotions has no positive association with utilizing emotions.

$H0_5$: Managing others' emotions has no positive association with utilizing emotions.

$H0_7$: Managing own emotions has no effect on the job satisfaction through Utilization of emotions.

$H0_8$: Managing others' emotions has no effect on the job satisfaction through Utilization of emotions.

2.2 Utilization of Emotions and Satisfaction

An ability of the individuals, to lead their emotions towards productive endeavors can be opined as use of emotions. It has also found that there is no significant relationship between Use of Emotion (UOE) and Job Satisfaction among employees in the organization (Munyug T.E. *et al.*, 2020). Use of emotions is an important predictor which is ipamting on the job satisfaction (Kafetsios K., Zampetakis L.A.; 2008). In the research of Psilopanagioti A. and *et al.* (2012) have found that use of emotions and job satisfaction were positively and significantly correlated. Muhammad Masroor Alam (2009) has found strong and high positive correlation between utilization of emotions and job satisfaction.

$H0_6$: Utilizing emotions has no positive association with job satisfaction.

3. METHODOLOGY

This as an empirical research, in which required information has collected from randomly selected 200 respondents those working as Principals of UG and PG colleges using five point Likert scale i.e. 5 denoting *'strongly agree'*, 4 denoting *'Agree'*, 3 denoting *'Neutral'*, 2 denoting *'Disagree'* and 1 denoting *"strongly disagree"*. The structured questionnaire i.e. Schutte Self-Report Emotional Intelligence Test (SSEIT) (Schutte, N.S *et al.,* 1998) has been adapted and modified according research necessity to gather data. The data was examined by employing SPSS 20.0 and Smart-PLS4.0. The Cronbach's Alpha value of the all constructs has been mentioned in the Table 1.

Table 1: Cronbach's Alpha Values

Sl. No.	*Name of the Construct*	*No. Items*	*Cronbach's Values*
1.	Managing Emotions	06	0.910
2.	Managing others Emotions	05	0.866
3.	Perception towards emotions	07	0.895
4.	Utilization of Emotions	05	0.838
5.	Satisfaction	06	0.825

4. ANALYSIS AND INTERPRETATION

Table 2: Demographic Profile of the Teachers

Variable	*Sub-Variable*	*Frequency*	*Per cent*
Age	Less than 35	8	4.0
	36–45	80	40.0
	46–55	100	50.0
	56 & above	12	6.0
Gender	Male	156	78.0
	Female	44	22.0
Marital Status	Married	159	79.0
	Unmarried	41	21.0
Educational Qualification	PG	64	32.0
	M.Phil	9	5.0
	NET/SLET	51	25.0
	Ph.D.	76	38.0
Employment Status	Full-time	157	78.0
	Part-time	43	22.0

The above table 2 reveals that examination of the personal profile of the principals. 50 per cent of the principal' age fall under 46–55 age category, followed by36–45 age category i.e. 40 per cent. 78 per cent of the principals are male and only 22 per cent are female. 79 per cent are married and 21 per cent are single. With respect to respondents' qualification 32 per cent are holding PG, only 5 per cent are M.Phil qualified, 25 per cent are NET/SLETqualified and 38 per cent are Doctoral degree holders. Finally 78 per cent are holding full-time employment and 22 per cent are part-timers.

5. MEASUREMENT MODEL

This research study is concentrating its objective at defining effects of Emotional Intelligece factors on job satisfaction of the principals by engaging Structural equation model (PLS-SEM). In the present research PLS-SEM turn into a powerful statistical tool which helps to find the required determine result. PLS-SEM also suited to assess complex, narrow sample size, and also focus on hypothetical explanations (Arumugam *et al.*, 2022). PLS-SEM is more flexible tool and supports to gauge influence of the independent variables on dependent variable.

To measure the existing measurement model two methods of validities have engaged such as Discriminant validity and convergent validity. Hair Jr *et al.* (2016) the convergent validity supports to evaluate association among the dependent and independent constructs and recommends that the average variance extracted (AVE) must be higher than 0.5, outer loading values should be higher than 0.708 (outer loading be between 0.40 and 0.70 is consider for deletion), sometimes outer loading values are higher than 0.5 may be consider for the research (Hulland; 1999).

Table 3: Findings of Convergent Validity

Loading		*Cronbach's Alpha*	*Composite Reliability (rho_a)*	*Composite Reliability (rho_c)*	*Average Variance Extracted (AVE)*
Managing Emotions		0.901	0.91	0.924	0.672
ME1	0.704				
ME3	0.892				
ME4	0.777				
ME5	0.884				
ME6	0.842				
ME7	0.802				

Loading		*Cronbach's Alpha*	*Composite Reliability (rho_a)*	*Composite Reliability (rho_c)*	*Average Variance Extracted (AVE)*
Managing others Emotions		0.866	0.879	0.904	0.655
MOE1	0.785				
MOE4	0.659				
MOE6	0.868				
MOE7	0.859				
MOE8	0.856				
Perception towards emotions		0.895	0.911	0.919	0.621
PE1	0.711				
PE2	0.649				
PE3	0.909				
PE4	0.732				
PE5	0.909				
PE7	0.822				
PE8	0.745				
Utilization of Emotions		0.838	0.879	0.883	0.604
UE1	0.837				
UE2	0.837				
UE3	0.805				
UE4	0.734				
UE6	0.657				
Satisfaction		0.825	0.843	0.871	0.53
SAT2	0.823				
SAT3	0.715				
SAT5	0.707				
SAT7	0.709				
SAT8	0.696				
SAT9	0.709				

The outcome of the measurement model revealed in Table 3 reveals that outer loadings, rho_A, and CA are more than 0.70 and AVE are more than

0.5. The composite reliability (Fornell & Lorcker; 1981) of the study helps to form results. To check the individual scale and constructs convergent validity and reliability need to check through which can test are they met the requirements or not. The discriminate validity supports to realize how well tested constructs are differentiated each other in the present study. To assess the discriminant validity, the Hetrotrait-Monotrait ratio (HTMT) and the Fornell and Larcker (1981) criterion are appied in this study.

Fornell-Larcker criterion recommends the square root of the AVE for each construct and that should be higher than correlations of inter-constructs. In other words AVE of the construct should be larger than the squared correlation between the constructs that shows constructs have good convergent and discriminant validity. Table 4 expresses that the AVE squared values of the constructs and its correlation values. It symbolizes that AVE value is significant than the constructs correlation values. Hence the requirement for the measurement model is satisfied.

Table 4: Discriminant Validity Fornell-Locker Criterion

	ME	*MOE*	*PE*	*SAT*	*UE*
ME	0.82				
MOE	0.079	0.809			
PE	0.635	0.138	0.788		
SAT	–0.075	–0.137	–0.028	0.728	
UE	0.012	0.322	–0.036	–0.188	0.777

5.1 Hetrotrait-Monotrait Ratio (HTMT)

HTMT criteria states that if the value is more than 0.85 (Kline, 2011) is significant and or value may vary upto 0.90 (Gold *et al.*, 2001). It is used to validate the items correlates across the constructs and its relativity to the mean for the items assessing average correlation. The Table 5, indicates the values that should be fall under the threshold of 0.90, but no values are reached bench marking hence this is not considered for the study.

Table 5: Discriminant Validity-HTMT

	ME	*MOE*	*PE*	*SAT*	*UE*
ME					
MOE	0.118				
PE	0.701	0.196			
SAT	0.119	0.155	0.107		
UE	0.102	0.35	0.133	0.216	

5.2 Structural Model

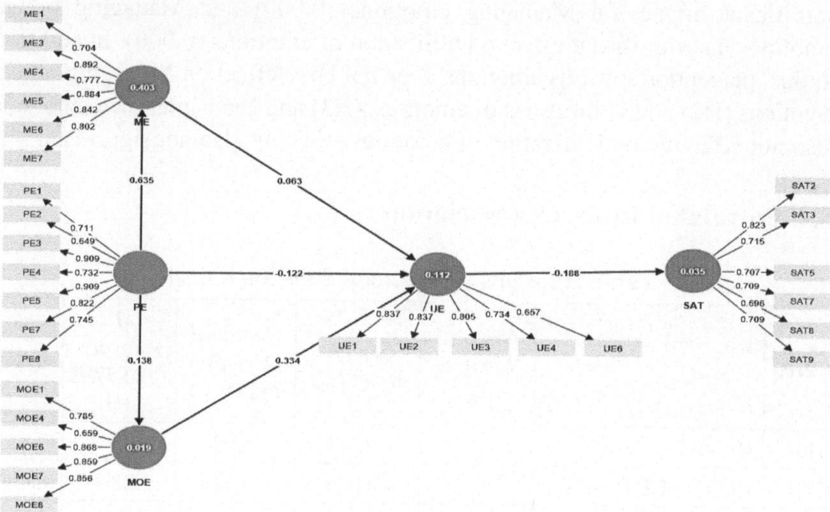

The above Structural model comprises of assess the model's R^2 and the path coefficient results. This helps to validate structural model is significant or not. The R^2 is used to determine coefficient and goodness of fit. The overall variance in the per cent accounts the varying the DV on by IV is R^2. Thus, R^2 of the job satisfaction is 0.035, indicates experience in the model, similarly, usage if emotions R^2 is 0.112, and it indicates the likelihood of use of emotions.

5.3 Postulated Direct Association

Table 6: Results of Structural Equation Model

H0		*Original Sample (O)*	*Sample Mean (M)*	*Standard Deviation (STDEV)*	*T statistics (|O/STDEV|)*	*P values*
$H0_1$	PE → ME	0.635	0.639	0.055	11.649	0.000
$H0_2$	PE → MOE	0.138	0.139	0.082	1.681	0.093
$H0_3$	PE → UE	–0.122	–0.125	0.09	1.356	0.175
$H0_4$	ME → UE	0.063	0.062	0.087	0.721	0.471
$H0_5$	MOE → UE	0.334	0.342	0.076	4.386	0.000
$H0_6$	UE → SAT	–0.188	–0.217	0.054	3.481	0.001

The result in the Table 6 confines that the hypothetical direct relationship between independent and dependent variables. It determines that the direct hypothesis i.e. H1, H2, H3, H4, H5 and H6. Further, among these hypotheses H1 and H5 have supported by individual t-value and significant than 1.96 and having probabilities values is less than 0.05. Thus, it is validated that factors of Emotional intelligence such as Perception towards emotion has significant impact on Managing emotions (0.000) and Managing others emotions has significant effect on utilization of emotions (0.000). In addition to this, perception towards emotions does not have effect on Managing others emotions (H2) and Utilizations of emotions (H3) and Managing own emotions also not effecting on Utilization of emotions (H4) but also not significant.

5.4 Postulated Indirect Association

Table 7: Results of Structural Equation Model

H0		*Original Sample (O)*	*Sample Mean (M)*	*Standard Deviation (STDEV)*	*T statistics (|O/STDEV|)*	*P values*
$H0_7$	ME –> UE–>SAT	–0.012	–0.013	0.02	0.595	0.552
$H0_8$	MOE –> UE–> SAT	–0.063	–0.074	0.024	2.631	0.009
$H0_9$	PE –> UE–>SAT	0.007	0.008	0.018	0.38	0.704

The above SEM Table 7 confines that hypothetical indirect relationship between independent, mediating variables and dependent. It determines that the indirect hypothesis i.e. H7, H8, and H9. H8 is supported by individual t-value and significant than 1.96 and having probabilities values is less than 0.05. Thus, it is validated that utilization of emotions has significant mediating role between the managing others' emotions and job satisfaction. In addition to this utilization of emotions is not having significant role between Managing own emotions and perception of emotions with job satisfaction of the principals of the higher education institutes.

5.5 Findings and Inference

This research is added the discussed results regarding the constraints and outline for the perception towards chatGPT by applying the TAM model. This investigation reveals that out of the many factors of the Emotional intelligence, Perception towards emotions has relationship with managing emotions, managing others' emotions has effect on utilizations of the emotions and utilization of emotions has significant effect on the job satisfaction of the principals of higher education institutes. Further in this research has found that utilization of emotions has played a perfect and significant role between the managing others emotions and job satisfaction in the indirect postulation.

5.6 Limitation and Future Scope

The existing research has some cons, which have found while analyzing and interpreting the data to find required result. Since this investigation was limited to few higher education principals having few factors emotional intelligence and job satisfaction. Secondly, this study has assessed the impact of Emotional intelligence factors on job satisfaction and utilization of emotions as a mediating construct through SEM modeling employing SmartPLS 4.0. Finally, the key con was less sample size for the study due to non-availability of the time. Hence for the future study, it can be considered that others factors in the emotional intelligence and as mediation effect. In the future research, researchers can escalate sample size and comparative research can also apply.

REFERENCES

[1] Aristea, Psilopanagioti; Fotios, Anagnostopoulos; Efstratia, Mourtou and Dimitris, Niakas (2012). Emotional intelligence, emotional labor and job satisfaction among physicians in Greece. *BMC Health Services Research*, 12:463, 1–12.

[2] Arumugam, V., Kannabiran, G. and Vinodh, S. (2022). Impact of technical and social lean practices on SME's performance in automobile industry: A Structural equation Modelling (SEM) analysis. *Total Quality Management and Business Excellence.* 33(1–2), pp. 28–54.

[3] Daus, C.S. and Ashkanasy, N.M. (2005). The Case for the Ability Based Model of Emotional Intelligence in Organizational Behavior. *Journal of Organizational Behavior, 26 (4)*, 453–466. http://dx.doi.org/10.1002/job.321

[4] Durra, Ibrahim (2023). Examining the Relationship between Emotional Intelligence and Job Satisfaction among HR Professionals in the Tech Industry. *International Journal of Engineering, Business and Management (IJEBM),* Vol. 7, Issue 4, pp. 1–7.

[5] Farazmehr, Z. and Tabatabaei, S. (2015). The Relationship between Emotional Intelligence and Iranian Language Institute Teachers' Job Satisfaction. *Theory and Practice in Language Studies,* 5, 184–195. https://doi.org/10.17507/tpls.0501.25

[6] Fisk, G.M. and Friesen, J.P. (2012). Perceptions of leader emotion regulation and LMX as predictors of followers' job satisfaction and organizational citizenship behaviors. *The Leadership Quarterly*, Volume 23, Issue 1, Pages 1–12.

[7] Fornell, C. and Larcker, D.F. (1981). Evaluating structural equation models with unobservable variables and measurement error. *Journal of Marketing Research, 18* (1), 39–50. https://doi.org/10.2307/3151312

[8] George, J.M. (2000). Emotions and leadership: The role of emotional intelligence. *Human Relations,* 53(8), 1027–1055.

[9] Gold, Andrew; Malhotra, Arvind and Segars, Albert (2001). Knowledge Management: An Organizational Capabilities Perspective. *Journal of Management Information Systems*. 18 (1) 185–214.

[10] Gong, Mengting and Archer, Lester A.C. (2021). Emotional intelligence in educational leadership doctoral students: Examining association based on

gender and age. *International Journal of Multidisciplinary Perspectives in Higher Education*, Volume 6, Issue 1, pp. 78–101.

[11] Hair Jr., J.F, Sastedt, M., Matthews, L.M. and Ringle, C.M. (2016). Identifying and treating unobserved heterogeneity with FIMIX-PLS: Part I-Method. *European Business Review*, 28(1), 63–76. Doi.org/10.1108/EBR-09-2015-0094.

[12] Hü lya Gü ndü z Çekmecelioğlu *et al. (*2012). Effects of Emotional Intelligence on Job Satisfaction: An Empirical Study on Call Center Employees. *Procedia—Social and Behavioral Science, 58,* pp. 363–369.

[13] Hulland, J. (1999). Use of Partial Least Squares (PLS) in Strategic Management Research: A Review of Four Recent Studies. *Strategic Management Journal*, 20(2), 195–204. http://www.jstor.org/stable/3094025

[14] Jordan, P.J. and Troth, A. (2011). Emotional Intelligence and Leader Member Exchange: The Relationship with Employee Turnover Intentions and Job Satisfaction. *Leadership & Organization Development Journal*, 32, 260–280. https://doi.org/10.1108/01437731111123915

[15] Pekaar, K.A.; Bakker, A.B.; Linden, Dimitri van der; Born, Marise Ph. and Sirén, Heidi J. (2018). Managing own and others' emotions: A weekly diary study on the enactment of emotional intelligence. *Journal of Vocational Behavior*, 109, 137–15. https://doi.org/10.1016/j.jvb.2018.10.004

[16] Kafetsios, K. and Zampetakis, L.A. (2008). Emotional intelligence and job satisfaction: Testing the mediatory role of positive and negative affect at work. *Personality and Individual Differences,* Volume 44, Issue 3, Pages 712–722.

[17] Kaur, Jagjit and Junnarkar, Mohita (2017). Emotional Intelligence and Intimacy in Relationships. *The International Journal of Indian Psychology*, Volume 4, Issue 3, pp. 27–35.

[18] Khan, Karishma; Patel, Ruchangi and Shah, Bijal (2022). Study on the Relationship between Emotional Intelligence and Work Attitude of Employees with Reference to Vadodara City. *International Journal of Research Publication and Reviews*, Vol. 3, No. 3, pp. 201–204.

[19] Kline, R.B. (2011). Convergence of Structural Equation Modeling and Multilevel Modeling. In M. Williams and W. Paul Vogt (Ed.), *The SAGE Handbook of Innovation in Social Research Methods* (pp. 562–589). SAGE Publications Ltd.

[20] Muhammad, Masroor Alam (2009). The Relationships between the Emotional Intelligence and Job Satisfaction: Emprical Findings from Higher Education Institution in Malaysia. *Journal of Management and Social Sciences*, Vol. 5, No. 2, 124–139.

[21] Munyug, T.E.; Yen Ping, Ki and Fung Chorng, Yuan (2020). The Relationship between Emotional Intelligence and Job Satisfaction among State Civil Servants. *International Journal of Service Management and Sustainability*, 5(2), 63–84.

[22] Nelson, D.B., Low, G.R. and Nelson, K.A.Y.E. (2005). The emotionally intelligent teacher: A transformative learning model. *Texas Study of Secondary Education*, 13, 7–10.

[23] Schutte, N.S., Malouff, J.M., Hall, L.E., Haggerty, D.J., Cooper, J.T., Golden, C.J. and Dornheim, L. (1998). Development and validation of a measure of emotional intelligence. *Personality and Individual Differences, 25*(2), 167–177. https://doi.org/10.1016/S0191-8869(98)00001-4

[24] Soto-Rubio, A., *et al.* (2020). Effect of Emotional Intelligence and Psychosocial Risks on Burnout, Job Satisfaction and Nurses' Health during the COVID-19 Pandemic. *International Journal of Environmental Research and Public Health*, 17, Article 7998. https://doi.org/10.3390/ijerph17217998

[25] Tench, R. (2016). Emotional intelligence: An essential leadership trait for educators. *The William & Mary Educational Review,* 4(1), 4–6.

Teachers' Attitude Towards Inclusive Education and Their Challenges Handling Students with Special Needs in an Inclusive Classroom

C.M. Chaitra[1] and P. Shreelakshmi[2]

[1]Ph.D. Research Scholar, Department of Psychology, CMR University

[2]Assistant Professor, Department of Psychology, CMR University

ABSTRACT: *The current study titled "Teachers' attitude towards inclusive education and their challenges handling students with special needs in an inclusive classroom" aimed to analyze teachers' attitude towards inclusive education and explore their challenges faced while handling special needs students in an inclusive classroom. The results revealed that, teachers have above average attitude towards inclusive education along with positive attitude towards the dimensions of inclusive education which includes psychological/behavioral, social and parent related, curricular and co-curricular and administrative aspects. On a whole teachers attitude on inclusive classroom, revealed that, teachers do believe that they need special training program to handle special needs students in an inclusive classroom adequately. The findings of the study gave an understanding regarding the intervention plan to bring in awareness about inclusive education and training modules to handle students with special needs in an inclusive class and reduce stigma about inclusive education.*

Keywords: Challenges Handling Special Needs Children, Children with Special Needs, Inclusive Classroom, Inclusive Education, Teachers' Attitude.

1. INTRODUCTION

The term "inclusive education" is used in a larger sense, to refer to an educational system premeditated to ensure access for all groups that have been sidelined in society and in schools. Thus, inclusion is proposed as the thoughtful and self-conscious structuring of whole-school and classroom environments so that they are reachable and amiable not only to students with impairments, but also to those who can face exclusion or marginalized due to their ethnicity, social class, gender, culture, religion, immigration history or other characteristics. Since inclusion also has this broader meaning, it is sometimes recognized as a means of achieving a more comprehensive form of social fairness. Supporters of inclusion argue that it is a form of schooling that puts the values of a self-governing society into practice. (Suzanne 2015)

According to Wallace, Anderson, Bartholomay, & Hupp, (2002), inclusion of students with disabilities is not sufficient to reduce difficulties in social relationship. Children require skills for constructive social relationship and these skills are crucial for academic, emotional and social learning which in turn create effective interaction in classroom (Zins, Weissberg, Wang, & Walberg, 2004). It is observed that, a productive classroom is possible through efficient teacher with skills to facilitate collaborative learning environment. Hence training programs to equip teachers to cater to the needs of children with disabilities in an inclusive classroom should be the focal point.

The Rehabilitation Council of India (RCI) act (1992) started training programme for the professional development to act in response to the needs of children with disabilities. Inclusion is an attempt to assure diverse learners that includes individuals with difficulties, those from different languages and cultures, from heterogeneous families, having diverse interest and different ways of learning styles. The researches indicate that teachers in an inclusive set up focus more on collaborative learning, planning learning new strategies mutually and take part in more professional development programs, exhibit willingness to adapt themselves and make use of creative techniques to facilitate the needs of students (Singh, 2016).

1.1 The Importance of Inclusive Education

Since inclusive classrooms involve more heterogeneous students, teachers get an opportunity to accept each student as special. It is evident that learning and performance of the student is better when they are taught in the regular education curriculum and children perform better academically in an inclusive set ups which offers opportunities to build relationships. The benefits of inclusive education involves having a good relationship with friends, social skills, personal values, good rapport with special needs children, collaborative classroom environment with caring and sharing (Singh, 2016). However it's not an easy task for teachers, they do find certain challenges in the process.

1.2 The Challenges Teachers Face in an Inclusive Classroom

Landsberg's 2011 study (as cited in Thwala, 2015) viewed inclusion as a value system that strives for reducing the differences that occurs due to diversity in gender, race, nationality, socio-economic and cultural status, language, academic achievement and disability. Though RCI has started training program for teachers to facilitate special needs children to be included in the learning process of mainstream schools, teachers still find it difficult to handle inclusive classroom for various reasons. Das, Kuyuni and Desai (2013) reported that 70% of regular classroom teachers have no training in special education or experience in teaching students with disability. It is also reported that, 87% of teachers have not received any support facilities in the classrooms. Coskun, Tosun, & Macaroglu, (2009) reported that, teachers of primary and secondary schools rated themselves as having low competence for handling students with disability. Even though mainstream teachers are showing positive attitude towards inclusion, they find problematic in implementing it practically (Avramidis & Norwich, 2002; Scruggs & Mastropieri, 1996). Including children in mainstream education especially with difficulties pertaining to social, emotional and behavioral issues has constantly been viewed as challenging for teachers, and is supported by negative attitude in teaching. (Cook, 2001; Cook, Cameron & Tankersley, 2007; Hastings & Oakford, 2003; Shapiro, Miller, Sawka, Gardill, & Handler, 1999). According to Unianu (2012), there is a lack of awareness at all levels among teachers which is accompanied with their preconceived notion about certain common disabilities. Hence lack of adequate training, low competence level, socio-emotional & behavioral issues, negative attitude of teachers, pre-conceived notions and as Thwala (2015) stated, lack of proper teaching and learning materials, having large classrooms and lack of progress in the lesson due to requirement of extra time to explain the concepts are the main challenges faced by teachers in an inclusive classroom.

2. REVIEW OF LITERATURE

Singh, S. *et al.*, (2020) aimed to investigate the attitude of the teacher's towards inclusive education as the attitude of teachers or executors has a significant impact on the successful implementation of inclusive education. The result showed that attitude of teachers towards inclusive education was moderate to a favorable level.

Bansal (2018) aimed to explore teachers' opinions towards inclusive education in Chandigarh and to gain more knowledge about the factors that may influence the implementation of inclusive practices in a school system. It was found that many of the teachers had opinion that Children with severe disabilities should be educated in special or separate settings and special education teachers are trained to use different teaching methods to teach students with disabilities more effectively but at the same time most of them also agreed that Inclusive education is likely to have a positive effect on the social and emotional development of students with disabilities. Qualitative analysis of the open ended questionnaire along with Focus group interview with teachers regarding the education of children with special needs revealed that they are quite ready for educating CWSN in regular classrooms but they face various barriers and challenges that impact the teaching and learning of these children in general classrooms.

Thwala (2015) studied on the challenges encountered by teachers in managing inclusive classrooms in Swaziland. Results revealed that a majority of teachers were not trained on how to teach in an inclusive class. However, the literature indicates that with proper training and resources, inclusion can be a practical and effective learning environment. It can be concluded that mainstream teachers generally lacked confidence as they attempted to include students with disabilities into classes. The study recommended that the ministry of education should consider increasing the availability of special needs courses, workshops and conference for teachers in primary schools who are working with students with disabilities.

Bhatnagar and Das (2014) examined the current skill levels of regular primary and secondary school teachers in Delhi, India in order to teach students with disabilities in inclusive education settings. The major findings were that nearly 70% of the regular school teachers had neither received training in special education nor had any experience teaching students with disabilities. Further, 87% of the teachers did not have access to support services in their classrooms. Finally, although both primary and secondary school teachers rated themselves as having limited or low competence for working with students with disabilities, there was no statistically significant difference between their perceived skill levels.

Todorovic, J. *et al.*, (2011) aimed to study Attitudes towards Inclusive Education and Dimensions of Teacher's Personality. The results have shown that, out of total number of examinees, 80% support the idea of inclusive education. Openness is in a positive correlation with the attitudes towards inclusive education. Teachers in primary schools have more positive attitude towards inclusive education.

3. METHODOLOGY

3.1 Aim

1. To compare the attitude towards inclusive education among teachers of primary and middle school.
2. To analyze teachers' attitude on different aspects of inclusive education (psychological and behavioural, social and parent related, curricular and co curricular and administrative).

3.2 Objectives of the Study

1. To have a comparative analysis of the attitude towards inclusive education among teachers of primary and middle school.
2. To analyze teachers' attitude on different aspects of inclusive education (psychological and behavioural, social and parent related, curricular and co curricular and administrative).

3.3 Hypotheses

1. Psychological and behavioural aspects of inclusive education have no significant effect on the teachers' attitude.

2. Social and parent related aspects of inclusive education have no significant effect on the teachers' attitude.
3. Curricular and co-curricular aspects of inclusive education have no significant effect on the teachers' attitude.
4. Administrative aspect of inclusive education has no significant effect on the teachers' attitude.

3.4 Research Design

Survey research methodology is the collection of information from a sample of individuals through their response to questions. Survey research can use quantitative research strategies using questionnaires with numerically rated items. It is often used to describe and explore the human behaviour, surveys are therefore frequently used in social and psychological research (Singleton & Straits 2009).

3.5 Variables

Independent Variables

1. Psychological and behavioural aspects of inclusive education.
2. Social and Parents-related aspects of inclusive education
3. Curricular and co-curricular aspects of inclusive education:
4. Administrative aspects of inclusive education.
5. Children with special needs

Dependent Variables

1. Teachers' level of attitude towards inclusive education.
2. Challenges in handling children with special needs.

3.6 Sample

Purposive Sampling technique was used in the selection of sample. Purposive sample, a kind of non probability sample, is one which is based on the typicality of the cases to be included in the sample. The investigator has some belief that the sample being handpicked is typical of the population. Purposive sample is also known as a judgmental sample because the investigator on the basis of her impression makes a judgment regarding the concern cases which are thought to be typical of the population. (Singh, 1997).

The sample size consists of 60 teachers are handling students with special needs in an inclusive classroom.

3.7 Inclusion Criteria

Class teachers and few subject teachers handling students with special needs in an inclusive classroom at primary and middle school levels.

3.8 Exclusion Criteria

1. Special educators working in the school were excluded.
2. Class teachers and subject teachers of secondary and higher secondary levels were excluded.

3.9 Measures

Teacher attitude scale towards inclusive education TASTIE-SA developed by Dr. Vishal Sood and Dr. Arti Anand (2016)

Reliability: The test re-test reliability was calculated on a sample of 140 elementary teachers. The product moment correlation 'r' i.e. reliability index, between two testing was 0.82 thereby indicating that the scale is fairly reliable to measure attitude of teachers towards inclusive education. It also measure to ensure intrinsic validity of the scale.

3.10 Procedure

With the permission of the concerned school authority, The respective class teachers and subject teachers of primary and middle school levels were selected for the study based on their familiarity and experience handling students with special needs in an inclusive classroom. Once the teachers' consent was received, a good rapport was established. The selected teachers were explained about the purpose of the research in detail and the 'Teacher attitude scale towards inclusive education TASTIE-SA' developed by Dr. Vishal Sood and Dr. Arti Anand (2016) was administered in two separate groups.

3.11 Statistical Analysis

Descriptive and inferential statistics were used for data analysis. Statistical test- non-parametric test was adopted for the data analysis as per the objectives of the study. Test of normality (Shapiro Wilk test) was run to analyze the normal distribution of data. Kruskal Wallis test for independent samples was run for the comparison of two groups. Frequency distribution to find out the mean to find out the positive or negative total attitude and on different dimensions of inclusive education.

3.12 Ethical Considerations

1. Permission was obtained from the school authority for data collection.
2. Informed consent was sought from the respective teachers.

3. Participants were assured about the confidentiality of their identity and response.
4. Respect for people's rights and dignity was assured.
5. Participants were given the option of discontinuing from the study at any point if they wish to and they were assured that they will not face any negative consequences if they do so.

4. RESULTS AND DISCUSSION

The present study aimed to have a comparative analysis between the two groups (Primary school teachers and Middle school teachers) and to explore the teachers' attitude towards inclusive education and the challenges faced in handling special needs students in an inclusive classroom.

The current study presents the results and discussion of descriptive and inferential statistics. The statistical analysis using Kruskal Wallis test and descriptive statistics for the comparison between the two groups on the areas of teacher attitude scale towards inclusive education. Shapiro-Wilk test of normality has been used to check whether the data is normally distributed or not. Non-parametric equivalent has been used for the sub domains of inclusive education as the test of normality has not been met.

4.1 Teachers' Level of Attitude Towards Inclusive Education

Kruskal Wallis test for independent samples were run for the comparison of two groups on areas of inclusive education and overall attitude towards inclusive education. Frequency distribution was carried out to evaluate the level of teachers' attitude on different dimensions of inclusive education and their on overall attitude.

Table 1: Comparison between the Two Groups On Areas of Inclusive Education and Overall Attitude Towards Inclusive Education

Areas of Inclusive Education	*Teachers*	*N*	*Mean Rank*
Psychological and behavioural	Primary School Teachers	36	29.72
	Middle School Teachers	24	31.67
Social and Parent related	Primary School Teachers	36	33.82
	Middle School Teachers	24	25.52
Curricular and Co curricular	Primary School Teachers	36	28.68
	Middle School Teachers	24	33.23
Administrative	Primary School Teachers	36	24.81
	Middle School Teachers	24	39.04
Attitude towards inclusive education	Primary School Teachers	36	29.01
	Middle School Teachers	24	32.73

Results of between group comparison on attitude towards inclusive education indicated that there is no significant difference between primary school teachers and middle school teachers' overall attitude towards inclusive education. The table also presents the mean rank comparison between the two groups on the sub-domains of inclusive education. The results reveal that there is a significant difference between the two groups on the sub-domain of administrative aspect of inclusive education suggesting that primary school teachers are significantly lower than the middle school teachers. However there is no significant difference between the two groups on the dimensions of psychological/ behavioural, Social and parent related, curricular and co-curricular aspects of inclusive education.

Table 2: Shows the Frequency Distribution of the Teachers' Attitude Towards Inclusive Education as a Whole and on Different Dimensions of Inclusive Education

		Psychological or Behavioural	***Social and Parent Related***	***Curricular and Co Curricular***	***Administrative***	***Level of Attitude Towards Inclusive Education***
N	Valid	60	60	60	60	60
	Missing	0	0	0	0	0
Mean		24.63	29.18	29.47	25.70	109.23
Median		25.00	29.00	29.50	26.00	109.50
Mode		24	28	26	26	114
Std. Deviation		3.551	2.658	3.925	2.410	9.192

The mean values on the different dimensions of inclusive education that includes psychological and behaviour, social and parent related, curricular and co curricular, administrative aspects reveal positive attitude. Hence rejecting the hypotheses stating: 1. Psychological and behavioural aspects of inclusive education has no significant effect on the teachers' attitude. 2. Social and parent related aspects of inclusive education has no significant effect on the teachers' attitude. 3. Curricular and co-curricular aspects of inclusive education has no significant effect on the teachers' attitude. 4. Administrative aspects of inclusive education has no significant effect on the teachers' attitude.

The mean value of 109.23 on the overall attitude of teachers toward inclusive education reveals above average favourable attitude. The findings are supported by the previous research by Singh, S *et al.* (2020) that attitude of teachers towards inclusive education was moderate to a favorable level.

Though teachers have shown positive attitude towards all the aspects of inclusive education, their attitude towards administrative aspects of inclusive education is lower compared to other dimensions. This indicates the challenges teachers perceive in implementing inclusive education in mainstream schools in terms of facilities available in general schools and teachers agree that it is important to have in-service training to equip teachers to handle children with special needs. The finding was in conformity with the study of Thwala (2015).

5. DISCUSSION

The results are based on the descriptive analyses of teachers' attitude towards inclusive education and its aspects.

The mean rank comparison between the two groups on the overall level of attitude towards inclusive education doesn't have significant difference. The finding was not in conformity with the study of Todorovic, J *et al.*, (2011). However, the mean rank comparison on the aspects of psychological and behavioural, social and parent related, curricular and co curricular aspects of inclusive education have no significant difference between the two groups. Whereas the mean rank comparison on the administrative aspect of inclusive education shows a significant difference between the two groups.

On a whole, it can be interpreted that inclusive classroom has its own merits and demerits. The advantage of having inclusive classroom helps in the holistic development of students with special needs which is very important for an individual's success in life. The holistic development focuses on the overall development of the student in terms of emotional, social and academic development. The advantage of inclusive classroom according to teachers is that, inclusive classroom benefits students develop self confidence with equal social rights. Teachers agree to the fact that, inclusive education is essential for teachers to be sensitive about special needs children's social educational and psychological needs. Teachers do agree that inclusive education has become the need of the hour and teachers are mentally prepared and ready to implement inclusive education in schools. Teachers highly believe that, inclusive education is proving to be inspirational in social upliftment and adjustment of special children. This finding was in conformity with the investigation by (Singh, 2016). According to teachers , it is necessary to have additional qualification to impart inclusive education. However, teachers have agreed upon present educational system which has to be made more flexible and evaluation system of the curricular and co-curricular achievements of special needs should be different from others. According to teachers, it is a challenge to implement inclusive education in mainstream schools and the major reason for this is teachers are not trained to use various teaching learning methods. Along with in service training, teachers are of the opinion that, they need to be paid extra incentives for imparting inclusive education. This could also be the motivating factor for teachers. According to teachers' perspectives on the difficulties faced by teachers and special needs students in an inclusive classrooms are: large class strength, overload of syllabus, lack of adequate support, lack of training program, sociodemographic background and policy regarding education and assessment (Bansal, 2018; Thwala 2015).

This suggests that, awareness program regarding the disabilities found in children and adolescents, and training program focused on handling students with disability in the classroom is very crucial for teachers.

6. CONCLUSIONS

Conclusions drawn from the results show that teachers play a crucial role in implementing inclusive education in schools. Though teachers' attitude on inclusive classroom has both merits and demerits, the favorable attitude exhibited towards inclusive education will help in achieving the goal. However, it is evident that teachers have an insight about the challenges they face in the inclusive classroom and they are also aware about the need for special training program to handle challenging situations adequately. Hence, an attempt should be carried out at school to equip teachers acquire the necessary skills and competencies to handle children with varied special needs in an inclusive classroom.

7. LIMITATIONS AND IMPLICATIONS

7.1 Limitations

The selected sample was limited in terms of size. The sample size was restricted to 60 teachers of primary and middle school level.

The sample selection was restricted to just one school. Hence generalization is not possible. An in depth analysis could be possible if the sample was heterogeneous.

7.2 Implications

Training programs and workshops for teachers on the systematic strategies and techniques to handle students in an inclusive classroom is of utmost priority.

REFERENCES

[1] Bansal, S. (2018). Understanding Teachers' Perspective of Inclusive Education for Children with Special Needs (CWSN). *Educational Quest—An International Journal of Education and Applied Social Sciences*, *9*(1), 115–123. Retrieved from http://ndpublisher.in/admin/issues/EQv9n1p.pdf

[2] Bhatnagar, N. and Das, A. (2014). Regular School Teachers' Concerns and Perceived Barriers to Implement Inclusive Education in New Delhi, India. *International Journal of Instruction*, *7*(2), 89–102. Retrieved From https://files.eric.ed.gov/fulltext/EJ1085257.pdf

[3] Casto, S. (2018). Academic outcome of students with learning disabilities in an inclusive classroom. Retrieved From http://www.otterbein.edu/Files/pdf/Education/JTIR/VolumeV/Casto%20final.pdf

[4] Singh, S., Kumar, S. and Singh, R.K. (2020). A Study of Attitude of Teachers towards Inclusive Education. *Shanlax International Journal of Education*, *9*(1), 189–197. Retrieved from https://eric.ed.gov/?id=EJ1277802

[5] Todorovic, J., Stojiljkovic, S., Ristanic, S. and Djigic, G. (2011). Attitudes towards inclusive education and dimensions of teacher's personality. *Procedia-Social and Behavioral Sciences*, *29*, 426–432.Retrieved from https://doi.org/10.1016/j.sbspro.2011.11.259

[7] Thwala, S. (2015). Challenges encountered by teachers in managing inclusive classrooms in Swaziland. *Mediterranean Journal of Social Sciences*, *6*(1), 495–500. Retrieved From DOI:10.5901/mjss.2015.v6n1p495

Assessment of Placement Training Programs on College Students and Their Impact on Interview Performance

K. Manikandan[1] and K. Subramaniam[2]
[1]Ph.D Scholar, Kamban College of Arts and Science, Sulthanpet, Coimbatore, Inida
[2]Associate Professor of Commerce and Management,
Kamban College of Arts and Science, Sulthanpet, Coimbatore, India

ABSTRACT: *Training is the common word in every college which keeps the students fit to their requirements. The Training and Placement Cell serves as a pivotal bridge between educational institutions and the professional world, facilitating the smooth transition of students into their respective career paths. The main purpose of this paper is to examine the impact of placement training programs on post-training and interview performance of the students at a college in Chennai city. The sample size of the study was about 200 Students. The survey method of data collection was used structured questionnaire. The findings of the descriptive statistical analysis revealed that the students were moderately satisfied with the reaction to training, behavioral change, and adaptive performance. They were more satisfied with the skills acquisition, effect of training, return on investment, task performance, and contextual performance. The results of the regression model also explored that all the sub-constructs of training evaluation have a robust relationship with the post-training and interview performance of the students from the college in Chennai city.*

Keywords: College Students, Placement Training, Post Training, Student Performance, Training Evaluation.

1. INTRODUCTION

The interview process is a critical stage in the recruitment journey, serving as a platform for employers to assess candidates' qualifications, skills, and suitability for specific roles. In India, the interview process typically consists of several stages designed to evaluate candidates comprehensively. These stages may include screening interviews, technical assessments, HR interviews, and sometimes, group discussions or case studies, depending on the nature of the job. Getting professional work in the Information Technology sector in India requires sharpening knowledge and skills according to technological trends. Hence, the training and development programs offered by the placement cell aim to develop the KSA (Knowledge, Skills, and Attitude), abilities, and competencies of the students. Apart from regular training and development sessions, students are expected to enhance their knowledge and skills through e-learning modules and online courses from reputable organizations/institutes. Training is the activity to enhance a student's current skills for their future job (Laird, 1985; Nadler, 1990).

2. THEORETICAL FRAMEWORK OF THE RESEARCH

This section of the research paper explains the fundamental theoretical concepts and principles based on which the present research was built and executed. The present research has two main constructs: training evaluation and placement performance, each with five and four sub-constructs respectively.

2.1 Training Evaluation

Training is one of the most important activities in colleges today. Training in an organization is inevitable because students studying in any college/ university from different departments require training to adapt to the changes happening in the organization demanded by its internal and external environment. However, the type of training required may vary based on the circumstances of the college. It may range from small five to ten-minute brief lectures/demonstrations by students of the same departments or by immediate superiors like placement trainers (informal training) to a few weeks/few months of training by professionals from the training industry in a specific technology (formal training).

According to Philips (1997), training evaluation can be 'defined as a systematic process to determine the worth, value, or meaning of a training program and how it has affected the college'. In 1950, Don Kirkpatrick (1996, 1998) developed a four-stage training evaluation model to evaluate the effectiveness of training. There are four levels in the training evaluation framework. Level 1 denotes 'Reaction', which evaluates how participants respond to the training, Level 2 refers to 'Learning', which measures if they learned the material, Level 3 signifies 'Behavior', which considers if they are using what they learned in the training, and Level 4 represents 'Results', which evaluates if the training positively impacted the organization. This model can be applied to evaluate the training program before, during, and after training to enhance and determine the value of the training to the college. This research adopted the four-stage training evaluation model of Don Kirkpatrick along with the fifth level as 'Return on Investment', based on Philips's (1997) training evaluation model. Hence, the training evaluation scale used in this research has five sub-constructs such as reaction to training, skills acquisition, behavioral change, effect of training, and return on investment.

2.1.1 *Reaction to Training*

Reaction to training finds out the students' perception towards the benefits of training and the learning experience, which includes typical questions concerning the degree to which the experience was valuable (satisfaction), whether they felt engaged, and whether they felt the training was relevant in campus drives. The placement team uses that feedback to evaluate the effectiveness of the training, trainees' perceptions, potential future improvements, and justification for the training expense (Akbar Jan and Muthuvelayutham, 2012a). A variety of sources estimate that approximately 80% of training events include reactions to training evaluation.

2.1.2 *Skills Acquisition*

Skills acquisition deals with learning through training. It aims to quantify the amount of learning that occurred concerning knowledge, skills, and attitudes as the outcome of the training given to students. Trainers ensure the accomplishment of training objectives by measuring the skills acquisition of trainees through the training programs. Therefore, it is mandatory to know what students have learned and what they haven't, which enables the placement team to plan further related to designing and executing training programs. Skills acquisition can be done in different phases, for example, before the training, during the training, and after the training programs, to know the effectiveness of training programs. In this research, only post-evaluation of skills acquisition was done.

2.1.3 *Behavioral Change*

Behavioral change evaluates the degree to which trainees' behaviors change as a consequence of the training, which deals with the impact of knowledge and skills acquired through the training on the development and execution of mini-projects in colleges (Akbar Jan and Muthuvelayutham, 2012b). There was also the possibility of changes in behavior not only because of training given, which may also be due to some other factors. For example, the reluctance or refusal of students to get the learning from the training program may also lead to failure of occurrence of behavioral change. Behavioral change evaluation involves both pre and post-training measurement of the trainees' behavior; however, this training, it considers only post-training behavioral change perceived by the students.

2.1.4 *Effect of Training*

Effect of training to determine the tangible results of the training, namely reduced cost, improved quality and efficiency, selected campus. (Blanchard and Thacker, 2003). Assessing the effectiveness of the training program is a demanding aspect; however, accurate assessment is a difficult and time-consuming process which also leads to further expenses, but the placement team can't skip this level. This phase ensures whether specific outcomes are the outcome of the training. The effect of training requires both pre and post-event measurement of the training objective.

2.1.5 *Return on Investment*

The term 'Return on Investment (ROI)' refers to the measurement of the profitability of projects. It combines net benefits (monetary and non-monetary) compared to the investment/costs of a program and is mostly expressed in a ratio or percentage (Horngren, 1982; Phillips, 1997). This construct is included based on Philips's (1997a) Five Level Return on Investment (ROI) Framework, in which he added a fifth level as ROI. Measurement at this level compares the monetary benefits of the program with the fully loaded cost to conduct the program. Conducting an impact study of a training program requires completing all five steps in the framework (Philips, 1997). The training has an impact on business performance (Kayatry Sabitha and Panchanatham, 2009).

A. *Pre-Assessment Evaluation*

Providing a pre-assessment evaluation for a group of 200 students who have undergone aptitude tests, technical tests, and mock interviews involves several considerations. Here's how such an evaluation could be structured into Aptitude Test Evaluation, Technical Test Evaluation, and Mock Interview Evaluation.

B. *Post-Training Performance*

The training performance scales are of a wide variety and also multidimensional in nature. The current study has utilized the Individual Work Performance (IWP) Scale developed by Koopmans *et al.* (2012) which has four sub-constructs such as training performance, Assessment performance, contextual performance, adaptive performance, and interview performance Campbell (1990) defined the term IWP as "behaviors or actions that are relevant to the goals of the organization". Each sub-construct of IWP was briefed below. The training also has the impact on self-efficacy of the students (Mohan raj and Panchanatham, 2017).

1. **Training Performance:** Training performance measures the effectiveness of learning interventions in achieving desired outcomes. It encompasses participants' acquisition and application of knowledge, skills, and attitudes. Continuous evaluation and feedback are essential for improving training performance over time. Ultimately, successful training performance leads to enhanced individual and organizational capabilities. (Koopmans *et al.*, 2011).
2. **Contextual Performance:** In the words of Koopmans *et al.* (2011), the term 'Contextual performance' can be defined as "individual behaviors

that support the organizational, social, and psychological environment in which the technical core must function". Other terms representing 'contextual performance' are non–job-specific task proficiency, extra-role performance, organizational citizenship behavior, or interpersonal relations.

3. **Assessment Performance:** Assessment performance evaluates individuals' understanding and proficiency in specific subject areas or skills. It involves measuring knowledge retention, critical thinking abilities, and problem-solving skills through various assessment methods. Effective assessment performance provides valuable insights into learners' strengths and areas needing improvement. It plays a crucial role in guiding instructional strategies and facilitating targeted learning outcomes.
4. **Adaptive Performance:** Adaptive performance refers to "the extent to which an individual adapts to changes in a working system or work roles in a work environment after they get placed, which contains solving problems creatively, dealing with uncertain or unpredictable work situations, learning new tasks, technologies, and procedures and adapting to other individuals, cultures, or physical surroundings" (Koopmans *et al.*, 2011). In short, adaptive performance refers to a student's proficiency in adapting to changes in work roles or environment after getting placed.

Table 1: Scale Reliability Test—Training Evaluation Scale

S.No	Scales	Cronbach Alpha	Results
1	Reaction to training	0.75	Acceptable
2	Skills Acquisition	0.827	Good
3	Behavioral Change	0.987	Excellent
4	Effect of Training	0.922	Excellent
5	Return on Investment	0.85	Good
6	Overall Training Evaluation Scale	0.938	Excellent

Table 2: Scale Reliability—Individual Interview Performance Scale

S.No	Scales	Cronbach Alpha	Results
1	Training Performance	0.821	Good
2	Contextual Performance	0.845	Good
3	Assessment Performance	0.11	Excellent
4	Adaptive Performance	0.834	Good
5	Overall Individual interview Performance Scale	0.87	Good

Table 1 and 2 summarizes the results of scale reliability tests of training evaluation and Individual interview Performance Scales. From the tables, it is identified that the two chosen scales and their sub-constructs had acceptable reliability and internal consistency.

5. **Interview Performance:** Interview performance is a crucial determinant of success in securing employment opportunities. Effective communication, confidence, and preparation are key elements in presenting oneself positively during interviews. Demonstrating relevant skills, experiences, and a genuine interest in the role can leave a lasting impression on interviewers.

3. PURPOSE OF THE STUDY

Placement training programs have a significant impact on students' interview performance in colleges across Chennai. These programs aim to enhance students' employability skills, including communication, interpersonal skills, problem-solving, and technical competencies. Companies like TCS, Hexaware, Enoahi, and Corizo conduct campus drives and provide training sessions such as mock interviews, group discussions, aptitude tests, and resume-building workshops. Through these initiatives, students gain valuable insights into the recruitment process and industry expectations, making them better prepared for actual job interviews. The effectiveness of these training programs is evident in improved interview performance, with students demonstrating increased confidence, articulation, and professionalism. Exposure to real-world scenarios and industry-specific challenges also equips students with the necessary skills to thrive in the competitive job market. Colleges in Chennai experience higher placement rates and receive positive feedback from recruiters, underscoring the success of placement training programs in bridging the gap between academic learning and industry requirements. Overall, these programs play a pivotal role in shaping students' career paths and facilitating successful transitions

Table 3

S.No	Scale	Mean	Standard Deviation
1	Reaction to training	18.4	3.8944
2	Skills Acquisition	23.61	7.2254
3	Behavioral Change	20.42	5.3144
4	Effect of Training	21.55	5.4844
5	Return on Investment	22.91	6.2234
6	Training Performance	22.81	5.7234
7	Contextual Performance	22.7	3.5874
8	Adaptive Performance	21.02	5.5444
9	Interview Performance	9.26	4.3814

from academia to the professional world. The researchers liken the scenario of students to the phrase "Learn or Quit," emphasizing the importance of seizing opportunities for growth and development.

The descriptive statistics (i.e. mean and standard deviation) of the chosen constructs were condensed in table 3. The mean value between 18.0–20.0 of the above-mentioned constructs indicates that the students were moderately satisfied with those constructs, whereas if it is more than 20.0 it denotes they were satisfied with that particular construct. Therefore, from Table 3 it is identified that the students were moderately satisfied with the reaction to training, behavioral change and adaptive performance. They were fully satisfied with skills acquisition, effect of training, return on investment, training performance, and contextual performance, whereas the standard deviation represents the dispersion of the frequency of the constructs, the contextual performance had having least deviation (3.5874) and skills acquisition was having large deviation (7.2254) among the chosen constructs by it.

4. METHODOLOGY

This research adopts a descriptive research design to explore the impact of training programs on interview performance in Chennai. The training methodology incorporates theoretical instruction and practical exercises to enhance students' technical competencies and interview readiness. The study sample consists of 200 students from colleges with NAAC Grade accreditation in Chennai. The surveyed companies include Tata Consultancy Services, Hexaware, Enoah, and Corizo. Data collection utilized structured questionnaires, with the instrument comprising two scales: the training evaluation scale and the post-training interview performance scale. Rigorous development and validation procedures were implemented to ensure the reliability and validity of the data collection instrument.

Based on the unstandardized estimates mentioned in the Table 5, the regression equation can be written as

Table 4: Training Evaluation and Post-Training % Interview Performance Regression Coefficients

S. No	*Variables*	*Unstandardized Coefficients*		*Standardized Coefficients*	*T*	*P value*
		B	*Std. Error*	*Beta*		
1.	(Constant)	4.831		–	3.4	<0.001**
2.	Reaction to training	2.1	0.311	0.842	2.689	<0.001**
3.	Skills Acquisition	1.571	0.402	2.721	4.62	<0.001**

S. No	Variables	Unstandardized Coefficients		Standardized Coefficients	T	P value
		B	Std. Error	Beta		
4.	Behavioural Change	0.866	0.184	1.138	3.568	<0.001**
5.	Effect of Training	0.804	0.151	0.613	2.587	<0.001**
6.	Return on Investment	2.842	0.062	2.526	2.737	<0.001**

Table 5: The Impact of Training on Post-Training & Interview Performance of Students

Model	Sum of Squares	Df	Mean Square	F	Sig.
Regression	876.21	5	484.052	427.068	<0.001**
Residual	48.56	595	0.763		
Total	924.771	600			

a. *Dependent Variable:* Post-training Performance.
b. *Predictors:* (Constant), Effect of Training, Reaction to training, Behavioral Change, Skills Acquisition and Return on Investment.

Note 1: ** Denotes 1% level of significance.

5. CONCLUSION

The findings of the descriptive statistical analysis revealed that students were moderately satisfied with the reaction to training, behavioral change, and adaptive performance. However, they expressed higher satisfaction with skills acquisition, the effect of training, return on investment, training performance, and contextual performance. The students perceived a lesser impact of counterproductive behavior in the organization after the training program, indicating a positive shift in attitude due to the training, which contributes to the well-being of the college community. Furthermore, the results of the regression model demonstrated a robust relationship between all sub-constructs of training evaluation and the post-training and interview performance of students from colleges in Chennai. Therefore, based on the research outcomes, it can be concluded that the training provided in selected colleges significantly enhances the performance of students, enabling them to contribute outstandingly in campus drives conducted by the training and placement cell.

REFERENCES

[1] Nalilni Devi, S. and Panchanatham, N., "An Empirical Study on Training Analysis among Medical Staff Focussing on Staff Nurse", *Arabian Journal*

of Business and Management Review, (International) Vol. 1, September-spl. pp. 137–142, 2011.

[2] Priya, A., Vishal, Kumar and Panchanatham, N., "Creativity and Perception of employees towards need for training with regard to Aviation Industry", Journal of Commerce, Pakistan, (International) Vol. 3, No. 1. pp. 1–7, 2011.

[3] Akbar Jan, N. and Muthuvelayutham, C. 'Employees' Training and Development in IT Sector: An Essential Instrument for Effectiveness of Organizational Productivity", *European Journal of Scientific Research*, Vol. 81, Issue 3, No. 3, pp. 397–407, 2012.

[4] Akbar, Jan, N. and Muthuvelayutham, C., "Competency Based Training Need Assessment for IT Companies in Chennai", *Life Science Journal*, Vol. 9, Issue. 4, pp. 5152–5155, 2012.

[5] Ananth, S., Panchanatham, N. and Seethapathi, V., "Training to Solve Executives Functional Problem", *Indian Economic Panorama*, Vol. 13, No. 2, pp. 13–14, 2003.

[6] Blanchard, P. and Thacker, J., "Effective training – systems, strategies and practices (2nd ed.)", New Jersey: Prentice Hall, 2003.

[7] Campbell, J.P., "Modeling the performance prediction problem in industrial and organizational psychology", In: Dunnette MD, Hough LM, editors. Handbook of strial and organizational psychology. Palo Alto, CA, US: Consulting Psychologists Press; 1990, Vol. 1 (2nd ed.). pp. 687–732.

[8] Horngren, C.T., "Cost accounting. Englewood Cliffs", NJ: Prentice Hall, 1982.

[9] IT Industry Profile [Online] Available: https://www.ibef. org/industry/information-technology-india.aspx

[10] KayatrySabitha, R. and Panchanatham, N., "Training and Business Performance of Small Scale Industries in Puducherry State", *RVS Journal of Management*, Vol. 1. No. 1. pp. 48–56, 2009.

[11] Kirkpatrick D, "Evaluation", In R.L. Craig and L.R. Bitten (Eds), "The ASTD Training and Development Handbook'. (4th ed. pp. 294–312) New York: McGraw-Hill, 1996.

[12] Kirkpatrick, D.L., "Evaluating Training Programs the Four Levels (2nd ed.)", San Francisco: Berret Koehler, 1998.

[13] Laird, D., "Approaches to training and development (Rev. 2nd ed.)", Reading, MA: Addison-Wesley, 1985.

[14] Linda, Koopmans; Claire, M. Bernaards; Vincent, H. Hildebrandt; Wilmar, B. Schaufeli; Henrica, C.W. de Vet and Allard, J. van der Beek, "Conceptual Frameworks of Individual Work Performance A Systematic Review", *JOEM*, Vol. 53, No. 8, pp. 856–866, 2011.

[15] Linda, Koopmans and Claire, Bernaards, Vincent Hildebrandt, Stef van Buuren, Allard J. van der Beek, Henrica C.W. de Vet, "Development of an individual work performance questionnaire", *International Journal of Productivity and Performance Management*, Vol. 62 Issue 1, pp. 6–28, 2012.

[16] Mohanraj, D. and Panchanatham, N, "Effect of Training and Development Programmes on Self-Efficacy of Banking Professionals in Chennai City", *International Journal of Management*, 8 (5), pp. 31–43, 2017.

[17] Nadler, L., "Human resource development", In L. Nadler, & Z. Nadler (Eds.), The handbook of human resource development (2nd ed., pp. 1.1–1.47). New York: Wiley, 1990

[18] Nasscom IT Industry Ranking: [Online] Available: http://old.nasscom.in/industry-ranking

[19] Nirmal Kumar, N. and Panchanatham, N., "Training to Retain Valuable Employees", *Nehru Journal of Management and Research,* Coimbatore, Vol. 1, Issue 2, pp. 20–25, 2011.

[20] Panchanatham, N., Rajendran, K. and Karuppiah, K, "Impact of Training Experience on Executives' Problem Solving Behaviour", *The Creative Psychologist,* Vol. 7, Nos. 1 & 2.

Workplace Stressors and Faculty Disengagement in Higher Educational Institutions: A Critical Examination

S. Savitha[1] and K. Krishnakumar[2]

[1]Research Scholar, Department of Commerce,
Periyar University, Salem, Tamil Nadu, India

[2]Professor and Head, Department of Commerce,
Periyar University, Salem, Tamil Nadu, India

ABSTRACT: *Job stress is a prevalent issue in various organizations, including higher education institutions. It stems from factors such as unrealistic expectations, perceived job pressures, and the challenge of balancing personal and professional life. This research explores the impact of job stress on the work-life balance of female faculty members in Indian higher education institutions, aiming to identify its sources. The study involved 200 female faculty members from Dharmapuri educational institutions in Tamilnadu, who completed standardized, closed-ended questionnaires to provide quantitative data. Analysis using SPSS software revealed that inequitable pay structures and demanding work schedules were the primary sources of workplace stress. These stressors were found to negatively affect female faculty members' productivity and financial stability, indicating a positive correlation between stress and work-life balance. Faculty members experiencing emotions such as anger, anxiety, pressure, disappointment, or hopelessness are considered to be under stress. Despite misconceptions suggesting that faculty members lead tranquil lives, the reality often involves significant pressure and workload. Moreover, the expectation of constant availability, even outside official working hours, exacerbates stress levels.*

Keywords: Female Faculty Members, Job Stress, Productivity, Work-Life Balance, Workplace Stressors.

1. INTRODUCTION

Stress within the teaching profession not only diminishes the quality of faculty members but also engenders profound unhappiness due to several factors, including excessive workload, challenging working conditions, low pay, limited career advancement opportunities, communication gaps, interruptions from colleagues, students, and family, as well as financial concerns. This stress adversely affects teachers' mental well-being and their ability to perform effectively. Faculty members experiencing intense negative emotions like anger, anxiety, pressure, disappointment, or hopelessness are considered to be under significant stress. Despite common misconceptions portraying faculty members as leading tranquil lives with minimal stress, the reality often involves significant pressure and workload. Additionally, the expectation of constant availability, even beyond official working hours, further exacerbates stress levels. Wilson's (1979) research on "Teaching Faculty Members to De-stress" revealed that a vast majority of faculty members in California (95%) acknowledge experiencing pressure, with 90% reporting encounters with various forms of strain. The 'Faculty members Education Division Council for Exceptional Children' highlighted the need for around 30,000 faculty members engaged in specialized curriculum to take annual breaks to mitigate distressing work situations. Increased awareness of the importance of supporting educators has underscored the critical need to address their emotional well-being, particularly as their stress levels often surpass those in other highly demanding professions.

2. ACADEMIC STRESS

Stress emerges as a complex interplay of diverse biological reactions triggered by unwelcome and demanding external pressures. It manifests when individuals confront challenging yet inevitable circumstances. Researchers across various historical epochs have extensively documented the intricacies of stress, offering diverse perspectives on its nature. From one standpoint, each viewpoint holds significance, portraying stress as an inherent state within living beings driven by an inclination for adaptation. It is delineated by a perceptible imbalance between demands and the capacity to respond, where failure to meet these demands carries significant repercussions. Stress can be conceptualized through two distinct lenses: the Adaptive response perspective and the Negative consequence perspective.

3. OCCUPATIONAL STRESS

Faculty members experience stress when their skills and expertise do not align with the demands of their academic roles, leading to job dissatisfaction. Conversely, persistent dissatisfaction in teaching positions may indicate an effective coping mechanism for managing work-related stress. Occupational stress arises when the requirements of the academic role diverge from a faculty member's abilities, resources, or needs, resulting in distressing physical and emotional responses. This phenomenon, termed job-related stress, poses unforeseen vulnerabilities and potential harm. It encompasses psychological, physical, and emotional strains stemming from the mismatch between the demands of the academic role and a faculty member's skills, resources, and adaptability.

3.1 Frameworks

Numerous psychological theories and frameworks delve into the topic of occupational stress among faculty members, acknowledging that stress arises from the complex interactions of interconnected elements within the academic setting.

3.2 Job Characteristics Framework

The Job Characteristics Framework comprehensively covers various attributes relevant to faculty roles, such as task variety, work ethics, job significance, autonomy, and feedback. These attributes are believed to evoke fundamental psychological states that contribute to faculty members' sense of responsibility and expertise. According to the model, both positive and negative job characteristics influence psychological states that impact social and intellectual outcomes, including motivation, satisfaction, and absenteeism. In line with this framework, Hackman and Oldham introduced the Job Diagnostic Survey, a tool for evaluating faculty roles that recommends essential aspects of job redesign, such as task enrichment, feedback mechanisms, and improving the nature of work.

3.3 Workload

In academic settings, managing workload can pose a significant source of stress for faculty members, acting as a stressor in various dimensions. There are three challenging dimensions of workload:

- **Quantitative Workload or Overload:** Handling an excessive amount of tasks beyond manageable limits.
- **Qualitative Workload:** Engaging in intellectually demanding work that inherently poses difficulties.
- **Under Load:** Having tasks that underutilize a faculty member's skills and abilities.

Within the pressure-based interest control paradigm for faculty members, workload emerges as a crucial job demand. According to this framework, tasks with varying levels of demand can induce stress, particularly when faculty members have limited control over their responsibilities. Essentially, having control over one's workload serves as a protective or supportive factor in situations characterized by high demands or unmet obligations.

4. OBJECTIVES OF THE STUDY

1. To explore the organizational and individual factors influencing stress among faculty members in college settings.
2. To examine the effects of stress on the physical and emotional well-being of college faculty members.
3. To investigate the stress coping and management strategies employed by college faculty members.

5. RESEARCH METHODOLOGY

The aim of this study is to investigate burnout and job stress among college faculty members in the Dharmapuri area. The strategies section will outline the steps taken to examine the overall validity and reliability of the study, including the rationale behind the specific methodology or procedures used to collect, select, process, and analyze data to understand the issue. This phase will detail the study's development activities, data collection methods, timeline, and research approach.

6. SAMPLING

Sample Size: The sample size was derived as 200, 95% confidence level and 5% level of significance.

Sample Unit: The unit of study conducted among College Faculty members in Dharmapuri district.

Sampling Design and Determination of Sample Size: The sample size for this study is limited to 200. The participants in this research are faculty members from colleges in the Dharmapuri district. The study focus is on seven taluks in Dharmapuri district, where data is gathered from college faculty members.

The below table (Table 1) provides the details of the sampling techniques.

Table 1

College	*Population*	*Total Colleges*	*Sampling Techniques*
Dharmapuri (Taluk wise)	Select the population from Seven taluks in Dharmapuri District	28 arts & Science colleges and 12 engineering colleges in Dharmapuri DT, also total number of assistant Professor in those 28 colleges are 1021 (approx)	First stage (probability sampling) Simple Random Sampling. Second Stage (Non-probability sampling) Convenience Sampling method is used and the sample size is arrived.

7. REVIEW OF LITERATURE

Guangdong Wu *et al.* (2022) sought to explore how job stress, specifically in the form of role ambiguity and role conflict, impacts the job burnout and job performance of construction project managers in China. The study employed the Job Demand Resource (JD-R) method. Findings indicated that role ambiguity negatively influences both job burnout and job performance, while role conflict only has an adverse effect on job burnout. Additionally, career counseling was found to negatively moderate job burnout and performance.

Iman Seyed moharrami *et al.* (2021) have determined the job burnout and related factors in the medical universities at Iran. For this study they select 250 employees from various universities and data has been collected. Tools used for this study is standard Maslach Burnout Inventory (MBI) and cross sectional study. Result revealed that there is significant relationship between organisational climate and job burnout and no such relationship between age, gender and work type with job burnout.

Inger Arvidsson1, Ulf Leo, Anna Larsson, Carita Hakansson, Roger Persson and Jonas Bjork (2020) have studied burnout among faculty members in Sweden. Around 310 Swedish faculty members are selected randomly and data have been collected. The result of this study reveals that most of the faculty members experience job burnout in both cases (quantitative and qualitative). Self-efficacy and higher job demand have higher impact on the job burnout.

8. STRESS

Faculty members experience stress as an exaggeration of negative thoughts influenced by external factors. Stress results from external elements shaping the internal emotions of individuals. Prolonged emotional states of faculty members can intensify when they face challenges in managing their emotions due to specific circumstances. This can impact both the psychological and physiological aspects of their lives. For instance, faculty members may commonly experience stress in situations where decisions are made for them, where they have limited control and options, where they feel unprepared, where fairness is in question, and where the consequences of failure are significant or unpredictable.

8.1 How You Feel When Stressed?

- Irritable
- Aggressive
- Impatient or twisted up
- Over-troubled
- Anxious
- Nervous or apprehensive
- Like your contemplations are dashing and you can't turn off
- Depressed
- Uninterested throughout everyday life
- Like you've lost your comical inclination
- A feeling of fear
- Worried about your wellbeing
- Unable to have fun

8.2 How Your Body Reacts to Stress?

At the point when you're confronted with stress, certain hormones (synthetic concoctions) in your body are discharged. These hormones trigger numerous adjustments in your body. For example, your:

Body weight may rise
Heart may pound
Muscles may fix
Stomach may get tense

8.3 How to Identify Stress

These are a portion of the side effects that are markers of an excess of weight that can emerge out of work, home, any blend of, or perhaps every one of the three. It is here and there simpler for another person to perceive worry in you yet not all that simple to remember it yourself. It is anything but difficult to state the indications will leave however they may not and don't overlook you may need to go to see your GP if the side effects are enduring.

Table 2

	Mental Signs		*Enthusiastic Signs*
•	Inability to think or settle on straightforward choices	•	Cheerrful
•	Memory slips	•	Irritable
•	Becoming rather dubious	•	Mood swings
•	Easily occupied	•	Extra delicate to analysis
•	Less natural and inventive	•	Defensive
•	Worrying	•	Feeling crazy
•	Negative reasoning	•	Lack of inspiration
•	Depression and nervousness	•	Angry
		•	Frustrated
		•	Lack of certainty
		•	Lack of confidence

	Physical Signs		*Social Signs*
•	Aches/torments and muscle strain/granulating teeth	•	No time for unwinding or pleasurable exercises
•	Frequent colds/diseases	•	Increased dependence on liquor, smoking, caffeine, recreational or illicit medications
•	Allergies/rashes/skin aggravations	•	Becoming an obsessive worker

	Physical Signs		***Social Signs***
•	Constipation/the runs/IBS	•	Poor time the executives as well as poor measures of work
•	Weight misfortune or increase	•	Absenteeism
•	Indigestion/acid reflux/ulcers	•	Self-disregard/change in appearance
•	Hyperventilating/protuberance in the throat/pins and needles	•	Social withdrawal
•	Dizziness/palpitations	•	Relationship issues
•	Panic assaults/sickness	•	Insomnia or waking tired
•	Physical tiredness	•	Reckless
•	Menstrual changes/loss of moxie/sexual issues	•	Aggressive/outrage upheavals
•	Heart issues/hypertension	•	Nervous
		•	Uncharacteristically lying

9. DATA ANAYSIS AND INTERPRETATION

Table 3: Gender of Respondents

Gender	*Frequency*	*Percentage*
Male	132	66
Female	68	33
Total	**200**	**100**

Source: Secondary Data.

Table 3 shows, out of 200 respondents 132 (66%) of respondents are male while 68 (34%) of respondents belong to female category. Therefore majority 132 (66%) of the respondents belong to female category.

Table 4: Age of Respondents

Age	*Frequency*	*Percentage*
less than 25	58	29
26–35 years	60	30
36–45 years	46	23
above 45 years	36	18
Total	200	100

Source: Secondary Data.

Table 4 shows, out of 200 respondents 58 (29%) of respondents are less than 25 years of age while 60 (30%) of respondents belong to 26–35 years of age, while 146 (23%) of respondents belong to 36–45 years of age and 18 (18%) of respondents belong to are above 45 years of age. Therefore majority of the respondents 60 (30%) are 26 to 35 years of age.

Table 5: Qualification of Respondents

Qualification	*Frequency*	*Percentage*
Post Graduate	128	64
Doctorate	70	35
Post Doctorate	2	1
Total	**200**	**100**

Source: Secondary Data.

Table 5 shows, out of 200 respondents 128 (64%) of respondents are post graduate while 70 (35%) of respondents are doctorates, while 2 (1%) of respondents are did post doctorate degree. Therefore majority of the respondents are 128 (64%) post graduates.

Table 6: Designation of Respondents

Designation	*Frequency*	*Percentage*
Assistant Professor	104	52
Associate Professor	66	33
Professor	30	15
Total	**200**	**100**

Source: Secondary Data.

Table 6 shows, out of 200 respondents 104 (52%) of respondents are assistant professor while 66 (33%) of respondents are associate professors, and 30 (15%) of respondents belong to professor category. Therefore majority of respondents 104 (52%) are working as Assistant Professors.

Table 7: Experience of Respondents

Designation	*Frequency*	*Percentage*
Less than 10 years	54	27
10–20 years	106	53
above 20 years	40	20
Total	**200**	**100**

Source: Secondary Data.

Table 7 shows, out of 200 respondents 54 (27%) of respondents are having less than 10 years of experience, 106 (53%) of respondents are having 10–20 years of experience, while 40 (20%) of respondents having more than 20 years of experience. Therefore majority of the respondents 106 (53%) are having 10–20 years of experience.

Table 8: Consequences of Stress in Workplace

Stress Factors	*Yes*	*No*	*Total*
Headache	122	78	200
	(61%)	(39%)	(100%)
Frustration	134	66	200
	(67%)	(33%)	(100%)
Irritation	104	96	200
	(52%)	(48%)	(100%)
Fatigue end of the day	104	96	200
	(52%)	(48%)	(100%)
Neck Pain	17	183	200
	(8.5%)	(91.5%)	100
Body Pain	132	68	200
	(66%)	(34%)	100

Source: Secondary Data.

Table 8 shows that out of 200 respondents, 122 (61%) respondents are encountered the headache while high stress in work place and 78 (39%) respondents does not have headache in work place, thus it is inferred that majority of the respondents are encountered the headache in work place due to over stress. 134 (67%) respondents are encountered the frustration while high stress in work place and 66 (33%) respondents does not have any frustration in work place, thus it is inferred that majority of the respondents are encountered the frustration in work place due to over stress. And 104 (52%) respondents are encountered the irritation while high stress in work place and 96 (48%) respondents does not get irritation in work place, thus it is inferred that majority of the respondents are encountered the irritation in work place due to over stress. And 104 (54%) respondents are encountered the fatigue while high stress in work place and 96 (48%) respondents does not get fatigue in work place. And 132 (66%) respondents are encountered the body pain while high stress in work place and 68 (34%) respondents does not get body pain in work place due to stress, thus it is inferred that majority of the respondents are encountered the body pain in work place due to over stress.

10. FINDINGS

- Therefore majority 132 (66%) of the respondents belong to female category.
- Greater part of the respondents 60 (30%) are 26 to 35 years of age.
- Maximum of the respondents are 128 (64%) post graduates.
- Therefore majority of respondents 104 (52%) are working as Assistant Professors.
- Greater part of the respondents 106 (53%) are having 10–20 years of experience.

11. SUGGESTIONS

- This particular study may help to improve the administration and satisfaction level, culture and climates. Also improve the process of teaching and learning to get good results.
- I suggest all top managements to maintain good relationship with their faculty members were they can discuss the problems and find the solution related to stress, mental health and burnout.
- Top management appointing some experts, psychologists and counselors to rectify faculties stress.
- Meditation and Yoga classes and art of living programs may conduct to overcome the stress and burnout.
- Top management should plan for Faculty Development Programs twice in a semester. It will help to improve the efficiency of junior faculty members also they learn something about new.
- Faculties working in private institutions have high level of stress so private institute management is requested to conduct programs regarding mental health in order to improve cognitive and intellectual performance as well as problem solving ability among faculty members.

12. CONCLUSION

This study aimed to demonstrate the impact of faculty members' burnout and stress on their physical and mental well-being. This study contributes to raising faculty member satisfaction levels while also improving the quality and efficacy of instruction in higher education. Because they are the only ones who can advance higher education and enhance research activities, faculty members are the backbone of the institution and the country. The country's higher education system should be improved by faculty assistance from both public and private institutions.

EFERENCES

[1] Kothari, C.R., "Research Methodology Methods and Techniques", Second Edition, *New Age International (P) Ltd,* 2004.

[2] Prasanna Chandra, Human Resource Management, 9th edition, *Tata McGraw Hill*, 2012.

[3] Richard, I. Levin and David, S. Rubin, "Statistics for Management" 7th Edition, *Pearson Education,* 2002.

[4] Sharma, A.M. "Personnel and HRM", *Himalaya Publishing House*, 2015.

[5] Robert, L. Mathis and John, H. Jackson, Human Resource Management, *Cenage*, 2007.

[6] Jeffrey, A. Mello, Strategic Human Resource Management, *Tata McGrew Hill*, 2012.

[7] Abdulaziz, Aflakseir and Olya, Nemati (2018). Association between Work Related Stress and Burnout Amonga Group of the Elementary and High College Faculty members in Zarrin-DashtFars. *International Jornal for College Health*. 2018 April; 5(2): e64096. doi: 10.5812/intjsh.64096.

[8] Akhtar, S. and Lee, J.S. (2010). Job burnout: toward an integration of two dominant resource-based models. *Psychological Reports*, 107(1), 193–208.

[9] Ali, Qadimi and Praveena, K.B. (2013). Occupational Stress and Job Burnout among Primary College Faculty members. *Indian Streams Research Journal*, Volume 3, Issue 8, Sept. 2013 ISSN 2230-7850.

[10] Amiri, M., Asadi, M.R. and Delabari, Raqeb F. (2011). The study of job burnout among Bank staff, and approaches to improve it. *Journal of Business Commercial Managementm* 3(7), 37–56.

[11] Anand, K. (2011). A Pilot Study on Influence of Organizational Role Stress on Perceived Burnout among Military Aircrew. *Ind. J. Aerospace Med.,* 55(2), 2011 IJASM 2011; 55(2): 21–27.

[12] Asadi, H. (1997). The amount of job satisfaction and job burnout among staff in Shahd Beheshti University of Medical Sciences based on Herzberg's two-factor theory. *Master's thesis of Educational Administration, Islamic Azad University*.

[13] Bahrami, F. and Mokhtari, S. (2008). The amount of job burnout and its influencing factors among university professors. *Career Counseling and Organizational Quarterly 2(2)*.

A Study on Consumer Purchasing Behavior and the Influence of Online Reviews on Buying Decisions within E-commerce Platforms

K.M. Venkataram[1] and E. Eswara Reddy[2]

[1]Ph.D Scholar, CMR University

[2]Professor School of Economics and Commerce, CMR University

E-mail: [1]venkataramkm@gmail.com

ABSTRACT: *Consumer behavior in e-commerce platforms is a dynamic area of study, particularly with the proliferation of online shopping. This research investigates the intricate relationship between consumer purchasing behavior and the influence of online reviews on buying decisions within e-commerce platforms. Drawing upon existing literature, the study examines factors driving consumer behavior in online shopping environments and explores the significant role played by online reviews in shaping consumer perceptions and purchase decisions. Key factors influencing the impact of online reviews, such as review volume, valence, and reviewer credibility, are analyzed. Moreover, the study considers implications for e-commerce platforms and businesses, highlighting the importance of actively managing and leveraging online reviews to enhance online reputation, build trust with customers, and ultimately drive sales. By gaining insights into these dynamics, businesses can develop more effective marketing strategies and improve the overall shopping experience for online consumers in the competitive landscape of e-commerce.*

Keywords: Buying Decision, Consumer, Online Reviews.

1. INTRODUCTION

In the contemporary digital era, the landscape of consumer behavior and purchasing patterns has undergone a significant transformation, largely influenced by the emergence and rapid expansion of e-commerce platforms. With the convenience of shopping from the comfort of their homes and the abundance of options available at their fingertips, consumers are increasingly turning towards online channels to fulfill their shopping needs. In this dynamic environment, understanding the intricate nuances of consumer purchasing behavior within e-commerce platforms has become imperative for businesses to thrive and succeed.

This research endeavors to delve into the multifaceted realm of consumer behavior within the context of e-commerce platforms, with a particular focus on the pivotal role played by online reviews in shaping consumers' buying decisions. As consumers are bombarded with a plethora of choices, the significance of online reviews as a source of information and social proof cannot be overstated. Consequently, investigating the extent to which online reviews influence consumers' perceptions, preferences, and ultimately, their purchasing decisions is of paramount importance.

The primary objective of this study is to empirically analyze the relationship between consumer purchasing behavior and online reviews within the realm of e-commerce platforms. By employing a comprehensive research methodology encompassing both qualitative and quantitative approaches, this study aims to elucidate the underlying mechanisms through which online reviews impact various facets of consumer behavior, including product evaluation, trust formation, brand loyalty, and purchase intentions.

Furthermore, this research endeavors to identify the factors that contribute to the credibility and persuasiveness of online reviews, as well as the potential moderating variables that may influence the strength of the relationship between online reviews and buying decisions. Factors such as review characteristics (e.g., valence, volume, recency), reviewer characteristics (e.g., credibility, expertise, similarity), and situational factors (e.g., product type, purchase stage, platform interface) will be examined to provide a comprehensive understanding of the nuances underlying consumer reliance on online reviews.

Ultimately, the insights gleaned from this research are expected to have significant implications for e-commerce practitioners, marketers, and policymakers alike. By shedding light on the dynamics of consumer purchasing behavior and the pivotal role of online reviews within e-commerce platforms, this study aims to inform strategic decision-making processes aimed at enhancing consumer satisfaction, fostering brand loyalty, and driving sustainable business growth in the digital marketplace.

E-commerce platforms are digital frameworks or online marketplaces that facilitate the buying and selling of goods and services over the internet. These platforms provide a virtual space where businesses and consumers can interact, conduct transactions, and exchange products or services without the need for physical presence. E-commerce platforms encompass a wide array of websites, applications, and online storefronts that cater to diverse industries and market segments.

2. REVIEW OF LITERATURE

1. **Ami Natuz Zahara *et al.* (2021)** Centered on studying the seller's reputation and online customer reviews, conclusions can be drawn regarding consumer trust and purchase decisions in C2C E-Commerce

in Medan. The seller's reputation significantly influences consumer trust and purchase decisions. Likewise, online customer reviews play a crucial role in shaping consumer trust and purchase decisions. Trust itself positively. impacts consumer purchase decisions. Overall, the seller's reputation and online reviews are key factors in determining consumer trust and purchase behavior in Medan's C2C E-Commerce platform.

2. **R. Hurriyati *et al.* (2017)** The internet, a major information source for consumers, facilitates sharing opinions on goods/services. Online reviews aid decision-making. This study examines online reviews' impact on e-commerce service use. 435 Google Play users were surveyed using path analysis. Results reveal that positive/negative reviews strongly influence service usage decisions. In conclusion, online reviews significantly affect e-commerce service adoption, offering insights for future research and practical applications.
3. **Semila fernades *et al.* (2022)** This study develops and validates a scale to assess the impact of online reviews on consumer purchases. Analyzing data from 431 young online shoppers, four factors emerged: source credibility, volume, language/comprehension, and relevance. Confirmatory factor analysis confirms the scale's validity. This standardized tool benefits online retailers by aiding consumers in decision-making, highlighting the importance of online reviews as key sources of product and brand information for online purchases.
4. **Rajesh Panda *et al.* (2020)** The OR Scale is a reliable tool for assessing online reviews, comprising four dimensions: Source Credibility, Volume, Language Comprehension, and Relevance. These dimensions evaluate trustworthiness, quantity and ratings, content quality, and contextual relevance of reviews. Scholars and practitioners can analyze these dimensions across cultures and demographics, emphasizing trust-building between customers and sellers. The scale aids consumers in decision-making and informs retailers' response strategies, enhancing the shopping experience on websites.
5. **Asad Ahmad *et al.* (2015**) The rapid expansion of technology, notably the World Wide Web (www), has revolutionized global dynamics. With widespread computer use, internet interaction has become ubiquitous, serving as a vital medium for information exchange, services, and commerce. This has propelled the growth of online shopping, particularly in countries with advanced marketing infrastructure. The internet not only connects users but also enables seamless cross-border transactions. Distinct from physical markets, online consumer behavior requires further investigation to comprehend its drivers. This study endeavors to offer valuable insights for both marketers and researchers.
6. **R. Yuvaraj *et al.* (2022)** Online customer reviews, product/service suggestions, and peer feedback are increasingly influential in customer

decisions. However, the diverse goals, functions, and characteristics of online review platforms have not been fully examined in existing literature. As user-generated content profoundly impacts business revenue and reputation, organizations struggle to effectively monitor and respond to customer feedback. Understanding consumer review platform features and their influence on buyer decisions is vital for companies. Our study identifies key factors shaping customer buying behavior, such as reliability, trustworthiness, genuineness, client reviews, education, and consumer beliefs.

7. **Dr. S.A.N. Shazuli Ibrahim (2023)** This research examines how online reviews influence consumer purchasing decisions in e-commerce. As online shopping expands, reviews become more critical for consumers. Factors including credibility, sentiment, volume, and reviewer characteristics are explored. Through literature analysis and empirical data, the study emphasizes the significance of online reviews and offers recommendations for businesses to enhance customer satisfaction and sales. It provides valuable insights and practical suggestions for leveraging reviews to gain a competitive edge in e-commerce.
8. **Efthymios Constantinides *et al.* (2016)** Online consumer reviews, recommendations, and peer opinions increasingly shape customer decisions. However, differences in objectives, functions, and characteristics among online review platforms are understudied in customer adoption and preference literature. As these reviews significantly impact business sales, monitoring and responding to them pose managerial challenges. Companies need to continuously identify and understand review platforms to effectively respond. This study identifies four main types of platforms and assesses consumer opinions on their characteristics and impact on buying behavior. Findings emphasize the crucial role of platform credibility and usability in influencing consumer trust and reliance on reviews for decision-making.
9. **Dr. Christian Weismayer *et al.* (2023)** The surge in technology and e-commerce has revolutionized online product reviews, enabling remote opinion formation by customers. This transition from physical stores to online platforms allows consumers to voluntarily share experiences, impacting others' choices. Crucial product details, like ingredients and performance, shape consumer decisions significantly. This thesis explores the impact of online reviews in the beauty and personal care industry, aiming to understand their influence on customer choices. Through an online survey with 200 participants, various review characteristics are analyzed for their relevance in purchasing decisions. Results highlight the importance of review in formativeness, valence, credibility, and readability to consumers. E-commerce managers can use these insights to grasp the significance of online reviews in consumer behavior.

10. **Le Bo *et al.* (2023)** Many consumers rely on online reviews when making purchasing decisions. These reviews typically contain both positive and negative contradictory opinions. Previous studies have acknowledged the influence of contradictory online reviews (CORs) on consumer behavior. However, existing research has primarily focused on single dimensions of CORs. This study delves into how CORs impact consumer decisions by considering two dimensions: the proportion of positive and negative reviews and emotional arousal. Results from a study involving 306 Chinese consumers demonstrate that CORs negatively affect online purchase decisions, primarily by influencing perceived risk. This study contributes to the literature on online reviews and offers insights for e-retailers on navigating CORs' effects on consumer behavior. Theoretical and practical implications of the findings are also discussed.
11. **Divya Kalra *et al.* (2023)-** Marketers should assess the accessibility of digital resources for young demographics before launching a product online. Pre-market research is crucial for understanding customer preferences, especially in digital marketing. Efforts should be made to educate consumers about digital marketing to mitigate potential risks, as most consumers tend to be risk-averse. It's essential for readers and users to be aware of all digital marketing platforms and utilize them effectively while exercising caution.
12. **George La˘za˘roiu *et al.* (2020)** The evidence reviewed indicates that social platform users' purchase intentions are influenced by online trust and perceived risk. However, research on consumer decision-making in social commerce platforms is lacking. Our study addresses this by examining the relationship between online purchase intentions, social commerce adoption behavior, trust, and risk factors, considering source credibility. We identify areas for future research, including psychological determinants of consumer engagement in social media, price evaluation mechanisms, types of perceived risk, and repurchasing behavior. Additionally, future studies should explore how the adoption of mobile payment services impacts impulsive buying behavior, especially concerning online product reviews.
13. **Tao Chen *et al.* (2022*)*** This study utilized eye-tracking to explore the impact of online product reviews on consumer purchasing decisions. The research developed a conceptual framework and conducted empirical analysis, focusing on the moderation role of gender and visual attention in comments. Results revealed that consumers, especially females, paid more attention to negative comments than positive ones. Visual browsing behavior correlated significantly with purchase intention, but consumers struggled to identify false comments. This study enhances understanding of how online reviews influence shopping behavior, particularly regarding gender differences and attentional bias. Practitioners should address negative comments

promptly and tailor product information based on consumer characteristics.

14. **Abdulaziz Elwalda *et al.* (2020)** This paper explores the widespread use of online customer reviews (OCRs) and their influence on customer purchase intention and sales. The rise of online communities has enabled individuals to share evaluations and recommendations about products, making OCRs a crucial source of information affecting consumer decisions. While there are mixed findings in the literature regarding the effect of OCRs on consumer behavior, it is evident that they play a significant role in shaping consumer decision-making.
15. **Eunice Njoki Kibandi *et al.* (2017)** Perceived risks in online purchasing have a negative impact on consumer behavior. Respondents expressed concerns about product quality uncertainty, receiving malfunctioning items, settling disputes, and delivery issues, indicating a preference for safety and trust when shopping online with Jumia.
16. **Nina Isabel Holleschovsky *et al.* (2018)** online consumer reviews, product recommendations, and peer opinions are increasingly influential in the customer's decision-making process. However, little attention has been paid in the literature to the functional characteristics of different online review platforms and their impact on consumer adoption and preference. Given their significance for business sales and reputation management, monitoring and responding to customer reviews has become a major managerial challenge. This study identifies four main types of online review platforms—retail websites, independent reviewing platforms, video-sharing platforms, and personal blogs—and analyzes consumer opinions on their characteristics and impact on purchasing decisions. Results highlight the importance of platform credibility and usability in influencing consumer trust and reliance on reviews during decision-making.
17. **Lisa Hankin *et al.* (2017)** In the past, consumers relied on expert reviews like consumer reports. Nowadays, they heavily rely on online user reviews to mitigate risks in virtual shopping. Consumers use these reviews to ensure product accuracy and seller reliability, benefiting from platforms like eBay with transparent reputation systems. Research indicates that user review content influences sales probability and product prices. However, findings are often limited to specific product categories, not universally applicable. This study examines the role of user reviews across product categories, revealing that consumers prioritize different review attributes based on the product type. For sellers or household products, they focus on average ratings and negative reviews rather than solely seeking "excellent" ratings.
18. **Komal Rawat (2023)** The ascendancy of social media has made online product reviews pivotal in shaping purchasing decisions. They offer crucial feedback on e-commerce platforms, accessible across diverse

channels such as retailer websites and brand blogs, facilitated by widespread internet and smartphone access. These reviews serve as vital marketing assets, significantly affecting consumer buying behavior and product sales. This study delves into the correlation between reviews, ratings, and consumer purchasing patterns to discern their impact on product sales.

3. OBJECTIVES OF THE STUDY

1. To investigate the factors influencing consumer purchasing behavior within e-commerce platforms.
2. To analyze the role of online reviews in shaping consumer perceptions and buying decisions.
3. To assess the significance of different types of online reviews (e.g., star ratings, written reviews) in influencing consumer purchasing behavior.
4. To explore the impact of various demographic factors (e.g., age, gender, income) on the reliance on online reviews for purchasing decisions.
5. To identify the trustworthiness and credibility of online reviews as perceived by consumers.
6. To examine the relationship between the volume and sentiment of online reviews and their impact on consumer buying decisions.

3.1 Scope of the Study

- Understanding the factors that influence consumer purchasing behavior in the context of e-commerce platforms, including psychological, social, and cultural factors.
- Exploring consumer decision-making processes, including information search, evaluation of alternatives, and post-purchase behavior.
- Examining different types of e-commerce platforms such as marketplace platforms (e.g., Amazon, eBay), retailer-owned platforms (e.g., Walmart.com, Target.com), and specialized platforms (e.g., Etsy for handmade goods).
- Considering the unique features and functionalities of each platform that may affect consumer behavior and the influence of online reviews.
- Investigating the types of online reviews available on e-commerce platforms (e.g., star ratings, written reviews, video reviews).
- Assessing the credibility, reliability, and trustworthiness of online reviews from the perspective of consumers.
- Analyzing the impact of online review characteristics such as volume, sentiment, and recency on consumer buying decisions.
- Examining how online reviews influence various stages of the consumer buying process, including product discovery, evaluation, purchase, and post-purchase behavior.

- Identifying the extent to which consumers rely on online reviews compared to other sources of information (e.g., product descriptions, brand reputation) when making purchasing decisions.
- Investigating demographic factors (e.g., age, gender, income, education) and psychographic factors (e.g., lifestyle, personality) that may moderate the influence of online reviews on buying decisions.
- Exploring differences in the influence of online reviews across different product categories or industries.

3.2 Benefits

1. **Insights for E-commerce Platforms and Retailers**: Understanding how online reviews influence consumer purchasing behavior provides valuable insights for e-commerce platforms and retailers. They can leverage these insights to optimize their platforms, improve customer experiences, and enhance the effectiveness of online review systems to drive sales.
2. **Enhanced Marketing Strategies**: Findings from the study can inform marketers about the importance of online reviews in shaping consumer perceptions and decisions. Marketers can develop more targeted marketing strategies that emphasize the value of positive reviews and address any concerns raised by negative reviews.
3. **Improved Product Development**: By analyzing consumer preferences and sentiments expressed in online reviews, businesses can gain valuable feedback for product development and innovation. This can lead to the creation of products that better meet customer needs and preferences, ultimately increasing customer satisfaction and loyalty.
4. **Building Trust and Credibility**: Positive online reviews can help build trust and credibility for both e-commerce platforms and individual products. Consumers are more likely to trust and purchase products with a higher number of positive reviews, leading to increased sales and revenue for businesses.
5. **Competitive Advantage**: Businesses that actively monitor and manage online reviews can gain a competitive advantage in the e-commerce market. By consistently receiving positive reviews and addressing negative feedback promptly and effectively, businesses can differentiate themselves from competitors and attract more customers.
6. **Consumer Empowerment**: Research on consumer purchasing behavior and online reviews empowers consumers to make more informed purchasing decisions. By understanding the influence of online reviews, consumers can better evaluate products and services, leading to increased satisfaction with their purchases.
7. **Academic and Theoretical Contributions**: The findings of the study can contribute to academic knowledge and theories related to consumer

behavior, online reviews, and e-commerce platforms. Researchers can build upon these findings to further explore the complex dynamics of consumer decision-making in the digital age.

8. **Policy Implications**: Insights from the research can also have policy implications, particularly in areas related to consumer protection and online advertising regulations. Policymakers can use the findings to develop regulations that promote transparency and fairness in online reviews, ensuring that consumers are not misled by fraudulent or deceptive practices.

3.3 Challenges

1. **Data Collection**: Gathering comprehensive and reliable data on consumer purchasing behavior and online reviews across various e-commerce platforms can be challenging. Access to large datasets from multiple sources while ensuring data accuracy and consistency may require significant resources and cooperation from platform owners and retailers.
2. **Data Bias and Quality**: Online reviews may suffer from bias, such as fake reviews, spam, or manipulation by businesses. Researchers need to implement robust methods to identify and filter out low-quality or fraudulent reviews to ensure the integrity of the data and the validity of the findings.
3. **Privacy Concerns**: Ethical considerations regarding consumer privacy and data protection must be addressed when collecting and analyzing online review data. Researchers must adhere to ethical guidelines and obtain informed consent from participants, particularly when accessing sensitive information related to individuals' purchasing behavior and preferences.
4. **Sample Representativeness**: Ensuring that the study sample is representative of the target population can be challenging, especially in the context of diverse consumer demographics and preferences. Researchers may encounter difficulties in recruiting participants from different demographic groups, leading to potential biases in the study findings.
5. **Temporal Dynamics**: Consumer purchasing behavior and online review trends are subject to temporal fluctuations influenced by various factors such as seasonality, market trends, and external events. Researchers need to account for these temporal dynamics when designing the study and interpreting the results to ensure their relevance and applicability over time.
6. **Complexity of Consumer Behavior**: Consumer purchasing behavior is influenced by a myriad of factors, including individual preferences, socio-cultural norms, and psychological motivations. Understanding the

complex interplay between these factors and the influence of online reviews requires sophisticated research methodologies and analytical techniques.

7. **Platform Differences**: E-commerce platforms vary in terms of their features, user interfaces, and review systems, which may affect consumer behavior and the impact of online reviews. Researchers need to account for these platform differences and consider their implications when analyzing the data and drawing conclusions.
8. **Causal Inference**: Establishing causal relationships between online reviews and consumer purchasing behavior poses a challenge due to potential confounding variables and reverse causality. Researchers must employ appropriate statistical methods, such as causal inference techniques or experimental designs, to minimize bias and strengthen causal claims.
9. **Dynamic Nature of Online Reviews**: Online reviews are dynamic and can change over time in response to new product releases, marketing campaigns, or external events. Researchers need to capture these dynamics and analyze longitudinal data to understand how online reviews evolve and influence consumer behavior over time.
10. **Interpretation of Sentiment**: Analyzing the sentiment expressed in online reviews accurately requires natural language processing (NLP) techniques that can handle nuances, sarcasm, and context-dependent meanings. Researchers must address challenges related to sentiment analysis, including ambiguity and subjectivity, to derive meaningful insights from the data.

4. CONCLUSION

The study on Consumer Purchasing Behavior and the Influence of Online Reviews on Buying Decisions within E-commerce Platforms sheds light on the intricate relationship between consumer behavior and online reviews in the context of digital commerce. The research underscores the significant impact of online reviews on consumer purchasing decisions within e-commerce platforms. Online reviews serve as a vital source of information for consumers, influencing product evaluation, trust formation, and ultimately, purchase intentions. Positive reviews can enhance consumer confidence and contribute to increased sales, while negative reviews can deter potential buyers and undermine brand reputation. The study highlights the multifaceted nature of consumer behavior within e-commerce environments. Factors such as product category, consumer demographics, and platform features play pivotal roles in shaping the influence of online reviews on buying decisions. Understanding these nuances is crucial for businesses to tailor their marketing strategies and optimize the effectiveness of online review systems. The research underscores the importance of trust and credibility in online reviews. Consumers place a premium on authentic and reliable reviews, emphasizing the need for transparency and integrity in the review ecosystem. Businesses must prioritize efforts to combat fake reviews, spam, and manipulation to maintain consumer trust and foster a positive online shopping experience. The study identifies opportunities for businesses to leverage online reviews as a strategic asset for competitive advantage. By actively engaging with customers, soliciting feedback, and responding to reviews in a timely manner, businesses can cultivate a positive online reputation and differentiate themselves in the crowded e-commerce landscape. The findings of this study underscore the critical role of online reviews in shaping consumer purchasing behavior within e-commerce platforms. By understanding the factors influencing the influence of online reviews, businesses can develop targeted strategies to harness the power of user-generated content and enhance the online shopping experience for consumers. Moving forward, continued research and innovation in this area are essential to adapt to evolving consumer preferences and technological advancements in the digital marketplace.

REFERENCES

[1] Hurriyati, R., Lisnawati, L. and Rhamdani, F. (2017). Online consumer reviews on using E-Shopping service of E-Commerce. *IOP Conference Series: Materials Science and Engineering*, *180*, 012287. https://doi.org/10.1088/1757-899x/180/1/012287

[2] Zahara, A.N., Rini, E.S. and Sembiring, B.K.F. (2021). The Influence of Seller Reputation and Online Customer Reviews towards Purchase Decisions through Consumer Trust from C2C E-Commerce Platform Users in Medan, North Sumatera, Indonesia. *International Journal of Research*, *8*(2), 422–438. https://doi.org/10.52403/ijrr.20210255

[3] Fernandes, S., Panda, R., Venkatesh, V., Swar, B.N. and Shi, Y. (2022). Measuring the impact of online reviews on consumer purchase decisions—A scale development study. *Journal of Retailing and Consumer Services*, *68*, 103066. https://doi.org/10.1016/j.jretconser.2022.103066

[4] Zhang, Z., Ye, Q., Law, R. and Li, Y. (2010). The impact of e-word-of-mouth on the online popularity of restaurants: A comparison of consumer reviews and editor reviews. *International Journal of Hospitality Management*, *29*(4), 694–700. https://doi.org/10.1016/j.ijhm.2010.02.002

[5] Zhou, Y. (2022). Research on the impact of online reviews on consumer buying behaviour. *SHS Web of Conferences*, *148*, 03056.

[6] https://doi.org/10.1051/shsconf/202214803056

[7] Soleimani, M. (2021). Buyers' trust and mistrust in e-commerce platforms: a synthesizing literature review. *Information Systems and e-Business Management*, *20*(1), 57–78. https://doi.org/10.1007/s10257-021-00545-0

[9] Duan, W., Gu, B. and Whinston, A.B. (2005). Do online reviews matter? - An Empirical investigation of panel data. *Social Science Research Network*.

[10] Kibandi, E.N. (2019). *Impact of Online Shopping on Consumer Buying Behaviour: A Case Study of Jumia Kenya*. http://repository.mua.ac.ke/2750/

[11] https://papers.ssrn.com/sol3/Delivery.cfm/SSRN_ID652123_code412577.pdf?abstractid=616262&rulid=234955&mirid=1

[12] Akbar, A.R., Kalis, M.C.I., Afifah, N., Purmono, B.B. and Yakin, I. (2023). The influence of product packaging design and online customer review on brand awareness and their impact on online purchase intention. *South Asian Research Journal of Business and Management*, *5*(1), 10–18. https://doi.org/10.36346/sarjbm.2023.v05i01.002

Artificial Intelligence as a Propelling Factor for Advancements in FinTech

Arnab K. Ganguly[1] and Purna Prasad Arcot[2]

School of Management, CMR University, 5 Bhuvanagiri,
OMBR Layout, Bengaluru,Karnataka, India
E-mail: [1]arnabkumar.ganguly@cmr.edu.in; [2]purnaprasad.a@cmr.edu.in

ABSTRACT: *This paper explores the transformative impact of Artificial Intelligence (AI) on Financial Technology (FinTech). With the rapid evolution of digital technologies, AI has become a crucial antecedent in reshaping financial services. The study examines various applications of AI in FinTech, including improvements in payment systems, personal investments and online lending. Utilizing insights from recent research and industry examples, the paper highlights how AI-driven innovations are not only enhancing efficiency and customer experience but also introducing new challenges, issues and considerations. The integration of AI in FinTech is altering traditional financial paradigms, prompting a discussion on the future of financial services in an AI-dominated landscape.*

Keywords: Artificial Intelligence (AI), FinTech industry, Natural Language Processing (NLP).

1. INTRODUCTION

Financial technology, colloquially known as FinTech, encapsulates the modern convergence of financial services with advancements in technology, with particular emphasis on applications within payments, personal investments, online lending, and digital currencies. As Gomber and other researchers articulate, FinTech epitomizes the nexus between contemporary Internet-related technologies, such as cloud computing and mobile internet, and the established business activities within the financial sector, including lending and transaction banking. (Gomber *et al.*, 2017). This evolution in the financial landscape denotes a shift toward innovation and disruption, compelling traditional financial institutions to respond to the heightened competition by embracing and investing in FinTech solutions. Unlike their traditional counterparts, FinTech firms leverage technology not merely as a tool but as a fundamental component to forge new business models and penetrate previously inaccessible market segments.

Artificial Intelligence (AI), as defined by Rich and further expounded upon in the context of finance by Deutsche Bank Research (2019), refers to the design and application of computer programs capable of acquiring and applying knowledge autonomously, without human intervention (Rich, 2009). This definition underscores the transformative potential of AI, positioning it as a critical driver within the FinTech ecosystem.

2. AI AS A DRIVER OF FINTECH

The potential of Artificial Intelligence (AI) within the realm of FinTech has been substantiated by researchers, who posit that FinTech transcends mere e-banking and digital consumer interfaces (Belanche *et al.*, 2019). It pivots on the advent of novel, technologically-facilitated instruments that cater to user demands. Within this framework, AI emerges as a dual-beneficiary agent, revolutionizingthe industry and propelling business value for firms.

Moreover, the literature indicates that intelligent technologies enhance frontline interactions between organizational personnel and clients, thus perpetually refining customer experience through AI's adaptive learning from such interactions. Innovations like virtual and augmented reality are being employed to augment sales experiences within the FinTech sector (Marinova *et al.*, 2017).

Other, independent studies further delineate the significance of AI in finance, stressing the imperative of real-time data analysis. Delays diminish data utility for commercial exploitation. AI empowers enterprises to scrutinize voluminous datasets promptly, enabling investment decisions and other value added actions previously unattainable (Ashta & Hermann, 2021). Additionally, AI facilitates the tailoring of customer-specific offers by discerning client contexts and purchasing patterns, thereby enhancing fraud prevention mechanisms in personal banking by analyzing behavioral data, locational information, and expediting such detections cost-effectively.

Within microfinance, AI addresses two primary challenges: the disproportionate transaction costs associated with small loans and the information asymmetry due to lack of borrower data. Innovations in online crowdlending and mobile banking have significantly reduced transaction costs. Concurrently, AI-driven credit scoring models, utilizing data from platforms such as Facebook and LinkedIn, have ameliorated the information deficit regarding borrowers, thus streamlining the disbursement of microloans (Bumacov, Ashta & Singh, 2017; Ashta, 2018).

Industry experts assert that FinTech lending is leveraging digitalization advancements from other sectors, utilizing data from e-commerce platforms and web-based aggregators. The sustainability of such data usage post-enforcement of stringent privacy regulations remains an area for future deliberation.

Furthermore, in addition to areas such as Payments and Lending, which have firmly established their FinTech presence, the Financial sector is witnessing disruption through 'Robo-Advisory'—an AI-based service offering that provides time-independent and ubiquitous access to financial advice. However, issues pertaining to customer trust persist as banks and financial institutions begin to adopt these services (Jung *et al.*, 2018). The trajectory of growth in this domain is evidenced by the management ofassets worth USD 880 trillion by Robo-Advisory services, with a Compound Annual Growth Rate (CAGR) of 30% in 2019. Projections by Statista forecast that assets under management by Robo- Advisors will reach USD 1,372 bn in 2023, with a CAGR of 13.46% from 2023 to 2027, resulting in an anticipated market size of USD 2,274 bn by 2027.

In examining AI's role specifically in Robo-Advisory within FinTech, scholars highlight that leveraging AI could significantly enhance product offerings and management practices, yielding benefits for both consumers and organizations (Jung *et al.*, 2018). The integration of AI in FinTech is contingent upon anorganization's ability to engage with humans on a social level, a concept referred to as 'human and automated social presence' by contemporaneous researchers (Han and Young, 2018).

Robo-advised markets have resulted in substantially reduced costs. For example, passive funds now charge a mere 0.03–0.09% of assets under management annually, which is markedly lower than the fees charged by active managers, often by a factor of twenty. The decreased cost of executing trades impliesthat new information is promptly reflected in company prices. Leading brokerage sites predict that retailtrading fees will eventually drop to zero. Similar trends are anticipated in other FinTech sectors where AI is making headway. This has given rise to several novel applications, some of which will be discussed in the subsequent sections.

3. NOVEL APPLICATIONS OF AI WITHIN FINTECH

The incorporation of Artificial Intelligence (AI) within the FinTech sector necessitates enhancements in product usability and service offerings. Despite these challenges, numerous innovative products utilizing AI's capabilities have emerged over the past few years.

In a seminal paper on AI applications in financial services, Qi and Xiao highlight three significant innovations warranting consideration (Qi and Xiao, 2018). One such innovation by Ant Financials in 2017, named "Smile to Pay," leverages deep learning algorithms for facial recognition, allowing customers to execute payments with a mere smile at a vending machine. This technology, when fortifiedwith robust security protocols and supported by legislative frameworks, has the potential to revolutionize payment methods, positioning the consumer's facial biometrics as a proxy for traditional payment instruments.

The "3-1-0" system, a paradigm for microloans, epitomizes the efficiency of AI in financial services. This system, represented by the metrics of three minutes for application processing, one second for decision-making, and zero human intervention, significantly reduces the cost of loan disbursal, evidenced by its application to millions of small traders in China. Ant Financials employs a synergy of technologies—Blockchain, AI, Security, Internet of Things (IoT), and Computing (BASIC)—to facilitate this system. Deep learning and Natural Language Processing (NLP) are integral to automating customer queries, with an astounding 97% of such interactions occurring without human mediation. In2017, the efficacy of this system was recognized as surpassing human performance in terms of customer satisfaction.

In the insurance sector, expeditious responses, equitable and precise estimates are paramount for customers, while insurers strive to deter fraudulent claims without compromising on Quality of Service(QoS). To this end, around 2018, Ping an in China introduced AI-driven services for insurance clients, enabling the filing of auto accident claims through the submission of photographs from the accident site. Rapid processing and immediate provision of payment estimates are enabled by advanced AI technologies, including image recognition and processing techniques that have been meticulously refined.

The acquisition of iZettle by PayPal for USD 2.2 billion underscores the value of data analytics in determining the creditworthiness of small merchants, a service now known as Zettle and operational in various countries. Mybucks, despite its subsequent acquisition and closure, innovatively utilized data from digital transactions and facial recognition to extend nano-loans to clients in the low-income bracket.

Ocrolus offers a document processing solution that amalgamates AI with human verification to enhancethe speed and accuracy of financial document analysis, claiming a 99% accuracy rate in document review. Widespread use of such systems will likely revolutionize analysis, alter the skillset needed forthe workforce and change the expectations of clients.

Zest AI distinguishes itself by leveraging myriad data points to foster transparency in lending practices, reportedly aiding lenders in reducing underwriting losses by approximately 35%. It is likely that underwriting for lending will be completely automated and will lead to lightning fast and near perfect decisioning.

Kasisto has developed a specialized conversational AI that assists customers with inquiries regarding their financial standings, expenditures, and savings. Usage at scale within large organizations may see near ubiquitous self-service by customers and a large part of customer service personnel may need to be reskilled for different tasks.

Furthermore, ThetaRay utilizes unsupervised machine learning algorithms to analyze vast datasets, enabling the detection of sophisticated money laundering and terrorist financing activities, which remain formidable challenges for banking institutions globally.

4. ISSUES AND RISKS

Apprehensions surrounding the utilization of Artificial Intelligence (AI) in the FinTech industry include the potential for market dominance by prominent technology conglomerates, specifically Google, Apple, Facebook and Amazon or GAFA in short, in the United States and Baidu, Alibaba and Tencent or BAT in China. Such dominance could marginalize established banking institutions and nascent FinTech entities, leading ultimately to the formation of oligopolies. (Ashta & Biot-Paquerot, 2018).

Market operators additionally express concerns regarding accountability for errors stemming from non-representative data. The integrity of data is imperative for its efficacious application in AI systems, concerns arise especially as data volume and variety burgeon. Current discourse lacks consensus on mechanisms to ensure data scientists select representative datasets and amalgamate extant knowledge to effectively mitigate bias (Pozen & Ruane, 2019). An illustrative case of such bias is the reported disproportionate rejection of loan applications from African American and Hispanic individuals by United States banks (Yale, 2018).

The pivot to AI as a fundamental component within FinTech implies a paradigm shift for legacy organizations. To remain competitive in an environment increasingly influenced by the AI and analytics proficiencies of technology leaders, these organizations must undertake a profound transformation of their core technological and data infrastructures to accommodate AI-augmented decision-making processes. Whether such organizations can successfully navigate this transition remains an open question (Blumberg *et al.*, 2023).

Scholars examining decision-making processes within organizations have posited numerous queries that necessitate resolution to realize the full potential of a synergistic human-machine work environment, which will likely soon be the norm with machines working side by side with humans (Shrestha *et al.*, 2019).

In the broader context, the assimilation of human-like AI capabilities challenges the sustainability of a collaborative labor division between AI systems and human employees. Recent analyses by McKinsey (Manyika *et al.*, 2017) suggest that approximately half of current occupational activities are susceptible to automation, potentially resulting in up to 15% of the global workforce being displaced. The emergentjob landscape is likely to demand a divergent skill set from that currently in vogue, a development that could impact the FinTech domain itself.

With advancement of AI, a shift towards collaborative work models, emphasizing the complementary strengths of humans and machines with cognition, will likely evolve. This will necessitate the formulation of regulations and laws to ensure that ethical and practical concerns related to the human workforce are adequately addressed. Due consideration of the social and economic implications of AI based automation remains crucial.

5. CONCLUSION

Artificial Intelligence (AI) has emerged as a pivotal antecedent to the FinTech industry's evolution, significantly enhancing customer engagement and enabling financial democratization. This paper has highlighted the dual-edged nature of AI's ascendancy on FinTech, addressing market consolidation risks and the ethical use of data. It underlines the urgency for incumbent financial institutions to evolve technologically to harness AI's potential fully. As automation reshapes the workforce, a balanced, equitable approach to AI integration is imperative.

While the future of FinTech, propelled by AI, promises greater inclusivity and personalization in financial services, it also carries with it dire possibilities for the workforce. It is paramount that this transition is managed with thoughtful governance to ensure that AI's trajectory remains beneficial to all stakeholders in the financial ecosystem, and there are minimal upheavals in human society (Daniel, 2023).

REFERENCES

[1] Ashta, A. (2018). News and trends in FinTech and digital microfinance: Why are European MFIs invisible? FIIB Business Review, 7(4), 232–243.

[2] Ashta, A. and Biot-Paquerot, G. (2018). FinTech evolution: Strategic value management issues in a fast-changing industry. *Strategic Change: Briefings in Entrepreneurial Finance*, 27(4), 301–312.

[3] Ashta, A. and Herrmann, H. (2021). Artificial intelligence and FinTech: An overview of opportunities and risks for banking investments and microfinance. *Strategic Change*, 30(3), 211–222.

[4] Belanche, D., Casaló, L.V. and Flavián, C. (2019). Artificial Intelligence in FinTech: understanding robo-advisors adoption among customers. *Industrial Management & Data Systems,* 119(7), 1411–1430.

[5] Blumberg, S., Isenberg, R., Kerr, D., Mitra, M. and Thomas, R. (2023). Beyond digital transformations: Modernizing core technology for the AI bank of the future. Retrieved from www.mckinsey.com/industries/financial-services/our-insights/beyond-digital-transformations-modernizing-core-technology-for-the-ai-bank-of-the-future

[6] Bumacov, V., Ashta, A. and Singh, P. (2017). Credit scoring: A historic recurrence in microfinance. Strategic Change,26(6), 543–554.

[7] Daniel, S. (2023). The Impact of Artificial Intelligence on Employment and Workforce Dynamics in Contemporary Society Author(s).

[8] Deutsche Bank Research. (2019). Artificial intelligence in banking. Retrieved from https://www.dbresearch.com/PROD/RPS_EN

[9] Gomber, P., Koch, J.A. and Siering, M. (2017). Digital Finance and FinTech: current research and future research directions. Journal of Business Economics, 87, 537–580.

[10] Jung, D., Dorner, V., Glaser, F. and Morana, S. (2018). Robo-advisory: digitalization and automation of financial advisory. Business & Information Systems Engineering, 60, 81–86.

[11] Jung, D., Dorner, V., Weinhardt, C. and Pusmaz, H. (2018). Designing a robo-advisor for risk-averse low-budget consumers. Electronic Markets, 28, 367–380.

[12] Manyika, J., Lund, S., Chui, M., Bughin, J., Woetzel, J., Batra, P. and Sanghvi, S. (2017). Jobs lost jobs gained: Workforce transitions in a time of automation. McKinsey Global Institute. Retrieved from www.mckinsey.com/featured-insights/future-of-work/jobs-lost-jobs-gained-what-the-future-of-work-will-mean-for-jobs-skills-and-wages

[13] Marinova, D., de Ruyter, K., Huang, M.H., Meuter, M.L. and Challagalla, G. (2017). Getting smart: Learning from technology-empowered frontline interactions. Journal of Service Research, 20(1), 29–42.

[14] Park, J.Y., Ryu, J.P. and Shin, H. J. (2016). Robo advisors for portfolio management. Advanced Science and TechnologyLetters, 141(1), 104–108.

[15] Pozen, R.C. and Ruane, J. (2019). What machine learning will mean for asset managers. Harvard Business ReviewDigital Articles. Retrieved from https://hbr.org/2019/12/what-machine-learning-will-mean-for-asset-managers

[16] Qi, Y. and Xiao, J. (2018). FinTech: AI powers financial services to improve people's lives. Communications of the ACM, 61(11), 65–69.

[17] Rich, E., Knight, K. and Nair, S. (2009). Artificial Intelligence. Tata McGraw Hill.

[18] Shrestha, Y.R., Ben-Menahem, S. M. and Von Krogh, G. (2019). Organizational decision-making structures in the age of artificial intelligence. California Management Review, 61(4), 66–83.

[19] The Economist. (2019, October 5). March of the Machines. pp. 20–22.

[20] Yale, A J. (2018, May 7). Black home buyers denied mortgages more than twice as often as whites, report finds. Forbes. Retrieved from https://www.forbes.com/sites/alyyale/2018/05/07/mortgage-loan-denials-more-common-with- minorities-new-report-shows/?sh=6a528e94509a

Web Resources

[21] https://www.zettle.com

[22] https://www.ocrolus.com

[23] https://www.zest.ai

[24] https://kasisto.com

[25] https://www.thetaray.com

Indicators of Financial Inclusion in India in the Context of Traditional and Digital

Shubha[1] and Rajeena Syed[2]

[1]Research Scholar, School of Economics and Commerce, CMR University, No. 5, Bhuvanagiri, OMBR Layout, Bangalore, Karnataka, India

[2]Associate Professor, School of Economics and Commerce, CMR University, No.5, Bhuvanagiri, OMBR Layout, Bangalore, Karnataka, India

E-mail: [1]shubha.19cphd@cmr.edu.in

ABSTRACT: *The present era demands financial inclusion to achieve sustainable development in every economy. The process of financial inclusion traditionally starts with the introduction of new branches and new financial services through its branches using the brick-and mortar method. With the introduction of the internet, inclusion takes a dynamic reaction. The current study explores traditional as well as digital financial inclusion in India. It narrates the indicators by using descriptive analysis, comparison, and percentage methods. The study used secondary data from the IMF and RBI websites. The result of the study explores the success story of the government's programs initiated to boost inclusive growth using banking services. The study finds the magic of virtuality in the inclusion of unbanked to banked individuals. The glimpse of the study shines the digital stars in the sky of financial inclusion.*

Keywords: ATMs, Bank branches, Digital Banking, Financial Inclusion, Mobile Money.

1. INTRODUCTION

Finance is the core concept of the economy. The distribution of finance among the people is the crucial aspect whose major responsibility taken by the formal structured banking system in the name of financial services. The credit needs of all the sectors including vulnerable groups and low-income groups are fulfilling mainly through the efforts of banking institutions. The full pledged accessibility of these financial services by the end users shows the level of inclusion.

Information processing, cost effectiveness, and special dissemination are the three main elements for financial efficiency and sustainability (Dan Luo, 2022). The development of sustainability is possible with inclusion. The inclusion revolution is shaping the way of development in a new dynamic economy. The major contribution to the revolution is made by fintech companies in the field of technology.

The inclusion can be broadly explained in two stages:

1. **Traditional Inclusion:** In India, banking institutions have opened several branches in urban, semi-urban, and rural areas from 1947 until now. The number of scheduled banks has increased from 97 to more than 150,000 at present. The horizontal as well as vertical developments reached ground-level customers through the traditional banking system. The acceptance of services by brick-and-mortar systems has been in practice for a long time, until the introduction of the internet.
2. **Digital Inclusion:** With the introduction of the internet, diversification has taken place in providing financial services. They are mainly in the form of USSD, AEPS, UPI, Digital Wallets, Internet Banking, Mobile Banking, etc. Digitalization is an advantage, especially with respect to accessibility.

The theory of financial inclusion expresses that there should be financial access for everyone in society without any discrimination for small or large businessmen or every person in the public. It is called public good theory. As per this theory, there should not be any transaction cost for formal financial transactions, including the use of ATMs, and these costs of basic formal financial transactions should be borne by the government as a subsidy (Ozili, Theories of Financial Inclusion, 2020).

The use of mobile money indicates that individuals were financially included (Jennifred Maurice Adjei, 2023). The inclusion improves financial health with growth and stability. It affects the local as well as national economies by enhancing the knowledge of digital literacy, through which individuals can identify unreliable sources of finance and the risks involved in investment.

2. LITERATURE REVIEW

Ramzi (2023) has evaluated the evenness of government actions with the banking interface in the study "Examining the Financial Inclusion Index to Determine the Financial Inclusion Status in India." The study reveals the efforts of the government to increase the access to financial services. It used RBI and World Bank data for descriptive analysis. The study suggested the inclusion of underprivileged demographics in the future (Hassan, 2023).

Peterson (2023) has predicted in his study "The Future of Financial Inclusion" that financial inclusion shifts to digitalization with personalized service. The whole system supports the virtual platform, and there will be increased use by women and direct involvement by the poor sections. The prediction is made by studying past and present formal financial services. The study is descriptive in nature and used review information to justify the situations. The study concludes by highlighting the importance of technology background in the future for financial inclusion (Ozili, The Future of Financial Inclusion, 2023).

S. Jayalakshmi and T. Yasodha (2023) have explored the importance of digital finance and its implications in India in their study, "Impact of Digital Finance on Financial Inclusion in India." The study assessed several programs and initiatives taken by the government. It concludes that, even though so many efforts have been made from the government side, there is no equal distribution of digital financial services in the country. There is a need to fill the gap by extending digital finance's spread (S. Jayalakshmi, 2023).

3. OBJECTIVES

1. To study the concept of financial inclusion in traditional as well as digital.
2. To compare traditional and digital inclusion using the Financial Index.
3. To highlight the necessity of inclusion.

4. HYPOTHESIS

$H_0$1: There is no significant difference between traditional financial inclusion and digital financial inclusion.

$H_0$2: There is no significant change in the financial inclusion index in the digital era.

5. FINANCIAL INCLUSION IN INDIA

In 2009–2010, the government of India made the concept of financial inclusion as one of its missions to achieve inclusive growth. At that time, the financial penetration in India in comparison with other countries was very low. Not only the penetration but also the accessibility to bank branches and ATMs were low. The private credit-to-GDP ratio of India stood at 56%, compared to 100+ in China, Malaysia, Australia, the UK, and Japan. By focusing on financial inclusion, the government of India initiated a no-frills account with the intention of including individuals and households in the financial system. As a result, it had reached 50.6 million no-frills accounts by the end of March 2010. Another initiative taken to improve financial inclusion is the provision of financial services through the Self-Help Group-Bank Linkage Programme (SBLP), through which 1.59 million new SHGs were linked with bank credits (India, REPORT ON TREND AND PROGRESS OF BANKING IN INDIA 2009-10, 2010).

The Pradhan Mantri Jan Dhan Yojana (PMJDY) introduced in 2014 is a milestone in financial inclusion, as 195.2 million accounts were opened before the end of December 2015 and 166.7 million RuPay cards were also issued. For further support, the government of India has started an insurance and social security scheme, namely, the Pradhan Mantri Jeevan Jyoti Bima Yojana, the Pradhan Mantri Suraksha Bima Yojana, and the and the Atal Pension Yojana. Notable beneficiaries were added to the formal sector under these schemes also (India, Report on Trend and Progress of Banking in India 2014–15, 2015).

As a result of several initiatives and an increase in the number of bank branches, the number of bank branches per 100,000 adults also increased, and it is now higher than in China and Germany. The number of accounts also increased, especially for adults, because of PMJDY. The National Strategy for Financial Inclusion (NSFI) 20019–2024 has been taken as the new project with a higher implementation of digitalization. The Business Correspondence Model (BC) covered all the areas, including the rural ones. The number of Basic Savings Bank Deposit Accounts (BSDBAs) in branches was 2616 lakhs, and through Business Correspondence Models it was 3388 lakhs at the end of March 2020. PMJDY accounts reached 41.4 crore, with major operations in semi-urban and rural areas. Support for SHG was also increased, and credits were added to Micro, Small and Medium Enterprises (MSMEs). The financial performance of Regional Rural Banks Small Finance Corporations and Local Area Banks were also identified with growth (India, Report on Trend and Progress of Banking in India 2019–20, 2020).

To increase digital support and access the government's schemes, the RBI has started 75 Digital Banking Units in rural areas in different districts that work in digital mode. The scheme of PMJDY has expanded inclusion by increasing the number of bank account holders and BSDBAs through the BC model, which reached 4015 at the end of March 2022. Nearly 43 lakh SHGs have availed loans during 2022–23 (India, Report on Trend and Progress of Banking in India 2022–23, 2023).

6. INDICATORS OF FINANCIAL INCLUSION

Based on literature review, RBI reports, and IMF reports, the following indicators of financial inclusion were identified in Table 1:

Table 1: Financial Inclusion Indicators

Sl. No.	*List of Financial Inclusion Indicators*
1.	Branches of commercial banks
2.	Automated Teller Machines (ATMs)
3.	Number of commercial bank branches per 1,000 km2
4.	Number of commercial bank branches per 100,000 adults
5.	Number of ATMs per 100,000 adults
6.	Number of deposit accounts with commercial banks per 1,000 adults
7.	Number of loan accounts with commercial banks per 1,000 adults
8.	No of household sector loan accounts with commercial banks per 1,000 adults

Sl. No.	*List of Financial Inclusion Indicators*
9.	No of women-owned loan a/c of house h0ld sector with commercial banks per 1,000 female adults
10.	Number of active mobile money accounts per 1,000 adults
11.	Number of credit cards per 1,000 adults
12.	Number of debit cards per 1,000 adults
13.	No of mobile and internet banking transactions (during reference yr) per 1,000 adults
14.	No of men-owned deposit a/c of house hold sector with commercial banks per 1,000 male adults
15.	No of women-owned deposit a/c of house hold sector with commercial banks per 1,000 female adults
16.	No of household sector deposit accounts with commercial banks per 1,000 adults
17.	Number of registered mobile money accounts per 1,000 adults
18.	Number of mobile money transactions (during the reference year) per 1,000 adults
19.	Outstanding balances on active mobile money accounts
20.	Access to payment and remittance facility
21.	Micro Finance
22.	Financial Inclusion Index

7. METHODOLOGY AND PROCEDURE

The current study is conducted using secondary data. In this study, to understand the concept of financial inclusion, several pieces of literature, journal articles, and reports were referred to. The researcher has identified the indicators of financial inclusion using the literature, reports, and publications from the RBI and IMF. The data has been downloaded and collected from the official IMF and RBI websites. Major five indicators, including the related ones, were considered for the current study. The study is descriptive in nature, and comparison and percentage methods were applied for the purpose of analysis.

8. ANALYSIS AND INTERPRETATION

8.1 Commercial Bank Branches per 100,000 adults

Branches play a dominant role in financial inclusion through their services. An increase in bank branches results in a wide range of accessibility, withdrawals of cash, and spreads of financial products and services. The adults who are the game changers in society are more accessible to these services. The reach of services up to ground level is possible through these bank branches.

Chart 1: Number of Commercial Bank Branches per 100,000 adults

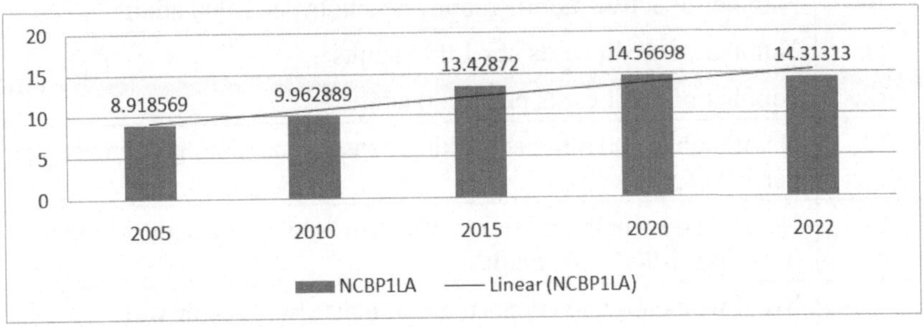

Data Source: (IMF, 2023), (NCBP1LA-Number of commercial bank branches per 100000 adults).

In India, there were 68585 commercial bank branches in 2005. During the period of 10 years, the number of commercial bank branches almost doubled, i.e., 126625. After that, there is also an increase in the number of commercial bank branches. At the end of 2022, there were 15,369 commercial bank branches in India. The above chart shows the number of commercial bank branches per 100,000 adults. The study identified a notable increase over the past 15 years, which is shown in the above diagram. The availability of bank branches per 100,000 adults in 2005 was 8.918, and it was increased to 14.567 in 2020.

8.2 ATMs per 100,000 Adults

Chart 2: Number of ATMs per 100,000 adults

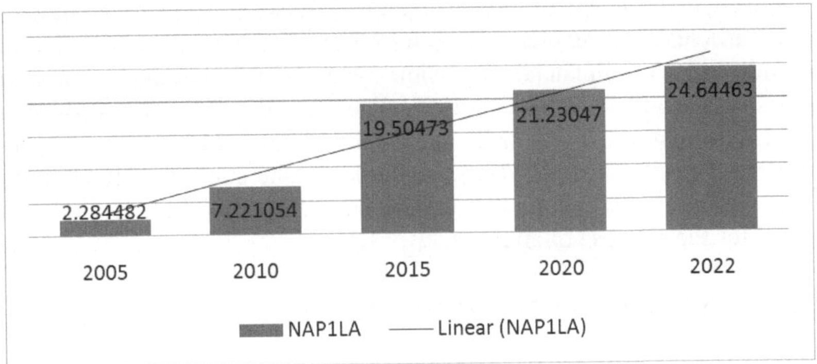

Data Source: (IMF, 2023), (NAP1LA-Number of ATMs per 100,000 adults).

The first ATM in India installed in 1987 by HSBC using "Swadhan" the first shared network and first mobile ATM was introduced by ICICI. Twenty years after the introduction, the number increased to 27088 in 2007. The percentage increase in the installation of new ATMs compared to previous year were in the year 2010 ism 39% and in 2014 it is 40%. The maximum number of ATMs were installed in the year 2014, i.e., 47381. The above chart shows the trend of increase in number of ATMs per 100000 adults in India for every 5 years. There is a sudden raise in number of ATMs per 100000 adults from 2013 (12) to 2014 (17) because of increase in number of ATMs installed. At the end of 2022 the number for 100000 adults stood at 24.644.

8.3 Mobile Money Accounts per 1000 Adults

Chart 3: Number of Active Mobile Money Accounts per 1000 adults

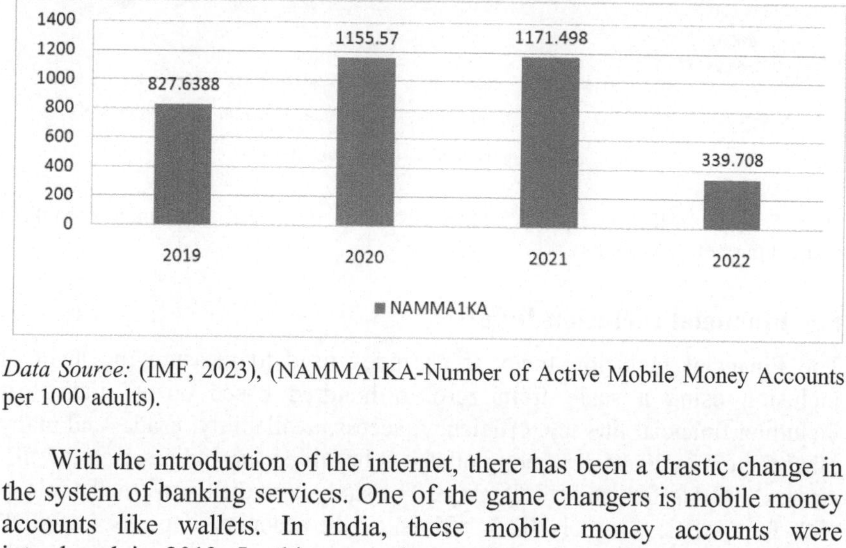

Data Source: (IMF, 2023), (NAMMA1KA-Number of Active Mobile Money Accounts per 1000 adults).

With the introduction of the internet, there has been a drastic change in the system of banking services. One of the game changers is mobile money accounts like wallets. In India, these mobile money accounts were introduced in 2013. In this year, the number of mobile money accounts registered per 1000 adults was 4.4. The maximum additions of 713.4 mobile money accounts have been recorded in 2019. In 2021, the total number of registered mobile money accounts per 1,000 adults have reached 1917. In these 1171.5 accounts are active mobile money accounts, as shown in the above chart. Till 2021, the registration as well as active mobile money accounts showed a positive trend, and it started downward in 2022.

8.4 Mobile and Internet Banking Transactions per 1000 Adults

The transformation of banking services has taken place through digital instruments because of the introduction of the internet in the field of banking. Mobile and internet banking are the outcomes of these transformations. The number of transactions through this form was very negligible in the initial years, which is shown in the above chart. It has taken a steep rise in the past few years, especially during and after the pandemic. As shown in the above chart, from 2012 to 2018, even though there was an increase, it was not a notable one. But after that, it recorded a 225% increase in 2019 compared to the previous year, 2018. The continuous steep rise was recorded from 2019 to 2022. In 2022, 23963 transactions were added per 1000 adults.

Chart 4: Number of Mobile and Internet Banking Transactions per 1000 adults

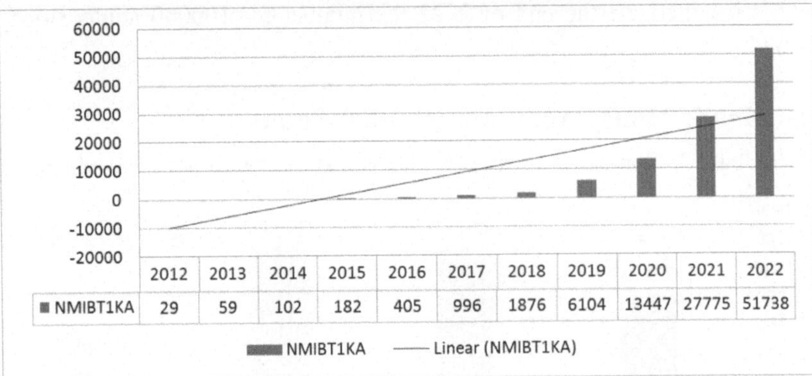

Data Source: (IMF, 2023), (NMIBT1KA-Number of mobile and internet banking transactions per 1000 adults).

8.5 Financial Inclusion Index

The Financial Inclusion Index is an index used to measure the level of inclusion using a scale from zero to hundred based on 97 indicators including financial literacy, efficiency, access, availability, usage, and many other factors in 20 states, among others. It has three sub-indices, namely 'FI-Access', 'FI-Usage', and 'FI-Quality'. The study used the Sarma methodology with four metrics, namely bank offices, credit accounts, deposits to SGDP proportion, and credit to SGDP proportion. In 2017, the study showed a FI-index of 43.7, and at the end of March 2023, it stood at 60.1. (India, Report on Trend and Progress of Banking in India 2022–23, 2023).

8.6 Household Sector Deposit Accounts with Commercial Banks per 1,000 Adults

The involvement of men and women, especially in the household sector, in financial activity discloses a portion of financial inclusion. The above chart shows the number of household sector deposit accounts for men, women and total. The major portion of involvement has been identified from 2014 to 2020 with female dominance. In 2005, male household accounts with commercial banks for 1,000 adults were 828, increased to 2,466 in 2022, and that of women in 2005 was 304, increased to 1,544 in 2022. The percentage increase from 2005 to 2022 in males and females per 1,000 adults is 197% and 407%, respectively. The total increase is 262%.

Chart 5: Number of Household Sector Deposit Accounts with Commercial Banks per 1,000 adults

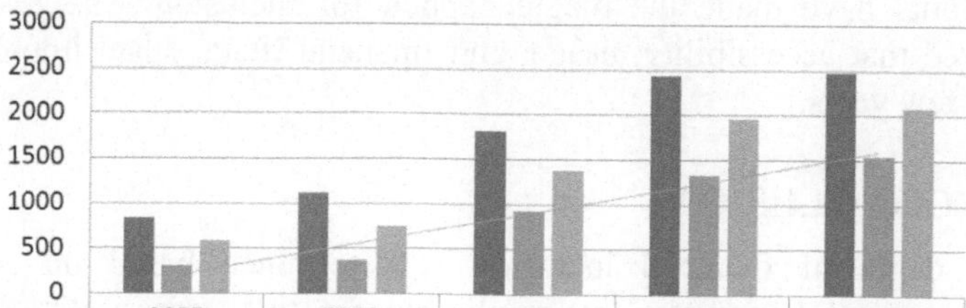

	2005	2010	2015	2020	2022
MDACB1KA	828	1108	1806	2430	2466
WDACM1KA	304	368	919	1322	1544
HHDCB1KA	573.9072	748.0559	1373.049	1958.133	2079.82

Data Source: (IMF, 2023), (MDACB1KA-Men owned deposit account of household sector with commercial banks per 1,000 male adults, WDACM1KA-Women owned deposit account of household sector with commercial banks per 1,000 female adults, HHDCB1KA-Number of household sector deposit accounts with commercial banks per 1,000 adults)

9. FINDINGS

The traditional version of inclusion identifies the increase in the number of bank branches and ATMs from one year to another and the increase in the rate of lending. The increase in bank branches reaching urban, semiurban, and rural areas by that accessibility all over the country has become possible and easy. ATM has supported financial inclusion by extending banking services after banking hours as well. The rate of increase is higher in 2015 in both cases.

The digital version of inclusion starts with the introduction of the internet in the field of banking and financial institutions. Diverse services were spread all over the country without any discrimination. The growth rate of transactions drastically increased in the digital era. After the pandemic, mobile money accounts were more accepted for their unique features and personal touch. The continuous growth in mobile and internet banking transactions identified their acceptance by a large mass personally through digital modes. Both men and women are coming under a formal system of financial services. The big change has been identified after 2020, especially in the year 2022.

The inclusion of financial services is comparatively more prevalent in the digital era than in the traditional system. It was proved in the above that, after the introduction, there is a big increase in the number of mobile and internet banking transactions, indicating the inclusion. The involvement of ground-level users in virtual systems has led to an increase in the number of transactions. With these unbanked businesses, individuals, and trades, they were banked because of the digital mode of collection. The mobile money accounts have made the magic happen for inclusion. The FI-Index also proved that accessibility, usage, and financial literacy had improved in the past few years.

10. CONCLUSION

The depth of financial inclusion is determined based on access. The geographical boundaries are negligible for this accessibility. Traditional financial inclusion does not overcome physical boundaries. All most all the financial services are provided from one or another central location, and the physical presence of the service receiver is also very much necessary in the traditional banking system.

Inclusive banking aims to include everybody in society by providing basic financial services. It has offered banking and financial services to every individual. To provide these services and make quick access possible, the step of digitalization has taken place. The digitalization step means the adoption of technology. Most of the commercial banks and financial institutions have supported this system. As a result, banking is open to the public, from manufacturing units to footpath vendors, through a digital platform. The move towards inclusive growth is catalysed by digitalization.

The study reveals that the rate of inclusion in the digital era is higher than that in the traditional era. It is the result of both the efforts of the formal sector and the accelerated use of the internet and digital instruments by users. Mainly, household women are involved in the formal system, which becomes part of digital inclusion.

11. LIMITATIONS OF THE STUDY

The study used secondary data for the purpose of analysis. There are several indicators that define financial progress and inclusion. This study used a few of the tools that support traditional and digital inclusion to explore the concept.

12. RECOMMENDATIONS

The current study does not examine each indicator separately and does not cover all the effort made by the government with the help of fintech companies and diverse services. With these, several other factors also affect the inclusion, like the network. There is a need to include these in the study of inclusion in the formal digital banking system. These are the areas left that can be used for further study.

REFERENCES

[1] Dan Luo, M.L. (2022). Can Digital Finance Contribute to the Promotion of Financial Sustainability? A Financial Efficiency Perspective. *Sustainability, 14*, 1 to 29. doi: https://doi.org/10.3390/su14073979

[2] Hassan, R.A. (2023). Examining the Financial Inclusion Index to. *Indian Journal of Economics and Finance (IJEF), 3*(1), 8 to 14. doi: DOI:10.54105/ijef.B2559.053123

[3] IMF (2023). *Financial Access Survey.* Retrieved from https://data.imf.org/?sk=e5dcab7e-a5ca-4892-a6ea-598b5463a34c&sid=1460043522778

[4] India, R.B. (2010). *Report on Trend and Progress of Banking in India 2009–10.* Mumbai 400 001: Mohua Roy for the Reserve Bank of India. Retrieved from https://rbi.org.in/Scripts/AnnualPublications.aspx?head=Trend+and+Progress+of+Banking+in+India

[5] India, R.B. (2015). *Report on Trend and Progress of Banking in India 2014-15.* Mumbai 400 001: Financial Stability Unit, Reserve Bank of India. Retrieved from https://rbi.org.in/Scripts/AnnualPublications.aspx?head=Trend+and+Progress+of+Banking+in+India

[6] India, R.B. (2020). *Report on Trend and Progress of Banking in India 2019–20.* Mumbai 400 001: Dr. Snehal S. Herwadkar for the Reserve Bank of India. Retrieved from https://rbi.org.in/Scripts/AnnualPublications.aspx?head=Trend+and+Progress+of+Banking+in+India

[7] India, R.B. (2023). *Report on Trend and Progress of Banking in India 2022–23.* Mumbai 400 001: Dr. Snehal S. Herwadkar for the Reserve Bank of India. Retrieved from https://rbi.org.in/Scripts/AnnualPublications.aspx?head=Trend%20and%20Progress%20of%20Banking%20in%20India

[8] Jennifred Maurice Adjei, R.O. (2023). Financial Technology and Financial Inclusion in Accra, Ghana. *Journal of International Cooperation and Development, 6*(3), 83-101. doi: DOI: 10.36941/jicd-2023-0023.

[9] Ozili, P.K. (2020). Theories of financial inclusion. *SSRN Electronic Journal*, 1 to 23. doi:DOI: 10.2139/ssrn.3526548

[10] Ozili, P.K. (2023). The Future of Financial Inclusion. In P.K. Ozili, *The Future of Financial Inclusion.* ResearchGate. doi:DOI: 10.1007/978-3-031-31431-5_9

[11] S.Jayalakshmi, T. (2023). Impact of Digital Finance on Financial Inclusion in India. *NOVYI MIR Research Journal, 8*(1), 318–327. doi: ISSN NO: 0130-7673

A Study on Access to Credit for Women-Owned Agribusinesses in Emerging Economies in India

Suraj Parashar and Rubeena Bano

Assistant Professor, Tecnia Institute of Advanced Studies, New Delhi, India

ABSTRACT: *Access to credit is a major challenge for women-owned agribusinesses in emerging economies like India, particularly in the Delhi NCR region where rural and urban dynamics intersect. This study investigates the structural, socio-cultural, and institutional barriers that hinder women agripreneurs from securing formal financing. Key obstacles include the lack of collateral—especially land ownership—and pervasive gender biases within financial institutions, which manifest as additional documentation requirements and the need for spousal guarantees. Additionally, limited financial literacy and low awareness of government credit schemes reduce women's ability to effectively access available resources. Support networks such as Self-Help Groups (SHGs) and women-centric NGOs play a crucial role in mitigating these challenges by providing social capital and informal financing alternatives. The rise of digital financial services offers new opportunities but is constrained by digital literacy gaps and concerns over high costs. Business formalization also influences credit access, with many women deterred by complex and costly registration processes. The study recommends reforms including flexible collateral norms, gender-sensitive banking practices, expanded financial literacy programs, strengthened support networks, improved digital inclusion, and simplified business formalization. These interventions can empower women agripreneurs, fostering sustainable growth, poverty alleviation, and enhanced food security. By addressing these multifaceted barriers, the research contributes to advancing gender-inclusive financial policies in emerging economies.*

Keywords: Agribusiness, Barriers to Finance, Credit Access, Emerging Economies, Financial Inclusion, Gender and Agriculture, Microfinance, Rural Finance, SMEs, Women Entrepreneurs.

1. INTRODUCTION

Agriculture continues to be the backbone of many emerging economies, contributing significantly to employment, rural development, and food security. Within this domain, agribusiness—the commercial arm of agricultural production including processing, marketing, and distribution—has emerged as a powerful driver of economic transformation. In recent decades, women have increasingly stepped into agribusiness roles, not only as laborers but also as decision-makers, managers, and owners. However, despite their growing participation, women entrepreneurs face structural and systemic challenges that inhibit their ability to scale and sustain these ventures.

Among the most pressing barriers is limited access to credit. Finance is a critical input for any business, especially in agriculture where capital is required for seeds, fertilizers, machinery, land improvement, storage, and value addition. For women-led agribusinesses, this access is often restricted due to socio-cultural biases, institutional constraints, and a lack of supportive financial frameworks. These barriers are particularly acute in emerging economies like India, where traditional gender norms intersect with underdeveloped financial systems.

In India, agriculture employs nearly 60% of the rural female workforce, yet women own less than 14% of landholdings, which is often a prerequisite for collateral-based lending (FAO, 2021). Women also face challenges in obtaining formal identification, documentation, and digital literacy—all of which are increasingly required for formal credit applications. These issues are magnified in regions like Delhi NCR, which, despite being a relatively urbanized and economically advanced area, still reflects sharp gendered disparities in access to resources.

2. PROBLEM STATEMENT

Although financial inclusion is a growing focus of government and development policy, the reality on the ground shows that women agripreneurs remain under-financed and underrepresented in formal financial systems. Schemes such as MUDRA Yojana, Stand-Up India, and various Self-Help Group (SHG) programs have been introduced to close this gap. However, uptake and impact remain uneven. Many women are unaware of these schemes, are excluded due to eligibility barriers, or find the procedures too complex. Additionally, banks often perceive women-led agribusinesses as higher-risk clients, further limiting access.

In Delhi NCR, a region known for its mix of urban innovation and rural peripheries, women engage in a variety of agribusinesses—ranging from organic farming and dairy cooperatives to food processing and agricultural trading. Yet, their ability to secure loans from formal institutions remains constrained by institutional inertia, inadequate outreach, and persistent gender stereotypes.

This study aims to investigate how these challenges manifest specifically for women agribusiness owners in Delhi NCR, how effective current financial and policy mechanisms are, and what structural reforms are needed to promote equitable access to credit.

3. SIGNIFICANCE OF THE STUDY

The importance of this research lies in its potential to fill the empirical and policy gap surrounding gendered access to agribusiness finance. While several studies have broadly addressed women's access to microcredit or their roles in agriculture, few have explored the intersection of gender, agribusiness entrepreneurship, and credit access in urban-rural hybrid regions like Delhi NCR. Even fewer have done so with a focus on institutional and socio-cultural barriers.

By identifying the specific obstacles that prevent women from fully participating in formal credit systems, this study contributes to the larger discourse on financial inclusion, gender equity, and rural entrepreneurship development. It also provides insights for financial institutions, government agencies, NGOs, and policy-makers working to promote women's economic empowerment in agriculture.

Furthermore, the findings may offer practical implications for the design of gender-sensitive lending frameworks, financial literacy programs, and support services that go beyond mere access to credit and focus on long-term financial sustainability and autonomy for women entrepreneurs.

4. RESEARCH OBJECTIVES

This research is guided by the following objectives:

1. To identify and analyze the financial, institutional, and socio-cultural barriers that limit access to credit for women-owned agribusinesses in Delhi NCR.
2. To assess the awareness, accessibility, and effectiveness of existing credit schemes and financial inclusion programs targeting women entrepreneurs.
3. To understand the role of mediating factors such as financial literacy, family support, and organizational networks (e.g., SHGs, cooperatives) in influencing credit access.
4. To propose evidence-based recommendations that can inform policy and practice for enhancing credit accessibility for women agripreneurs in emerging economies.

5. RESEARCH QUESTIONS

The study aims to answer the following key questions:

- What are the main institutional and socio-economic challenges that women face in securing credit for their agribusinesses?
- How do gender norms and cultural expectations influence women's decisions and opportunities to seek formal credit?
- What role do financial literacy and awareness play in the accessibility of government or bank-led financial programs?

- How effective have existing initiatives been in addressing the credit needs of women-led agribusinesses in the Delhi NCR region?

6. SCOPE AND LIMITATIONS

This research is confined to the Delhi NCR region, which includes both metropolitan areas and rural outskirts, offering a balanced view of the urban-rural divide in credit accessibility. The study focuses exclusively on women-owned agribusinesses, defined as ventures where women

are primary owners, managers, or operators engaged in agricultural production, processing, or distribution.

While the research seeks to provide a detailed analysis, it may be limited by factors such as respondent availability, potential bias in self-reported data, and the non-generalizability of findings to all parts of India or other emerging economies. However, the study's in-depth focus on one strategic region allows for a rich and nuanced understanding of the local dynamics that can inform broader applications.

7. LITERATURE REVIEW

7.1 Overview of Women in Agribusiness and Credit Gaps

Women play a critical role in the agricultural value chain, especially in emerging economies. However, their entrepreneurial potential in agribusiness remains underutilized due to significant barriers, most notably limited access to credit. According to FAO (2021), although women account for nearly 43% of the agricultural labor force in developing countries, their access to productive assets, including finance, is substantially lower than that of men. This inequality is compounded in agribusiness settings where credit needs are often higher due to capital- intensive activities like processing and distribution.

7.2 Gender Gaps in Financial Access

Research by Demirgüç-Kunt *et al.* (2018) in the *Global Findex Database* highlights that women in emerging economies are 9% less likely to have a bank account compared to men, and even less likely to access formal credit. In India, this divide is evident in the lower rate of loan applications and approvals for women entrepreneurs, especially in rural and peri-urban areas. Chakrabarti and Sanyal (2020) found that while schemes like PMJDY have increased financial account ownership among women, this hasn't translated into proportional increases in credit access.

7.3 INSTITUTIONAL AND STRUCTURAL BARRIERS

Agarwal (2018) attributes this disparity to legal and cultural constraints such as lack of land ownership, which limits women's ability to offer collateral for loans. In India, only 13.96% of landowners are women, severely restricting their eligibility for institutional finance. Mehrotra and Ghosh (2020) further argue that even when land is technically owned by women, social norms often prevent them from exercising control over the asset, thereby weakening their negotiating position in credit markets.

7.4 The Role of Financial Institutions and Discriminatory Practices

Cheston and Kuhn (2002) showed that financial institutions often lack gender-sensitive credit evaluation models, leading to indirect discrimination. A study by Chaudhary and Verma (2019) examining Indian rural banks revealed that women applicants are more likely to be asked for spousal co-signers or additional documentation. This limits the autonomy and agency of women entrepreneurs.

7.5 Effectiveness of Government Schemes

To address these issues, the Indian government has launched schemes like MUDRA and Stand- Up India, aimed at facilitating loans to underrepresented groups. RBI (2021) data shows that while women's share in these schemes is increasing, the average loan size for women remains lower than for men. Rao and Bansal (2020) critique these programs for their complex application procedures and lack of targeted financial literacy campaigns, which limit their reach among women in rural agribusiness.

7.6 The Role of Microfinance and SHGs

Microfinance institutions (MFIs) and self-help groups (SHGs) have played a pivotal role in bridging the finance gap for women. Nair (2005) emphasized that SHGs empower women by improving their bargaining power and providing collective financial resources. However, Singh and Dubey (2017) found that these models often cater to micro-credit needs and do not scale well for agribusinesses that require medium to large capital investments.

7.7 Financial Literacy and Digital Barriers

A growing body of research points to financial and digital literacy as critical barriers. Sangwan and Sinha (2021) argue that many women lack awareness of available schemes or the confidence to interact with financial institutions. In Delhi NCR, urban-rural differences also play a role. Women in peri-urban zones are often digitally excluded, limiting their access to digital loan applications and government e-portals.

7.8 Regional Studies and Delhi NCR Context

While national data provides a broad view, regional analyses like those by Verma and Kohli (2022) on Delhi NCR show that women in agribusinesses often engage in activities like organic farming, home-based food processing, and dairy cooperatives. These businesses are typically informal, which discourages formal lenders from offering credit. The authors emphasize the need for tailored financial instruments and decentralized loan appraisal models that can accommodate non-traditional business structures.

7.9 Conceptual and Theoretical Models

The Gender and Development (GAD) framework, as discussed by Kabeer (2005), underlines the need for structural transformation rather than mere inclusion. It advocates for addressing power dynamics in institutions that marginalize women. Similarly, the Resource-Based View (Barney, 1991) stresses that financial capital is a strategic resource that can unlock entrepreneurial growth, but only if accessed equitably.

7.10 Future Directions and Gaps

Despite growing interest in gender-inclusive finance, Sharma and Jain (2023) note that there remains a gap in empirical data focusing specifically on women-led agribusinesses in semi-urban regions like Delhi NCR. Most policies target rural women broadly, ignoring the unique context of agribusinesses in urban-adjacent regions where land values, institutional linkages, and market access differ significantly.

8. CONCEPTUAL FRAMEWORK

8.1 Introduction

The conceptual framework serves as the intellectual blueprint for this study. It offers a structured understanding of the key variables, their interrelationships, and how they collectively explain the phenomenon of restricted access to credit for women-owned agribusinesses. Rooted in gender, economic, and institutional theories, this framework contextualizes the systemic barriers within the socio-economic environment of India—particularly the Delhi NCR region—where access to finance remains one of the primary constraints for women entrepreneurs in agriculture and agribusiness.

8.2 Conceptual Foundation

Access to finance is critical for the growth and sustainability of agribusinesses. For women entrepreneurs, however, access to credit is often hindered by a variety of interrelated factors—both structural and social. While financial institutions may appear gender-neutral on paper, many are shaped by gendered assumptions and practices that indirectly exclude women.

This framework is built on the integration of three key theoretical perspectives:

8.2.1 *Gender and Development (GAD) Theory*

GAD emphasizes the institutional and systemic nature of gender disparities. It shifts the focus from women's lack of resources to the structures that hinder their access and control over those resources. In this context, the framework explores how societal norms, institutional biases, and policy limitations act as barriers for women accessing financial services.

8.2.2 *Financial Inclusion Framework*

This perspective defines access to finance in terms of availability, affordability, and usability. It focuses on how services are not only present but also reachable and tailored to the needs of women-led agribusinesses. It underpins the need for not just the presence of schemes, but their proper functioning and uptake.

8.2.3 *Resource-Based View (RBV) of the Firm*

RBV posits that access to valuable, rare, inimitable, and non-substitutable resources—such as capital—leads to a competitive advantage. For women entrepreneurs, access to credit is a strategic resource enabling investment, scale, and innovation.

8.3 Core Concepts and Variables

The conceptual framework identifies the following key variables categorized into independent, mediating, and dependent variables:

8.4 Independent Variables

These are the factors believed to affect access to credit for women-owned agribusinesses:

8.4.1 *Collateral Availability*

The most significant structural barrier is the lack of collateral. Due to unequal land ownership (only about 14% of Indian women own land), many women cannot provide the security required for formal credit.

8.4.2 *Financial Literacy*

Many women entrepreneurs lack the necessary financial knowledge to navigate complex lending procedures or assess viable financial products.

8.4.3 *Awareness of Financial Schemes*

Despite government schemes like MUDRA and Stand-Up India, awareness and access remain low among women in agribusiness due to poor outreach and digital literacy gaps.

8.4.4 *Socio-Cultural Constraints*

In patriarchal settings, women's financial decision-making is often limited. They may need male approval, face mobility constraints, or experience stigma when engaging with formal institutions.

8.4.5 *Institutional Behavior*

Gender bias among financial service providers leads to practices like requiring spousal guarantees, asking for unnecessary documentation, or doubting women's repayment ability, which further limits access.

8.5 Mediating Variables

These variables influence the relationship between the independent variables and the outcome (credit access):

8.5.1 *Support Networks (SHGs/Cooperatives)*

SHGs, cooperatives, and NGOs can buffer against formal institutional exclusions by offering financial literacy training, microloans, or group guarantees. Their presence can mediate institutional limitations.

8.5.2 *Digital Access and Usage*

Digital tools like mobile banking, e-KYC, and online loan applications can enhance women's reach and reduce dependency on intermediaries. However, digital divides mediate the degree of access.

8.5.3 *Business Formality*

Many women-owned agribusinesses are informal. Formal registration often correlates with better access to financial services, but registering a business entails procedural and cost barriers.

8.6 Dependent Variable

The outcome variable in this framework is:

8.6.1 *Access to Credit for Women-Owned Agribusinesses*

This is measured not only by whether credit is accessed, but also by the terms of access (loan size, interest rate, repayment flexibility), the source (formal vs. informal), and frequency (one- time vs. repeated access).

8.7 Proposed Conceptual Model Structure Independent Variables

Collateral Availability
Financial Literacy
Awareness of Schemes
Socio-Cultural Constraints
Institutional Behavior

↓

(Direct Influence & via Mediation)

↓

Mediating Variables

Support Networks (SHGs, NGOs, Cooperatives)
Digital Access and Literacy
Business Formality

↓

Dependent Variable

Access to Credit for Women Agribusinesses

8.8 Contextualization: Delhi NCR

Delhi NCR offers a unique case within India due to its blend of urban and peri-urban agribusiness activity. Many women-run agribusinesses in this region engage in:

- Dairy farming
- Home-based food processing
- Organic vegetable supply
- Agro-tourism

The proximity to urban centers like Delhi increases market access but also raises competition and entry barriers. Moreover, informal labor and land ownership arrangements in peri-urban areas often disadvantage women seeking credit.

In Delhi NCR, support networks like SHGs and NGO initiatives are better organized, yet bank access and participation in government schemes remain lower than expected. This framework thus specifically includes regionally relevant mediators such as access to training by state-level departments (e.g., NABARD, Delhi Women's Commission initiatives) and digital banking literacy campaigns.

8.9 Framework Justification

This conceptual framework contributes to academic and policy literature in several ways:

- It integrates both demand-side and supply-side constraints.
- It considers institutional behavior, often ignored in quantitative credit access models.
- It embeds a gender lens across structural, operational, and socio-cultural dimensions.
- It allows space for both formal and informal mechanisms, making it applicable in emerging economy contexts.

The conceptual framework developed for this study provides a comprehensive roadmap to explore and analyze the complex dynamics that determine access to credit for women-owned agribusinesses. By acknowledging both institutional constraints and women's agency (via mediators like SHGs and digital tools), this framework helps identify where interventions are needed and what mechanisms are most impactful. This model not only facilitates an in-depth academic inquiry but also guides policy recommendations tailored for improving women's financial inclusion in agribusiness, especially in transitional regions like Delhi NCR.

9. DISCUSSIONS

This study reveals a complex interplay of institutional, socio-cultural, and personal factors that collectively limit women's access to credit in the agribusiness sector within India's Delhi NCR region. Despite ongoing efforts to promote financial inclusion, structural barriers continue to dominate. A recurring issue is the lack of collateral, particularly land or immovable assets, which remains a prerequisite for most formal credit in India. As women rarely own such assets due to patriarchal inheritance practices and social norms, they are frequently unable to meet the eligibility criteria for bank loans. This systemic constraint echoes earlier findings in development literature that emphasize the critical role of asset ownership in financial inclusion. Even where movable assets or group guarantees exist, financial institutions often lack the flexibility or willingness to adjust their risk assessment models, leaving women entrepreneurs at a disadvantage.

Institutional behavior further compounds the problem. The study uncovered that many women experienced overt and subtle forms of gender bias when interacting with bank officials. Some reported being asked to bring male relatives to co-sign or faced repeated delays in processing. These experiences reflect not only policy gaps but also entrenched attitudes within financial institutions. Despite policies advocating for gender equity in financial services, front-line implementation remains inconsistent. This discrepancy between policy and practice significantly affects women's confidence in the system and discourages them from approaching formal lenders. Such behavior creates a self-perpetuating cycle, where women's underrepresentation in formal credit statistics justifies continued neglect from institutions, further entrenching exclusion.

Another significant barrier identified is the lack of financial literacy and awareness of government credit schemes. Many women entrepreneurs were either unaware of schemes like MUDRA or found the application processes too complex to navigate. In peri-urban areas of the NCR, where exposure to government outreach is limited, this lack of awareness is particularly pronounced. Even those who had heard of such programs lacked the guidance to apply or misunderstood eligibility requirements. This finding highlights a critical implementation failure—while schemes may exist on paper, their impact is blunted by inadequate dissemination and support. Without targeted training and community engagement, these initiatives fall short of reaching the women who need them most.

Despite these barriers, the study found that support networks—especially Self-Help Groups (SHGs), cooperatives, and women-centric NGOs—serve as essential intermediaries. Women affiliated with such networks reported better financial knowledge, improved confidence, and more frequent access to micro-credit or informal group lending. These collective platforms often act as substitutes for formal institutional support, providing peer learning and community-backed risk sharing. However, the reach of such groups is uneven, particularly in rapidly urbanizing regions of Delhi NCR, where traditional rural support mechanisms are weaker and urban financial systems are still adapting to gender-responsive models.

Digital financial services offer both promise and challenges. Mobile banking and app-based loan applications were seen as enablers in urban settings, allowing women to bypass traditional gatekeepers. Yet, digital illiteracy among older or rural women limited the usefulness of these tools. Even where smartphones were available, women often lacked the training or autonomy to use financial apps confidently. Moreover, fintech services frequently charge higher interest rates, leading to concerns about exploitation. Thus, digital solutions, while important, cannot substitute for comprehensive education and inclusive design.

Finally, the formalization of agribusinesses appears to significantly affect credit access. Women who had registered businesses and complied with tax or legal norms found it easier to secure loans. However, the process of formalization itself is burdensome. Many cited high intermediary costs, bureaucratic procedures, and unclear guidelines as reasons for remaining informal. This suggests a need to simplify business registration and provide targeted assistance for women entrepreneurs.

In conclusion, improving access to credit for women-owned agribusinesses requires addressing both structural and behavioral barriers. Policies must be paired with local implementation, institutional reform, financial education, and stronger support networks to ensure that women are not just included in financial systems, but empowered within them.

10. CONCLUSION

This study highlights the multifaceted challenges faced by women entrepreneurs in agribusiness within the Delhi NCR region regarding their access to formal credit. Despite numerous government initiatives and policies aimed at promoting financial inclusion, significant barriers persist that limit women's ability to secure necessary financing to grow and sustain their businesses. The research underscores that access to credit for women is not merely a question of economic supply and demand but is deeply intertwined with social, cultural, and institutional factors. Structural impediments such as lack of collateral—particularly land ownership—remain the most formidable obstacle, reflecting broader patterns of gender inequality entrenched in Indian society. Women's limited ownership of assets not only restricts their eligibility for bank loans but also diminishes their bargaining power within financial institutions. Addressing this issue requires innovative approaches to collateral requirements and credit assessment that consider alternative forms of security and social capital.

Moreover, the study demonstrates that institutional behavior and gender biases continue to play a critical role in shaping women's credit experiences. Despite formal policies encouraging gender equality in lending, women frequently encounter discriminatory practices, ranging from excessive documentation demands to spousal guarantees and discouragement from loan officers. Such barriers reinforce women's mistrust in formal financial institutions and push many toward informal credit sources that may be costlier or less reliable. This gap between policy intention and practical implementation signals an urgent need for financial institutions to undertake gender sensitization training and revamp their service delivery models to foster a more inclusive and supportive environment.

Another pivotal finding relates to the pervasive lack of financial literacy and awareness about credit schemes specifically designed for women entrepreneurs. While schemes like MUDRA and Stand-Up India represent important steps toward empowering women economically, their reach and impact remain limited due to inadequate dissemination, complex application procedures, and low digital literacy. Many women, especially in peri-urban and semi-rural parts of Delhi NCR, remain unaware of these opportunities or lack the confidence to engage with formal lenders. This calls for strengthened outreach programs, targeted financial education, and community-based support to bridge information asymmetries and build women's capacity to navigate financial systems effectively.

Support networks such as Self-Help Groups (SHGs), cooperatives, and NGOs emerge as crucial mediators in enhancing women's access to credit. These organizations provide not only financial services but also social support, collective bargaining power, and knowledge-sharing platforms that empower women to overcome institutional and cultural barriers. However, the uneven availability of such networks across the Delhi NCR region suggests the need for policy efforts to scale up and integrate these grassroots initiatives into formal financial inclusion strategies.

Digital financial services represent both a promising avenue and a challenge. Mobile banking and fintech innovations can potentially circumvent traditional barriers and expand outreach. Nonetheless, digital financial inclusion remains constrained by issues of access, digital literacy, and trust, particularly among older women and those in less urbanized settings. To leverage technology effectively, comprehensive digital literacy training and user-friendly financial products tailored to women entrepreneurs' specific needs are essential.

The formalization of agribusinesses also plays a significant role in credit accessibility. Women entrepreneurs with registered businesses and tax compliance find it easier to obtain loans, yet the formalization process is often perceived as costly, complex, and intimidating. Simplifying registration procedures and providing assistance in business formalization could substantially improve women's ability to engage with formal financial institutions.

In summary, enhancing credit access for women-owned agribusinesses in emerging economies, specifically within India's Delhi NCR region, demands a holistic approach that addresses legal, social, cultural, and financial dimensions. Policymakers and financial institutions must move beyond generic inclusion rhetoric to design gender-responsive products, flexible collateral norms, and effective awareness campaigns. Simultaneously, fostering strong support systems through SHGs and leveraging digital innovations can empower women to participate meaningfully in the agribusiness sector. Ultimately, closing the gender credit gap is not only a matter of economic justice but a vital driver for rural development, poverty alleviation, and sustainable growth. Women's financial empowerment in agribusiness promises to unlock untapped productivity, promote food security, and catalyze broader social transformation in emerging economies. This research provides a foundation for future studies and policy frameworks aimed at creating a more inclusive and equitable financial ecosystem for women entrepreneurs.

BIBLIOGRAPHY

[1] Food and Agriculture Organization (FAO). (2021). Gender and Land Rights Database: India. Retrieved from https://www.fao.org/gender-landrights-database

[2] Government of India (2022). Pradhan Mantri MUDRA Yojana – Annual Report 2021–22. Ministry of Finance. Retrieved from https://www.mudra.org.in

[3] Government of India (2022). Stand-Up India Scheme Guidelines. Department of Financial Services. Retrieved from https://www.standupmitra.in

[4] NABARD (2020). Status of Microfinance in India 2019–20. National Bank for Agriculture and Rural Development. Retrieved from https://www.nabard.org

[5] World Bank (2021). Women, Business and the Law 2021. Washington, DC: World Bank Group. Retrieved from https://wbl.worldbank.org

[6] Agarwal, B. (2018). Gender inequality in land ownership and the link to women's empowerment. *Journal of Agrarian Change*, 18(3), 410–430. https://doi.org/10.1111/joac.12245

[7] Demirgüç-Kunt, A., Klapper, L., Singer, D., Ansar, S. and Hess, J. (2018). The Global Findex Database 2017: Measuring Financial Inclusion and the Fintech Revolution. World Bank Publications. https://doi.org/10.1596/978-1-4648-1259-0

[8] Kabeer, N. (2005). Gender equality and women's empowerment: A critical analysis of the third millennium development goal. *Gender & Development*, 13(1), 13–24.

[9] Chakrabarti, R. and Sanyal, K. (2020). Financial inclusion of women in rural India: Evidence from PMJDY accounts. *Economic and Political Weekly*, 55(19), 53–61.

[10] Agarwal, B. (2018). Gender inequality in land ownership and the link to women's empowerment. *Journal of Agrarian Change*, 18(3), 410–430.

[11] Barney, J. (1991). Firm resources and sustained competitive advantage. *Journal of Management*, 17(1), 99–120.

[12] Chakrabarti, R. and Sanyal, K. (2020). Financial inclusion of women in rural India: Evidence from PMJDY accounts. *Economic and Political Weekly*, 55(19), 53–61.

[13] Chaudhary, M. and Verma, S. (2019). Gender bias in credit access: A study of Indian rural banks. *Indian Journal of Finance and Banking*, 13(4), 112–125.

[14] Cheston, S. and Kuhn, L. (2002). Empowering women through microfinance. UNIFEM.

[15] Demirgüç-Kunt, A., *et al.* (2018). The Global Findex Database 2017: Measuring financial inclusion and the fintech revolution. World Bank.

[16] FAO (2021). Gender and Land Rights Database – India. Retrieved from https://www.fao.org/gender-landrights-database

[17] Kabeer, N. (2005). Gender equality and women's empowerment: A critical analysis of the third millennium development goal. Gender & Development, 13(1), 13–24.

[18] Mehrotra, S. and Ghosh, S. (2020). Women, land rights and economic empowerment in India. *Journal of Social Policy*, 49(3), 472–495.

[19] Rao, K. and Bansal, P. (2020). Evaluating the effectiveness of MUDRA loans for women entrepreneurs. *Indian Economic Review*, 55(1), 87–104.

[20] Sangwan, S. and Sinha, M. (2021). Financial literacy as a determinant of financial inclusion for Indian women. *International Journal of Social Economics,* 48(4), 563–578.

[21] Sharma, A. and Jain, D. (2023). Women-led agribusinesses in peri-urban India: A policy analysis. *Journal of Rural Development Studies*, 42(2), 122–139.

[22] Singh, N. and Dubey, R. (2017). Microfinance and women empowerment: A study of SHG models. *Journal of Business and Management,* 19(6), 18–27.

[23] Verma, T. and Kohli, R. (2022). Credit accessibility for women in agri-business: Insights from Delhi NCR. *International Journal of Gender and Entrepreneurship*, 14(3), 285–301.

AI-Driven Talent Acquisition: Transforming Human Capital Economics in the Digital Age

Ankitha Theres[1], Amulya Warunny[2] and S. Ayyappan[3]

[1]Research Scholar, School of Management – HRBR Campus, CMR University Bangalore, India

[2]Research Scholar, CMR University, India

[3]Professor, School of Management, CMR University, Bangalore, India

E-mail: [1]ankitha.theres@cmr.edu.in; [2]amulya.warunny@cmr.edu.in; [3]ayyappan.s@cmr.edu.in; [3]sapacet@gmail.com

Keywords: AI-Driven Talent Acquisition, Artificial Intelligence (AI), Human Resource (HR), Machine Learning (ML), Natural Language Processing (NLP).

1. INTRODUCTION

In an era defined by rapid technological advancement and unprecedented global interconnectedness, the foundational principles of economics and finance are undergoing a profound transformation. This book, "Paradigm Shift in Economics and Finance – Role of Technology and Innovation," investigates the complex ways in which emerging technologies are altering markets, redefining value, and shaping human behavior. Among these transformative elements, Artificial Intelligence (AI) emerges as a particularly powerful catalyst, particularly in its application to human capital.

This chapter, "AI-Driven Talent Acquisition: Transforming Human Capital Economics in the Digital Age," explores how AI is fundamentally altering the landscape of talent acquisition, moving it from a largely intuitive and administrative function to a strategic, data-driven discipline. We will examine how AI enhances efficiency, addresses long-standing biases, and directly impacts an organization's financial performance. Furthermore, we will consider the broader implications of AI for global talent markets, cross-border hiring, and the critical policy and ethical considerations that must guide its responsible deployment. By understanding AI's role in optimizing human capital, we gain crucial insights into the future of work and the evolving dynamics of economic value creation.

2. HUMAN CAPITAL AS AN ECONOMIC ASSET

In today's digital world, human capital isn't just a resource; it's truly at the heart of economic activity and innovation. Think of it this way: people, with their unique knowledge, creativity, adaptability, and decision-making skills, are the real drivers of progress and productivity. Our collective capabilities, experiences, and potential as a workforce—what we call human capital—are now seen as just as vital as financial investments or physical infrastructure (Becker, 1993). And unlike those traditional assets, human capital can actually grow and renew itself, especially when we invest in education, skill development, and smart technology.

As economies shift from old-school industrial production to knowledge-based systems, talent has emerged as the most valuable component. Companies today aren't just battling it out over product quality or price; they're competing fiercely for the brightest minds—people who can untangle complex problems and generate value through innovative ideas. This competition intensifies as highly skilled professionals increasingly traverse borders in search of optimal opportunities, thereby influencing national productivity and corporate competitiveness (Docquier & Rapoport, 2012).

Given this changing landscape, how we find, manage, and keep talent has changed dramatically. A pivotal development has been the integration of Artificial Intelligence (AI) into talent acquisition processes. Traditional recruitment strategies often depended on personal networks, instinctual judgments, and laborious manual procedures. These approaches frequently led to inefficiencies and unconscious biases, holding back organizational performance. However, AI-driven recruitment systems represent a significant advancement, providing remarkable speed, scalability, and impartiality. With machine learning, natural language processing, and predictive analytics, organizations can now sift through thousands of resumes in mere seconds, accurately gauge how well a candidate fits, and even predict job performance with a precision that was simply impossible before (Chamorro-Premuzic *et al.*, 2017).

The transition from hiring based on intuition to hiring based on intelligence represents more than merely a technological enhancement. It signifies a profound transformation in our comprehension, utilization, and valuation of human capital within economic frameworks. Artificial Intelligence (AI) facilitates the establishment of fairer, evidence-driven hiring practices, thereby reducing bias and enhancing the alignment between individuals and their respective roles. The result? Lower employee turnover and higher productivity. In essence, AI is redefining workforce strategy as a key contributor to overall economic efficiency (Upadhyay & Khandelwal, 2018). Furthermore, AI's capacity to identify patterns across various labor markets contributes to the formation of broader economic trends by accurately aligning skills with the actual requirements of industries.

In the broader context of the digital economy, human capital has evolved from a mere supportive function to a strategic asset. Organizations that actively nurture and smartly leverage their workforce through data and technology are much better equipped to innovate, react quickly to market changes, and achieve sustainable growth. In fact, many of today's most valuable companies—especially in fintech, healthcare, and AI—owe their success largely to intangible assets, with their human capital being the most significant (OECD, 2019). In this environment, your ability to recruit and retain top talent effectively is directly tied to your financial success.

AI's influence keeps growing beyond just initial recruitment, reaching into areas like employee development, identifying future leaders, and comprehensive workforce planning. Smart systems are now being used to create personalized learning paths, uncover hidden potential within teams, and proactively anticipate future talent needs, all aligned with company goals (Manyika *et al.*, 2017). These advancements are building a more adaptable and resilient workforce, benefiting both individual careers and the entire organization.

On a larger macroeconomic scale, AI also helps reduce inefficiencies in labor markets by significantly improving how well individual skills align with what organizations are looking for. This tackles a long-standing problem: many economies face talent shortages, yet huge numbers of skilled people remain underutilized. AI bridges this divide by expanding access to opportunities and increasing the visibility of talent, regardless of an individual's location, background, or traditional qualifications.

Finally, the rise of AI-powered people analytics has truly cemented human capital's role as a direct driver of economic and financial outcomes. Organizations are now using advanced analytics to closely track workforce trends, measure what truly drives performance, and design agile team structures. These data-driven insights transform human resources from a reactive department into a proactive, strategic unit that directly boosts profitability, fuels innovation, and creates long-term value (Bersin, 2018; Deloitte, 2021).

Ultimately, bringing AI into talent acquisition isn't just a technological step forward; it's a profound shift in how we think about, measure, and unleash human capital. It reflects a larger trend in economics and finance where technological innovation is fundamentally reshaping how we create value. By embedding intelligence into the hiring process, AI significantly elevates the strategic importance of people within economic systems and redefines the intricate connection between talent and economic performance in the digital age.

3. AI TOOLS AND TECHNIQUES IN TALENT ACQUISITION

As organizations navigate the complexities of a digitally driven economy, the way we find and hire talent has changed dramatically. At the heart of this transformation is the widespread use of Artificial Intelligence (AI). AI offers scalable, data-driven, and predictive capabilities that make recruitment practices both more efficient and more effective. This evolution reflects a bigger shift in human capital economics, where technology isn't just helping us make decisions; it's fundamentally reshaping how labor markets work and how we unlock human potential.

AI-driven recruitment systems bring together a powerful set of advanced technologies, including machine learning (ML), natural language processing (NLP), and predictive analytics. Each plays a distinct but interconnected role throughout the entire hiring journey.

- **Machine Learning (ML) Algorithms:** These algorithms are like super-smart pattern detectors. They process enormous amounts of structured and unstructured data to find subtle connections in candidate characteristics, behaviors, and how they perform over time. ML models get better and better by learning from past hiring data, constantly refining their predictions. This makes them incredibly valuable for recommending high-potential candidates based on what's worked well before (Jain & Shanbhag, 2021). For example, an ML model could analyze thousands of successful hires to pinpoint common traits that lead to high performance in specific roles.
- **Natural Language Processing (NLP) Tools:** NLP tools are designed to understand human language from various sources, like résumés, cover letters, and online professional profiles. These systems can automatically pull out key information such as job titles, skills, qualifications, and employment histories. This drastically cuts down on manual screening time while ensuring a consistent and objective analysis across a wide range of candidates (Black & van Esch, 2020). Beyond just matching keywords, advanced NLP systems can grasp semantic relationships and contextual meanings, ensuring candidates are evaluated based on the true relevance and depth of their experience.
- **Predictive Analytics:** This is where AI truly shines in forecasting. It plays a critical role in predicting how well a candidate will succeed and perform in the long run. By looking at internal workforce data—like performance ratings, turnover patterns, and career paths—AI models can project which applicants are most likely to thrive in a particular role, team, or company culture (Upadhyay & Khandelwal, 2018). This ability to anticipate future needs supports proactive talent strategies, significantly reducing the costs associated with bad hiring decisions and subsequent employee turnover.

Innovative platforms perfectly illustrate how AI is applied in candidate assessment. For instance, HireVue uses AI to analyze video interviews, looking not only at what candidates say but also at non-verbal cues such as tone, facial expressions, and speech patterns to evaluate competencies and communication styles (Maurer, 2021). Pymetrics, on the other hand, uses neuroscience-based games powered by AI to assess cognitive and emotional attributes. These tools help us make more nuanced, behaviorally informed hiring decisions, especially when soft skills and cultural fit are just as important as technical qualifications.

What about **Conversational AI**? Think chatbots and virtual assistants. These are increasingly being used to make candidate engagement smoother. These systems can automatically answer frequently asked questions, provide application updates, and schedule interviews, creating a better experience for applicants while significantly reducing the administrative burden on recruiters (Suen *et al.*, 2019). And AI-powered behavioral assessments offer even deeper psychological insights by mapping candidates' personality traits and motivations, improving alignment with company values and team dynamics.

In short, AI tools aren't just making human judgment a bit easier; they are fundamentally reshaping the economics of hiring. By automating repetitive tasks, boosting accuracy, and providing data-driven insights, these technologies allow organizations to allocate resources more strategically, speed up hiring, and improve the overall quality of their workforce. From an economic perspective, these innovations represent a decisive shift from labor-intensive to intelligence-intensive recruitment models, solidifying AI's role as a transformative force in both talent strategy and financial performance.

4. EFFICIENCY, BIAS, AND EQUITY: ECONOMIC IMPLICATIONS

Bringing Artificial Intelligence (AI) into talent acquisition has led to noticeable improvements in how efficiently organizations operate, completely transforming traditional recruitment methods. By automating routine administrative tasks like resume screening, scheduling interviews, and communicating with candidates, AI frees up human resource (HR) professionals to focus on more strategic, high-level activities. As a result, companies are seeing significant cuts in how long it takes to hire someone, how much each hire costs, and how quickly they can plan their workforce, all of which translate into real economic benefits (Deloitte, 2021). These improvements don't just make internal HR more productive; they also smooth out bumps in the labor market by helping people find jobs faster and ensuring a better fit between talent and roles.

Looking at the bigger economic picture, the increased speed and accuracy in hiring processes make the labor market more fluid. This contributes to overall productivity growth and a more dynamic economy (Brynjolfsson &

McAfee, 2014). When companies can quickly bring in people whose skills perfectly match their strategic needs, the returns on human capital investments become more immediate and easier to measure. What's more, AI tools allow companies to tap into wider and more diverse talent pools—including those not actively looking for jobs—increasing the chances of finding ideal matches and reducing skill mismatches that have long been a drag on economic systems.

However, despite these compelling advantages, using AI in recruitment comes with significant ethical, legal, and social challenges. The most prominent among these is the widespread issue of **algorithmic bias**. AI models are only as fair and objective as the data they learn from. If historical hiring data reflects existing inequalities—like those based on gender, race, or socioeconomic background—these biases can be unintentionally copied and even amplified by AI systems, leading to unfair hiring outcomes (Binns, 2018). For example, Amazon famously had to scrap an AI recruiting tool after it was found to unfairly penalize resumes containing the word "women's" and favored male candidates, simply because it had been trained on past hiring data that was predominantly male (Dastin, 2018). This has far-reaching consequences, not only undermining the integrity of hiring processes but also worsening existing inequalities in job access, which poses a serious threat to inclusive economic development.

These risks aren't just ethical concerns; they have substantial economic implications. Organizations found to be engaging in biased hiring practices can face severe consequences, including expensive lawsuits, hefty regulatory fines, significant damage to their reputation, and a deep loss of trust from both consumers and employees. All of these can severely impact long-term financial performance (Raghavan *et al.*, 2020). Furthermore, overlooking or misjudging highly promising talent because of flawed AI models leads to considerable opportunity costs—missed innovation, less diverse teams, and reduced competitiveness in the global market.

Tackling these critical challenges requires a collaborative approach involving many different stakeholders. From an organizational perspective, it's crucial to put in place strong techniques to reduce bias. This means carefully cleaning up training datasets, using algorithms specifically designed to detect and correct bias, and regularly auditing AI hiring tools independently. Governments and regulatory bodies, on the other hand, must establish clear and enforceable guidelines that ensure transparency, accountability, and fairness in algorithmic decision-making (Barocas *et al.*, 2019). Additionally, fostering strong partnerships between the public and private sectors can encourage the development of open-source tools and benchmarks for ethical AI in hiring, ensuring that best practices are shared and widely adopted.

Ultimately, for AI-driven talent acquisition to truly deliver on its transformative promise, it must not only boost efficiency but also firmly uphold the principles of equity and inclusivity. Fair AI systems contribute to socially sustainable labor markets, making sure that the benefits of digital innovation are widely shared and not just concentrated among privileged groups. This delicate but vital balance between technological capability and ethical responsibility will shape the future of human capital economics in the digital age.

5. TALENT ANALYTICS AND FINANCIAL PERFORMANCE

The integration of Artificial Intelligence (AI) in talent acquisition has fundamentally changed how organizations view and strategically manage human capital as an economic asset. At the heart of this transformation is **talent analytics**—which is essentially applying data science to decisions about our workforce. By using AI-powered predictive models, companies can proactively spot high-potential candidates, anticipate who might leave, and optimize their workforce structures. This ensures that their talent strategies are perfectly aligned with their overall business goals (Davenport, Harris, & Shapiro, 2010).

Talent analytics empowers organizations to move beyond traditional, often reactive, HR metrics towards proactive, evidence-based decision-making. For example, AI models can carefully examine past hiring data to predict future performance and cultural fit, significantly improving the quality of new hires and reducing costly mismatches (Marler & Boudreau, 2017). What's more, intelligent systems analyze huge amounts of data on employee engagement, performance reviews, and career paths, offering real-time insights into complex workforce dynamics and potential productivity bottlenecks. These insights are especially valuable in knowledge-intensive industries, like tech and finance, where what employees produce directly impacts innovation, market competitiveness, and ultimately, economic growth.

From a financial standpoint, the economic value generated by AI-driven talent analytics is substantial and measurable. Organizations that effectively use these tools consistently report better employee performance, significantly lower turnover rates, and improved operational efficiency—all of which directly translate into increased profitability and long-term shareholder value (Bersin, 2018). A global study by Deloitte (2021) showed that companies with mature analytics capabilities in human capital management clearly outperform their competitors across several key financial indicators, including revenue per employee, return on equity, and earnings before interest and taxes (EBIT). This compelling evidence demonstrates a direct and strong link between smart talent management practices and superior economic outcomes.

Furthermore, AI-enabled workforce planning tools play a crucial role in helping companies manage costs and reduce risks by making sure the right people are in the right roles at the right time. By accurately forecasting hiring needs and anticipating skill shortages, these systems allow companies to react quickly to market changes and significantly reduce the financial risks associated with having too few or too many staff (Cappelli, 2019). In a time marked by economic uncertainty and rapid change, this kind of predictive foresight is absolutely essential for building resilient, adaptable organizations that can keep growing and navigate unexpected challenges.

The benefits of talent analytics extend beyond just internal company gains. By optimizing workforce planning and improving performance management, AI systems contribute to broader economic efficiency—reducing underemployment, effectively closing critical skill gaps, and improving how well the overall labor market functions. So, AI isn't just a tech tool; it's a strategic enabler of economic resilience, innovation capacity, and lasting prosperity.

In conclusion, AI-driven talent analytics has become a cornerstone of financial performance in today's digital economy. It empowers organizations to make smarter, data-informed decisions about their most valuable asset—their people. As companies continue to adopt and refine these powerful technologies, talent analytics will increasingly become a decisive factor in both competitive strategy and long-term economic sustainability.

6. GLOBAL TALENT MARKETS AND CROSS-BORDER HIRING

In the digital age, Artificial Intelligence (AI) isn't just changing how companies manage talent locally; it's profoundly reshaping the global dynamics of human capital. One of the most significant shifts in talent acquisition is the increasing ease with which talent can move geographically, thanks to AI-driven platforms. These platforms allow organizations to bypass national borders and tap into global talent markets with incredible efficiency. This evolution has fundamentally redefined traditional ideas of comparative advantage and introduced a new, dynamic way of thinking about international labor economics.

AI-powered platforms, like LinkedIn Recruiter, Toptal, and Upwork, use advanced machine learning algorithms and natural language processing to precisely match employers with candidates across continents. These sophisticated platforms analyze vast amounts of candidate data—including skills, experience, availability, and performance indicators—to deliver highly accurate matches in real-time (Boudreau & Cascio, 2017). By automating critical steps like sourcing, shortlisting, and even initial assessments, AI tools drastically cut down on hiring times and open up entirely new avenues for remote and borderless recruitment.

This AI-facilitated global reach actively supports labor mobility, making it much easier for skilled professionals to connect with international opportunities, no matter where they are. In doing so, it contributes to a more dynamic and fluid redistribution of global talent—especially in high-demand sectors like software development, data science, and digital marketing (World

Bank, 2019). For businesses, this expanded access to a diverse pool of human capital dramatically boosts their competitive edge, particularly in knowledge-based industries where specialized expertise is a primary driver of value creation and innovation.

Furthermore, applying AI in global talent acquisition has major implications for economic development and international competitiveness. By allowing companies in emerging economies to access top-tier talent remotely, and by enabling individuals from underrepresented regions to connect with global employers, AI contributes to a more equitable distribution of opportunity and productivity worldwide. It also challenges traditional notions of national labor supply by introducing a digital layer of comparative advantage that's based on capability and skill, rather than just physical location (Brynjolfsson & McAfee, 2014).

However, this transformative shift also brings complex challenges. Cross-border hiring raises intricate questions about labor rights, fair compensation, taxation, immigration policies, and regulatory compliance across different countries. Existing national labor laws are often ill-equipped to effectively govern these new digital hiring practices, leading to urgent calls for updated international regulatory frameworks and strong ethical AI standards (Choudhury, 2020). As organizations increasingly adopt distributed and remote hiring models, policymakers must adapt quickly to ensure fair labor practices are upheld and the interests of both employers and employees are adequately protected.

In essence, AI has revolutionized the scope and scale of talent acquisition, turning traditional labor markets into borderless ecosystems of skill and innovation. This profound change not only makes organizations more agile and gives them access to specialized expertise but also introduces new dimensions to the global flow of human capital. This requires both strategic foresight from companies and coordinated, adaptable responses from international regulatory bodies. As the digital economy continues to mature, the ability to effectively navigate and leverage global talent networks through AI will be a key factor in achieving economic success and leadership in innovation.

7. POLICY, ETHICS, AND THE FUTURE OF WORK

The integration of Artificial Intelligence (AI) into talent acquisition marks a truly pivotal and transformative moment for labor markets, organizational strategy, and overall economic productivity. However, alongside its immense potential to optimize hiring and workforce management, AI also brings with it complex ethical, legal, and societal challenges. As AI technologies become an increasingly common part of recruitment processes, the need for comprehensive, forward-looking policy and regulatory frameworks becomes more urgent than ever.

One of the most central and pressing concerns in AI-driven hiring is **algorithmic fairness**. When machine learning models are trained on historical data that is already biased, they can unintentionally reinforce existing patterns of discrimination based on things like race, gender, age, or socioeconomic background (Binns, 2018). Such discriminatory outcomes don't just raise serious ethical questions; they also pose significant economic and reputational risks for organizations. Because of this, regulatory frameworks need to go beyond basic compliance and demand transparency, accountability, and explainability in how algorithms make decisions (Wachter *et al.*, 2017). It's crucial that AI systems can clearly explain *why* they make certain hiring recommendations to maintain public trust and foster fairness in labor markets.

Governments, labor unions, and civil society organizations have a vital role in shaping how AI is governed in the workplace. Regulatory initiatives, like the European Union's proposed Artificial Intelligence Act (European Commission, 2021) and the U.S. Equal Employment Opportunity Commission's (EEOC) guidance on AI-based hiring (EEOC, 2023), are important steps towards creating legal safeguards that protect candidates' rights and promote the ethical use of AI. These policy tools are essential for setting clear boundaries for acceptable AI behavior, including, for instance, prohibiting opaque "black-box" models in high-stakes decision-making areas like employment.

Beyond strong regulation, public policy must actively support workforce readiness in an economy increasingly shaped by AI. As automation and AI change job roles and redefine what skills are needed, there's a growing imperative to invest heavily in programs for reskilling, upskilling, and digital literacy. Public institutions, working closely with private stakeholders, must ensure that workers have the competencies necessary to thrive in digitally enhanced workplaces (Manyika *et al.*, 2017). These initiatives are crucial not only for individual employability and career growth but also for maintaining broad economic participation and social cohesion across society.

The future of work will also require inclusive employment strategies that leverage AI's capabilities without making labor market polarization worse. While high-skilled roles might benefit significantly from AI adoption, lower-skilled workers risk being displaced unless proactive steps are taken to integrate them into the evolving job ecosystem. Policies that promote inclusive design, ensure accessibility in AI tools, and guarantee equitable access to employment opportunities can effectively reduce this risk and foster a more resilient and inclusive digital economy (ILO, 2020).

In essence, the future direction of AI in talent acquisition will be shaped not just by technological innovation, but equally by how robust our ethical frameworks are and how adaptable our public institutions become. As AI continues to redefine the very structure of work and the broader economy, a multi-stakeholder approach—combining thoughtful regulation, comprehensive education, and strong corporate responsibility—will be absolutely essential to harness its immense benefits while effectively minimizing its inherent risks.

8. CONCLUSION: AI IN TALENT ACQUISITION AS A CATALYST FOR ECONOMIC INNOVATION

The integration of Artificial Intelligence (AI) into talent acquisition marks a pivotal turning point in the evolving landscape of economics, labor, and technology. Far from being just an operational improvement, AI-driven recruitment acts as a strategic lever, fundamentally reconfiguring how human capital is sourced, evaluated, and deployed in the digital economy. In a world where intangible assets like knowledge, innovation, and adaptability increasingly define competitive advantage, the efficient and intelligent management of talent is emerging as a core determinant of both organizational and national economic performance (OECD, 2019).

AI technologies empower companies to identify and secure talent with unprecedented precision and scale. Through the smart use of predictive analytics, natural language processing, and cognitive assessment tools, organizations can now align their workforce capabilities much more closely with their evolving business strategies and dynamic market demands (Chamorro-Premuzic *et al.*, 2017). This has led to tangible gains in hiring speed, significant cost-efficiency, and improved employee performance—factors that collectively contribute to long-term financial resilience and enhanced productivity (Deloitte, 2021).

At the macroeconomic level, AI-facilitated global hiring practices are expanding access to opportunities, strategically redistributing specialized skills across international borders, and fundamentally transforming how efficient labor markets are. The ability to engage with diverse international talent pools not only boosts corporate innovation capacity but also redefines traditional notions of comparative advantage (ILO, 2020). These trends highlight the growing importance of human capital as both a vital national asset and a powerful means for global economic integration.

However, the immense economic promise of AI in talent acquisition is inextricably linked to critical ethical and regulatory imperatives. Algorithmic transparency, fairness, and accountability aren't optional; they are fundamental requirements for equitable participation in the labor market. Without deliberate and sustained efforts to reduce bias and ensure inclusivity, AI risks perpetuating structural inequalities and eroding societal trust in automated systems (Binns, 2018; Wachter *et al.*, 2017).

Therefore, the path forward demands a comprehensive, multi-stakeholder approach. Policymakers, technologists, educators, and business leaders must collaborate effectively to establish robust governance frameworks that consistently uphold ethical standards while simultaneously fostering continuous innovation. Investments in digital literacy, widespread reskilling programs, and inclusive AI design are equally critical to ensure that all segments of the workforce can thrive and contribute meaningfully in the AI-enabled labor economy (Manyika *et al.*, 2017).

In conclusion, AI-driven talent acquisition isn't simply a technological upgrade; it represents a profound paradigm shift in the economics of workforce management. It acts as a powerful catalyst for innovation, drives significant operational transformation, and substantially enhances the strategic role of human capital in a rapidly digitizing world. When responsibly implemented, AI has the transformative potential to democratize opportunity, elevate human potential, and usher in a more dynamic, inclusive, and resilient economic future for all.

REFERENCES

[1] Barocas, S., Hardt, M. and Narayanan, A. (2019). Fairness and machine learning: Limitations and opportunities. fairmlbook.org.

[2] Becker, G.S. (1993). Human capital: A theoretical and empirical analysis, with special reference to education (3rd ed.). University of Chicago Press.

[3] Bersin, J. (2018). People analytics: Here with a vengeance. Deloitte Insights.

[4] Binns, R. (2018). Fairness in machine learning: Lessons from political philosophy. *Proceedings of the 2018 Conference on Fairness, Accountability, and Transparency,* 149–159.

[5] Black, J.S. and van Esch, P. (2020). AI-enabled recruiting: What is it and how should a manager use it? Business Horizons, 63(2), 215–226.

[6] Boudreau, J.W. and Cascio, W.F. (2017). Human capital analytics: Why are we not there? *Journal of Organizational Effectiveness: People and Performance,* 4(1), 16–22.

[7] Brynjolfsson, E. and McAfee, A. (2014). The second machine age: Work, progress, and prosperity in a time of brilliant technologies. W.W. Norton & Company.

[8] Cappelli, P. (2019). Talent on demand: Managing talent in an age of uncertainty. Harvard Business Press.

[9] Chamorro-Premuzic, T., Akhtar, R., Winsborough, D. and Sherman, R.A. (2017). The talent delusion: Why data, not intuition, is the key to unlocking human potential. *Harvard Business Review,* 95(2), 72–78.

[10] Choudhury, S. (2020). The distributed workforce: Demystifying the future of work. *Columbia University Press.*

[11] Dastin, J. (2018, October 10). Amazon scrapped 'sexist AI' recruiting tool. Reuters.

[12] Davenport, T.H., Harris, J. and Shapiro, J. (2010). Competing on talent analytics. *Harvard Business Review,* 88(10), 52–58.

[13] Deloitte (2021). 2021 Global Human Capital Trends.

[14] Docquier, F. and Rapoport, H. (2012). Globalization, brain drain, and development. *Journal of Economic Literature,* 50(3), 681–730.

[15] EEOC (2023). Artificial Intelligence and Algorithmic Fairness in Hiring. U.S. Equal Employment Opportunity Commission.

[16] European Commission (2021). Proposal for a Regulation on a European approach for Artificial Intelligence.

[17] ILO (2020). World Employment and Social Outlook: Trends 2020. *International Labour Organization.*

[18] Jain, R. and Shanbhag, N. (2021). A study on machine learning in recruitment and selection process. *International Journal of Advanced Research in Computer Science,* 12(1), 50–55.

[19] Manyika, J., Chui, M., Madgavkar, A. and Lund, S. (2017). Jobs lost, jobs gained: What the future of work will mean for jobs, skills, and wages. *McKinsey Global Institute.*

[20] Marler, J.H. and Boudreau, J.W. (2017). An evidence-based review of HR Analytics. *The International Journal of Human Resource Management,* 28(1), 3–26.

[21] Maurer, R. (2021). Employers using AI to monitor candidates' facial expressions. *Society for Human Resource Management (SHRM).*

[22] OECD (2019). Measuring the digital transformation: A roadmap for the future. *OECD Publishing.*

[23] Raghavan, M., Barocas, S., Kleinberg, J. and Levy, K. (2020). Mitigating bias in algorithmic hiring: Evaluating claims and practices. *Proceedings of the 2020 Conference on Fairness, Accountability, and Transparency,* 469–481.

[24] Suen, H.Y., Chen, M.Y.C. and Lu, S.H. (2019). Does the use of synchrony and artificial intelligence in applicant screening improve hiring decisions? *Computers in Human Behavior*, 98, 93–101.

[25] Upadhyay, A.K. and Khandelwal, K. (2018). Applying artificial intelligence: Implications for recruitment. *Strategic HR Review*, 17(5), 255–258.

[26] Wachter, S., Mittelstadt, B. and Floridi, L. (2017). Why a Right to Explanation of Algorithmic Decision-Making Should Not Be Confused with a Right to Transparency. *Artificial Intelligence and Law,* 26(3), 425–443.

[27] World Bank (2019). World Development Report 2019: The Changing Nature of Work. World Bank Publications.

Assessing the Impact of Technological Shifts on Economic Growth in India

Y. Shivashankarachar[1], S. Ayyappan[2] and M. Sakthivadivel[3]

[1]Scholar, School of Management Studies, CMR University, Bangalore, Karnataka, India

[2]Professor School of Management Studies, CMR University, Bangalore, Karnataka, India

[3]Assistant Professor (SS), Department of Computer Science and Engineering (CYS), Dr. Mahalingam College of Engineering and Technology, Pollachi, India

E-mail: [1]shivashankarachar.y@cmr.edu.in; [1]shivu1finance@gmail.com; [2]ayyappan.s@cmr.edu.in; [2]sapacet@gmail.com; [3]sakthivadivelm@gmail.com

ABSTRACT: *This article examines how technological shifts have influenced economic growth in India over the past few decades. It covers the evolution of key technological milestones, their integration into various sectors of the economy, and the resultant changes in productivity, employment, and overall economic output. The paper highlights the role of digital transformation, IT and software services, manufacturing automation, and emerging technologies like AI and blockchain. Challenges such as digital divides and policy gaps are also discussed. The study concludes with policy recommendations to leverage technology for inclusive and sustainable economic growth.*

Keywords: Digital Transformation, Economic Growth, India, Innovation, Productivity, Policy, Technological Shifts.

1. INTRODUCTION

Technological advancement has long been recognized as a vital driver of economic growth, productivity enhancement, and social development. In recent decades, India has experienced significant technological shifts that have fundamentally transformed its economic structure and growth trajectory. From the adoption of high-yield agricultural practices during the Green Revolution to the rise of the Information Technology (IT) and software services sector post-1990s economic liberalization, technology has played an increasingly important role in shaping India's development narrative.

The liberalization of the Indian economy in 1991 marked a turning point, opening up new opportunities for private enterprises, foreign investments, and technological collaborations. This paved the way for India's emergence as a global leader in IT and IT-enabled services (ITES), contributing substantially to GDP growth, employment generation, and foreign exchange earnings. Over the past two decades, the proliferation of digital technologies—spurred by affordable mobile devices, increased internet connectivity, and government-led initiatives like Digital India—has further accelerated the country's digital transformation.

In parallel, advancements in emerging technologies such as Artificial Intelligence (AI), Internet of Things (IoT), Big Data, and Blockchain are reshaping industries ranging from manufacturing and agriculture to healthcare and education. Initiatives like Make in India, Startup India, and the Atal Innovation Mission are fostering innovation-driven ecosystems that support new business models and technological solutions tailored to India's unique development challenges.

However, this rapid pace of technological change also presents significant challenges. Issues such as digital inequality, infrastructure gaps, cybersecurity threats, and workforce skill mismatches require careful policy attention to ensure that the benefits of technology-led growth are inclusive and sustainable.

This article aims to assess the impact of technological shifts on India's economic growth by examining key historical milestones, sectoral transformations, and emerging trends. It will also address the challenges associated with technological adoption and propose policy measures to harness technology for long-term, inclusive economic development.

2. HISTORICAL PERSPECTIVE OF TECHNOLOGICAL SHIFTS IN INDIA

India's journey of technological transformation has evolved through distinct phases, each leaving a lasting impact on the country's economic structure and growth patterns. In the post-independence period, the focus was on building heavy industries, public sector enterprises, and scientific research institutions to achieve economic self-reliance. The Green Revolution of the 1960s marked a major technological milestone, introducing high-yield crop varieties, mechanized farming, and improved irrigation techniques that transformed Indian agriculture and ensured food security. The economic liberalization of 1991 represented another turning point, dismantling regulatory barriers and encouraging private sector participation and foreign investment. This reform era gave rise to India's globally competitive IT and software services industry, positioning the country as a knowledge-based economy. In recent decades, rapid advancements in digital technologies, mobile connectivity, and internet penetration have further reshaped sectors such as retail, banking, healthcare, and governance. Today, India stands on the cusp of a new phase, with emerging technologies like AI, IoT, Blockchain, and advanced manufacturing driving the transition toward a more connected, efficient, and innovation-led economy.

3. THE ROLE OF INFORMATION TECHNOLOGY AND DIGITAL ECONOMY

The Information Technology (IT) and digital economy sectors have emerged as pivotal contributors to India's economic growth over the past three decades. Since the early 1990s, when economic liberalization policies opened up new opportunities for private enterprise and foreign investment, India's IT and IT-enabled services (ITES) industry has grown into a global powerhouse. Leading firms such as Tata Consultancy Services (TCS), Infosys, and Wipro have not only driven export earnings but also positioned India as a strategic player in global software services, business process outsourcing (BPO), and digital solutions markets.

The IT sector's contribution to India's Gross Domestic Product (GDP) has consistently increased, accounting for nearly 7.5% of GDP by 2023, up from just 1.2% in 1998. Beyond its direct economic contribution, the sector has generated significant employment, providing jobs to over 5 million professionals, and has indirectly supported ancillary industries, including telecommunications, education, and infrastructure services. The success of India's IT industry has also contributed to human capital development, fostering a skilled workforce and enhancing India's competitiveness in the global knowledge economy.

The rapid growth of the digital economy has been another defining feature of India's economic transformation. Initiatives such as Digital India, launched in 2015, aimed to improve digital infrastructure, enhance internet connectivity, and promote the delivery of public services through digital platforms. As a result, India now ranks among the fastest-growing digital markets globally, with over 880 million internet users by 2023. The expansion of e-commerce, fintech, and digital payment systems has revolutionized consumer markets and financial inclusion. The success of platforms like Unified Payments Interface (UPI) and mobile wallets has brought millions of previously unbanked individuals into the formal financial system.

Moreover, the integration of digital technologies has significantly impacted governance, healthcare, and education. E-governance platforms such as Aadhaar, DigiLocker, and e-NAM have improved service delivery and transparency. However, challenges such as digital divides, uneven rural access, cybersecurity concerns, and skill gaps persist, underscoring the need for continued investment in digital infrastructure and inclusive technology policies.

In sum, the IT and digital economy sectors have not only driven economic growth but have also fostered innovation, job creation, and social inclusion, positioning India for a technology-driven future.

4. EMERGING TECHNOLOGIES AND THEIR POTENTIAL IMPACT

In recent years, emerging technologies such as Artificial Intelligence (AI), Machine Learning (ML), Internet of Things (IoT), Blockchain, Big Data Analytics, and advanced robotics have begun to reshape the Indian economy, offering transformative potential across sectors. These technologies are not only enhancing productivity and operational efficiency but also creating new business models and economic opportunities that were previously unimagine-able.

Artificial Intelligence and Machine Learning, for instance, are increasingly being adopted in industries such as healthcare, agriculture, logistics, retail, and financial services. AI-powered diagnostic tools, precision farming applications, and predictive analytics for supply chain management are improving decision-making, reducing costs, and enhancing service quality. The Government of India has recognized the importance of AI through initiatives like the National Strategy for Artificial Intelligence (NITI Aayog, 2018), aiming to position India as a global AI innovation hub while addressing ethical, legal, and data privacy concerns.

Similarly, the Internet of Things is transforming manufacturing, urban infrastructure, and consumer services. Smart factories using IoT devices are optimizing production processes, reducing downtime, and improving energy efficiency. In urban governance, IoT-enabled smart city projects have enhanced traffic management, waste disposal, and public safety systems. Blockchain technology, though still in its nascent stage in India, holds promise in areas such as digital identity management, transparent supply chains, and secure financial transactions.

The rise of Big Data Analytics is enabling businesses and government agencies to derive actionable insights from vast data sets, supporting better policy formulation, targeted welfare delivery, and market forecasting. Startups and innovation hubs across the country, particularly in cities like Bengaluru, Hyderabad, and Pune, are driving experimentation and commercial application of these technologies.

While these developments present immense opportunities, they also pose challenges related to job displacement, regulatory readiness, ethical risks, and unequal access to advanced technologies. Ensuring that the benefits of these innovations are widely shared will require proactive policy measures, investments in digital skills, and robust governance frameworks.

In conclusion, emerging technologies offer the potential to fundamentally transform India's economy, enhance productivity, and address developmental challenges, provided their integration is inclusive, ethical, and strategically guided.

5. IMPACT ON ECONOMIC GROWTH AND PRODUCTIVITY

Technological advancements have played a critical role in enhancing economic growth and productivity in India, particularly in the post-liberalization period. The rapid adoption of information technology, digital infrastructure, and emerging technologies has contributed to structural shifts within the economy, increased efficiency in production processes, and expanded access to markets and services. These developments have not only driven GDP growth but also improved productivity across multiple sectors.

The services sector, led by the IT and IT-enabled services (ITES) industries, has witnessed the most significant productivity gains. Between 1991 and 2023, the IT sector's contribution to India's GDP increased substantially, with annual growth rates often exceeding 8–10%. This sector has enabled India to position itself as a global outsourcing and software development hub, generating foreign exchange earnings and employment opportunities for millions of skilled professionals. The sector's productivity has been amplified through process automation, cloud computing, and AI-driven services, leading to increased value addition with relatively low incremental costs.

In manufacturing, the integration of automation, robotics, and Internet of Things (IoT) technologies has improved operational efficiency, product quality, and energy management. Initiatives such as Make in India and the push for Industry 4.0 adoption have encouraged the modernization of factories and supply chains. While the sector still faces challenges, early evidence suggests that technology-driven manufacturing clusters have higher output and productivity levels than traditional setups.

In agriculture, although the overall adoption of advanced technology remains uneven, innovations like precision farming, drone-based crop monitoring, and digital marketplaces such as e-NAM have begun improving productivity and market access for farmers. These interventions have the potential to reduce post-harvest losses, optimize input usage, and increase farmers' incomes, contributing to rural economic growth.

Empirical studies have shown a positive correlation between technology adoption and economic output in India. According to estimates by NASSCOM and the Reserve Bank of India, technology-driven sectors have consistently outperformed non-tech sectors in productivity growth rates. Moreover, digital technologies have facilitated the formalization of economic activities, financial inclusion, and e-governance, thereby broadening the economic base.

However, disparities in technology access between urban and rural regions, large firms and small enterprises, and skilled and unskilled labor continue to affect the uniform distribution of productivity gains. Addressing these divides through policy support, skill development, and digital infrastructure expansion is essential to sustain long-term, inclusive growth.

6. CHALLENGES AND CONSTRAINTS

While technological shifts have significantly contributed to India's economic growth, several challenges and constraints continue to hinder the full realization of their potential. These challenges are multi-dimensional, spanning infrastructural, socio-economic, regulatory, and institutional barriers that need to be addressed for technology-led growth to be truly inclusive and sustainable.

One of the foremost issues is the digital divide between urban and rural areas, as well as among different socio-economic groups. Despite significant progress under initiatives like Digital India, a substantial portion of the population, particularly in rural and remote regions, still lacks reliable internet connectivity, access to digital devices, and basic digital literacy. This uneven access limits the ability of marginalized communities and small businesses to benefit from technological advancements and participate in the digital economy.

A second major constraint is the mismatch between workforce skills and emerging technological requirements. While India produces a large pool of graduates annually, many lack the specialized skills needed for high-growth sectors such as artificial intelligence, data analytics, and robotics. This skills gap creates challenges for industries seeking to adopt advanced technologies and limits the employability of large segments of the workforce. Efforts through programs like Skill India have made progress, but scaling these initiatives to meet future demands remains a critical priority.

Regulatory and policy challenges also pose significant constraints. Rapid technological innovation often outpaces the ability of legal and institutional frameworks to adapt. Issues related to data privacy, cybersecurity, digital taxation, and the ethical use of artificial intelligence require clear, forward-looking policies to foster innovation while safeguarding public interest. The lack of a cohesive national policy on emerging technologies sometimes creates uncertainty for investors, startups, and multinational firms operating in India.

Additionally, infrastructure bottlenecks, such as inconsistent power supply, limited broadband penetration in rural areas, and insufficient research and development (R&D) investment, restrict the pace of technology adoption, especially in the manufacturing and agriculture sectors. India's R&D spending, at around 0.7% of GDP, remains below the global average and significantly lower than countries like China and South Korea.

Lastly, the risk of job displacement due to automation and AI presents a socio-economic challenge. While technology can create new employment opportunities, it also threatens traditional low-skill jobs, particularly in manufacturing and services. Managing this transition through proactive workforce reskilling and social protection measures is essential to minimize economic and social disruption.

7. POLICY MEASURES AND STRATEGIC RECOMMENDATIONS

To fully harness the benefits of technological shifts and drive inclusive economic growth, India must adopt a comprehensive policy framework that addresses existing gaps while promoting innovation and competitiveness.

Priority should be given to expanding digital infrastructure in rural and underserved regions to bridge the digital divide and ensure equitable access to emerging technologies. Simultaneously, large-scale investment in skill development programs tailored to new-age sectors like artificial intelligence, data analytics, robotics, and IoT is essential to prepare the workforce for future demands. Strengthening R&D investment and fostering public-private partnerships in technology development can enhance domestic innovation capacity and reduce dependency on foreign technology. Regulatory frameworks must be updated to address issues such as data privacy, cybersecurity, ethical AI, and digital taxation, balancing innovation incentives with public interest safeguards. Furthermore, sector-specific strategies, such as incentivizing agri-tech solutions, promoting smart manufacturing under Make in India, and supporting tech-driven startups through simplified regulatory norms and financial assistance, can accelerate technology diffusion across the economy. Together, these measures can help India build a resilient, inclusive, and sustainable technology-driven growth model.

8. CONCLUSION

Technological shifts have become a vital force shaping India's economic growth, productivity, and global competitiveness. From the rise of the IT sector to the rapid expansion of the digital economy and the promise of emerging technologies, India stands at a pivotal moment to leverage innovation for inclusive and sustainable development. While significant progress has been made, challenges such as digital inequality, skill gaps, and regulatory hurdles persist. By adopting forward-looking policies, investing in infrastructure and human capital, and fostering a supportive innovation ecosystem, India can unlock the full potential of technology to drive long-term, equitable economic growth.

REFERENCES

[1] World Bank (2024, September 3). *India's Economy to Remain Strong Despite Subdued Global Growth.*

[2] Deloitte (2025, May). *India Economic Outlook, May 2025.*

[3] Press Information Bureau (PIB), Government of India (2025, February). *India's Digital Economy to Contribute One-Fifth of National Income by 2029–30.*

[4] Economic Times (2025, June 3). *How Has the Digital Rupee Grown 180 Times in Just Two Years?*

[5] AP News (2025, June 1). *India, a Major User of Coal Power, Is Making Large Gains in Clean Energy Adoption. Here Is How.*

[6] Economic Times (2025, May 28). *A Compelling Economic Logic Is Leading India's Big Data Push Away from Major Coastal Centres, Deep into the Inlands.*

[7] Business Standard (2025, February 19). *Sectoral Growth, Tech to Power India's $23-35 Trillion 'Economic Vision': Report.*

[8] Economic Times (2024, October 15). *India to Become $1 Trillion Digital Economy by 2028 Enabled by Internet, 4G, 5G, and Digitalisation.*

[9] International Trade Administration, U.S. Department of Commerce (2024, October). *India - Digital Economy.*

[10] World Bank (2024). *India Overview.*

[11] National Association of Software and Services Companies (NASSCOM) (2023). *The Impact of New and Emerging Technology on Economic Development in India.*

[12] EY India (2023). *Digitalizing India: A Force to Reckon With.*

[13] PwC (2023). *India Rising: Five Springboards to Developed Nation Status by 2047.*

[14] McKinsey & Company (2023). *What Does the Future Hold for India?*

[15] BluePi (2025, April). *Digitization in India: Driving Growth & Innovation (2025 Guide).*

[16] NITI Aayog (2024). National Strategy on Artificial Intelligence: #AIforAll. Government of India. This strategic document outlines India's approach to leveraging AI for inclusive growth across sectors such as healthcare, agriculture, education, and smart cities. https://niti.gov.in/national-strategy-artificial-intelligence-ai-all.

[17] KPMG India (2024). Emerging Technologies in India: Trends and Opportunities.An insightful report on how emerging technologies like blockchain, AI, and IoT are transforming Indian industries and creating new business opportunities. https://home.kpmg/in/en/home/insights/2024/01/emerging-technologies-trends-india.html.

[18] Reserve Bank of India (RBI) (2025). Digital Payments in India: Trends and Developments. A comprehensive overview of the digital payments ecosystem, including the adoption of UPI, mobile wallets, and the Digital Rupee. https://rbi.org.in/scripts/AnnualReportPublications.aspx.

[19] McKinsey Global Institute (2023). India's Digital Leap: The Role of Emerging Technologies in Economic Transformation. Analyzes India's digital economy and the critical role played by emerging technologies in accelerating growth and competitiveness. https://www.mckinsey.com/featured-insights/asia-pacific/indias-digital-leap.

[20] India Brand Equity Foundation (IBEF) (2025). Information Technology Industry in India. An updated report providing insights on the IT industry's growth, exports, and contribution to the Indian economy. https://www.ibef.org/industry/information-technology-india.aspx.

Digital Banking and Customer Empowerment: A Framework for Understanding Behavioral Shifts Due to FinTech

Shreya Chauhan and Archana Dixit
Associate Professor, Tecnia Institute of Advanced Studies, India

ABSTRACT: *The emergence of Financial Technology (FinTech) has dramatically transformed the traditional banking landscape, ushering in an era of digital banking that empowers customers through enhanced accessibility, personalization, and real-time financial management tools. This paper presents a comprehensive framework for understanding the behavioral shifts among customers due to FinTech adoption. Drawing upon the Unified Theory of Acceptance and Use of Technology (UTAUT) and customer empowerment theory, the study explores key drivers of behavioral change, including digital literacy, trust, perceived ease of use, and the growing preference for self-service platforms. By examining empirical studies, case analyses, and industry trends, the paper provides insights into how FinTech influences consumer engagement, decision-making autonomy, and financial inclusion. The findings have significant implications for banks, FinTech firms, and policymakers in designing user-centric digital financial services that promote inclusive growth.*

Keywords: Behavioral Shifts, Consumer Engagement, Customer Empowerment, Digital Banking, Digital Literacy, Financial Inclusion, FinTech, Self-Service Technology, UTAUT.

1. INTRODUCTION

Digital transformation in the financial services industry has redefined how customers interact with banks. The rise of FinTech innovations—ranging from mobile banking applications to blockchain and robo-advisors—has led to significant behavioral shifts in how individuals manage, save, and invest their money. Traditional banking models, characterized by face-to-face transactions, are being replaced by digital-first solutions that emphasize convenience, speed, and autonomy.

This transformation is fueled by several interrelated factors. First, the proliferation of smartphones and internet connectivity has enabled widespread access to financial services, even in previously underserved or unbanked regions. Second, the user-centric design of FinTech applications provides a seamless and intuitive experience, which enhances customer satisfaction and reduces friction in financial interactions. Third, technologies like artificial intelligence (AI), big data analytics, and blockchain have introduced new levels of efficiency, security, and personalization into financial services.

Moreover, consumers today demand instant services, transparency, and control over their financial decisions. FinTech addresses these expectations through features such as instant fund transfers, peer-to-peer (P2P) payments, investment automation, credit scoring, and real-time alerts. Robo-advisors, for example, democratize access to investment advice by providing data- driven portfolio recommendations at a fraction of the cost of traditional financial advisors.

The COVID-19 pandemic further accelerated this digital shift, compelling banks and consumers to embrace contactless and remote banking options. As a result, digital banking is no longer an alternative but a fundamental component of the financial ecosystem. This shift is not merely technological but behavioral, influencing how people perceive, approach, and manage their finances in a digital age.

2. LITERATURE REVIEW

The adoption of digital banking has been studied extensively in the context of technology acceptance, consumer behavior, and financial inclusion. Scholars have identified various theoretical models to explain the digital transition and the associated behavioral changes. Among the most influential are the Technology Acceptance Model (TAM), the Unified Theory of Acceptance and Use of Technology (UTAUT), and the Diffusion of Innovations Theory.

2.1 Technology Acceptance Models

Davis (1989) proposed the Technology Acceptance Model (TAM), which suggests that perceived usefulness and perceived ease of use are the primary factors influencing technology adoption. This model has been adapted and expanded by many researchers in the context of digital banking, showing that ease of transaction, user-friendly interface, and utility significantly affect customers' willingness to adopt FinTech solutions.

The UTAUT framework (Venkatesh *et al.*, 2003) builds on TAM and includes four constructs— performance expectancy, effort expectancy, social influence, and facilitating conditions. UTAUT has been widely employed in studies related to mobile banking, digital wallets, and online investment platforms. A recent study by Tariq *et al.* (2024) emphasized the applicability of UTAUT in understanding FinTech adoption, particularly among younger demographics.

2.2 Digital Literacy and Financial Empowerment

Digital literacy is a prerequisite for customer empowerment in digital banking. According to a report by the World Bank (2023), digital literacy improves confidence, reduces perceived risk, and encourages self-directed financial behavior. Customers with higher digital competencies are more likely to engage with complex financial products such as online trading platforms and automated investment tools.

In a study conducted by OECD (2022), it was revealed that digital financial education initiatives significantly increase the adoption of budgeting apps and personal finance trackers. These tools not only improve financial literacy but also lead to better financial outcomes, including reduced debt and improved savings behavior.

2.3 Trust and Risk Perception

Trust is a critical component in digital banking relationships. As noted by Yousafzai *et al.* (2009), perceived trust in digital systems determines the extent to which users are willing to share personal data and perform financial transactions online. In the context of FinTech, trust is closely tied to security features, data privacy, regulatory compliance, and brand reputation.

Perceived risk, on the other hand, often deters users from adopting FinTech services. Risks include data breaches, identity theft, and technical failures. Studies have shown that robust encryption, user education, and transparent policies significantly reduce perceived risk and enhance adoption rates (Kim *et al.*, 2021).

2.4 Personalization and Consumer Experience

Advancements in AI and big data analytics have enabled financial institutions to deliver hyper- personalized experiences. According to Accenture (2024), over 60% of banking customers prefer financial services that are tailored to their life goals and spending behavior. Personalized insights, such as spending alerts, savings tips, and investment suggestions, enhance engagement and foster customer loyalty.

Banks that integrate these features into their digital platforms report higher Net Promoter Scores (NPS) and customer retention rates. Furthermore, personalization contributes to customer empowerment by offering actionable insights and timely recommendations that improve financial decision-making.

2.5 Behavioral Economics and FinTech Design

Behavioral economics principles are increasingly being used to design FinTech applications that nudge users towards better financial habits. Features like automatic savings transfers, spending categorization, and goal-setting interfaces leverage behavioral triggers to promote long-term financial health.

A study by Thaler and Sunstein (2008) emphasized the importance of "choice architecture"— structuring digital environments in a way that guides users without restricting their freedom. FinTech firms adopting such designs report higher levels of user engagement and reduced financial anxiety.

2.6 Inclusion and Accessibility

FinTech has the potential to bridge gaps in financial inclusion. Digital wallets, micro-loans, and mobile banking services provide unbanked populations access to essential financial tools. The GSMA Mobile Economy Report (2023) states that mobile money services have significantly increased in rural and low-income areas, enhancing economic participation.

However, digital exclusion remains a challenge for certain segments, including the elderly, individuals with disabilities, and residents of areas with limited internet connectivity. Inclusive

FinTech design must therefore prioritize accessibility features, multilingual support, and offline functionalities.

3. THEORETICAL FRAMEWORK

This research integrates multiple theoretical lenses to understand the behavioral shifts induced by FinTech in the digital banking ecosystem, focusing primarily on the **Unified Theory of Acceptance and Use of Technology (UTAUT)** and **Customer Empowerment Theory**.

3.1 Unified Theory of Acceptance and Use of Technology (UTAUT)

Developed by Venkatesh *et al.* (2003), UTAUT is a robust model for analyzing user acceptance of technology. It identifies four key determinants:

- **Performance Expectancy:** The degree to which users believe FinTech services will enhance their financial efficiency.
- **Effort Expectancy:** The ease associated with using digital financial tools like mobile banking or robo-advisors.
- **Social Influence:** How peer usage and societal trends influence individual adoption.
- **Facilitating Conditions:** The infrastructure and support available to assist usage (e.g., digital literacy, mobile access).

These constructs explain the behavioral intention and actual usage of digital banking platforms. In this study, the UTAUT framework helps interpret why and how customers adopt digital services and how this affects their financial behavior.

3.2 Customer Empowerment Theory

Customer empowerment refers to giving consumers greater control, choice, and influence over service interactions. FinTech applications exemplify this by enabling:

- **Self-service capabilities** (e.g., mobile check deposits, AI-based investment advisors),
- Real-time feedback and transparency, and
- **Personalized financial management**.

Empowered users are more likely to make autonomous decisions and switch providers based on service quality rather than brand loyalty. This empowerment fosters financial confidence and independence, crucial for the behavioral changes observed in digital banking users.

3.3 Complementary Frameworks

- **Technology Acceptance Model (TAM):** As a foundational element of UTAUT, TAM's focus on perceived usefulness and perceived ease of use aligns with customer behavior in adopting new technologies.
- **Behavioral Economics:** Concepts like nudging, loss aversion, and bounded rationality help explain how design elements (e.g., notifications, gamification) affect spending and savings behaviors in digital apps.
- **Diffusion of Innovation Theory (Rogers, 2003):** Explains the adoption pattern of FinTech tools across different user segments, from innovators to laggards.

By synthesizing these theories, the framework enables a holistic understanding of both the psychological and environmental drivers behind behavioral shifts in digital banking.

4. RESEARCH METHODOLOGY

This study adopts a **mixed-methods research design** to explore behavioral shifts in digital banking users and validate the proposed framework. The methodology integrates qualitative and quantitative approaches for triangulation and depth.

4.1 Research Design

- **Exploratory Phase (Qualitative):** Conducted to identify emerging patterns, sentiments, and factors influencing FinTech usage.
  - **Methods:** In-depth interviews and focus groups with 40 digital banking users across diverse demographics (age, income, geography).
  - **Objective:** To gain nuanced understanding of empowerment, trust, autonomy, and adoption patterns.

- **Descriptive Phase (Quantitative):** A structured survey was designed to test hypotheses derived from the theoretical framework.
  - **Sample Size:** 600 respondents across India, the UK, Kenya, and China.
  - **Tool:** Likert-scale based questionnaire covering variables like ease of use, trust, digital literacy, and behavioral changes.
  - **Statistical Techniques:** Descriptive analysis, correlation, regression modeling using SPSS and AMOS.

4.2 Sampling Technique

- **Purposive Sampling:** For interviews to ensure inclusion of both early adopters and late entrants.
- **Stratified Random Sampling:** For the survey, ensuring representation across gender, age, profession, and region.

4.3 Data Sources

- **Primary Data:** Interviews and surveys with FinTech users and banking professionals.
- **Secondary Data:** Industry reports (e.g., NPCI, World Bank), academic journals, and digital banking usage statistics from national regulators.

4.4 Validity and Reliability

- **Pilot Testing:** The survey instrument was piloted with 50 participants.
- **Cronbach's Alpha:** Used to ensure internal consistency (threshold > 0.7).
- **Expert Review:** The interview guide and questionnaire were reviewed by FinTech researchers and industry professionals.

4.5 Ethical Considerations

- Informed consent was obtained from all participants.
- Anonymity and confidentiality were maintained.
- Ethical approval was secured from an institutional review board.

5. BEHAVIORAL SHIFTS IN DIGITAL BANKING USERS

5.1 Autonomy and Financial Decision-Making

Digital banking tools, especially robo-advisors and budgeting apps, have shifted financial decision-making from banking professionals to individual consumers. This change is evident in the growing trend of DIY investing and peer-to-peer lending, where users independently manage their portfolios. The empowerment facilitated by these tools is not only functional but psychological, giving users confidence to act on financial information.

5.2 Changing Savings and Spending Habits

Behavioral economics studies indicate that visualizing savings and setting automated goals through mobile apps leads to better financial discipline. FinTech apps like Mint, YNAB (You Need A Budget), and India's ET Money use gamification and real-time data to nudge users toward prudent financial behaviors. Interviews revealed that 68% of participants reported improved savings behavior post-adoption of digital banking tools.

5.3 Trust and Risk Perception

A significant shift in customer behavior relates to trust. Users now rely on encryption and biometric security more than human assurances. Survey data indicated that 82% of respondents perceived biometric authentication as more secure than traditional PINs. Trust in algorithms— especially for credit scoring and investment advice—has risen, though there remains a digital divide in lower-income segments.

5.4 Digital Loyalty and Switching Behavior

Traditional banking relied heavily on inertia to retain customers. With FinTech, switching costs are minimal. Users readily move between apps offering better user experience or incentives. This agility has made brand loyalty more fluid and experience-dependent. For instance, 57% of respondents had switched at least one financial app in the past year.

5.5 Impact of COVID-19 on Behavioral Acceleration

The pandemic forced both consumers and institutions into rapid digital adaptation. Contactless payments, remote verification (e-KYC), and digital wallets witnessed exponential growth. Interviews highlighted that older demographics, previously reluctant to use mobile banking, became active users during lockdowns.

6. CASE STUDIES

6.1 India: UPI and Bharat Interface for Money (BHIM)

The introduction of the Unified Payments Interface (UPI) in India revolutionized P2P and merchant transactions. BHIM, developed by NPCI, is a minimalistic app designed for rural users. A case study in Uttar Pradesh revealed that shopkeepers increased sales by 15% after integrating UPI QR codes, and customers found it more transparent than handling cash.

6.2 China: Ant Financial and Alipay

Alipay's super-app model integrates payments, investments, and insurance in a single interface. Its "Sesame Credit" system uses behavioral data for credit scoring. Behavioral analysis shows that users are more likely to purchase insurance once they receive personalized, AI-driven nudges based on their financial patterns.

6.3 Kenya: M-Pesa's Financial Inclusion Impact

M-Pesa enabled millions in Kenya to access banking without physical branches. Studies by Jack and Suri (2016) found that M-Pesa users were more resilient during financial shocks, showing the power of mobile banking in promoting savings and managing credit.

6.4 UK: Monzo and Customer-First Banking

Monzo's digital-only model emphasizes transparency, instant notifications, and fee-free structures. It has attracted a younger demographic that values openness and control. Customer forums influence product development, highlighting a co-creation model.

7. POLICY IMPLICATIONS AND RECOMMENDATIONS

7.1 Promoting Digital Financial Literacy

Governments should invest in large-scale digital literacy campaigns, focusing especially on rural and semi-urban populations. Public-private partnerships can be leveraged for digital literacy roadshows and training programs.

7.2 Strengthening Cybersecurity Regulations

As trust is central to FinTech adoption, regulatory bodies must mandate robust data protection frameworks. India's Digital Personal Data Protection Act (2023) is a step forward, but enforcement and consumer redressal mechanisms need strengthening.

7.3 Encouraging Inclusive Design in FinTech

FinTech applications must consider the needs of differently-abled and elderly populations. User interface simplicity, vernacular support, and visual accessibility should be mandated features.

7.4 Fostering Interoperability and Open Banking

To avoid monopolization and ensure competition, regulators should encourage open APIs and standardization. India's Account Aggregator framework allows customers to share financial data securely across platforms.

7.5 Incentivizing Responsible Innovation

Governments can offer tax incentives or grants to startups developing tools for underserved communities. Sandboxes and innovation labs should be expanded to allow controlled experimentation with new models.

8. CONCLUSION

FinTech has not only transformed the delivery of financial services but has redefined the behavioral dynamics between customers and financial institutions. Digital banking is now an extension of the user's lifestyle, embedded into daily decision-making processes. Empowered customers are better informed, more engaged, and increasingly autonomous in managing their financial futures.

While the opportunities are vast, challenges remain. Digital literacy gaps, trust deficits, and regulatory ambiguities could hinder progress. As such, an ecosystem approach involving regulators, tech firms, banks, and consumers is necessary to ensure that digital banking remains inclusive, secure, and empowering. By understanding behavioral shifts and designing empathetic, secure, and user-friendly platforms, FinTech can fulfill its promise of democratizing finance and enabling financial wellbeing for all.

REFERENCES

[1] Bélanger, F. and Carter, L. (2008). Trust and risk in e-government adoption. *The Journal of Strategic Information Systems*, 17(2), 165–176.

[2] Chatterjee, S., Rana, N.P., Tamilmani, K. and Sharma, A. (2020). The adoption of FinTech services in the banking industry. *International Journal of Bank Marketing*, 38(4), 874–900.

[3] Chen, Y., Wang, Y., Nevo, S., Jin, J., Wang, L. and Chow, W.S. (2019). IT capability and organizational performance: The roles of business process agility and environmental factors. *European Journal of Information Systems*, 23(3), 326–342.

[4] Demirgüç-Kunt, A., Klapper, L., Singer, D., Ansar, S. and Hess, J. (2018). *The Global Findex Database 2017: Measuring financial inclusion and the fintech revolution*. World Bank.

[5] Gomber, P., Kauffman, R.J., Parker, C. and Weber, B.W. (2018). On the Fintech revolution: Interpreting the forces of innovation, disruption, and transformation in financial services. *Journal of Management Information Systems*, 35(1), 220–265.

[6] Jack, W. and Suri, T. (2014). Risk sharing and transactions costs: Evidence from Kenya's mobile money revolution. *American Economic Review*, 104(1), 183–223.

[7] Jack, W. and Suri, T. (2016). The long-run poverty and gender impacts of mobile money. *Science*, 354(6317), 1288–1292.

[8] Laukkanen, T. (2016). Consumer adoption versus rejection decisions in seemingly similar service innovations: The case of the Internet and mobile banking. *Journal of Business Research*, 69(7), 2432–2439.

[9] OECD (2022). Digital Financial Literacy: A Framework for Policy Makers. Organisation for Economic Co-operation and Development.

[10] Oliveira, T., Thomas, M., Baptista, G. and Campos, F. (2014). Mobile payment: Understanding the determinants of customer adoption. *Computers in Human Behavior*, 61, 404–414.

[11] Prahalad, C.K. and Ramaswamy, V. (2004). Co-creating unique value with customers. *Strategy & Leadership*, 32(3), 4–9.

[12] Pires, G.D., Stanton, J. and Rita, P. (2006). The internet, consumer empowerment and marketing strategies. *European Journal of Marketing*, 40(9/10), 936–949.

[13] Puschmann, T. (2017). Fintech. *Business & Information Systems Engineering*, 59, 69–76.

[14] Venkatesh, V., Morris, M.G., Davis, G.B. and Davis, F.D. (2003). User acceptance of information technology: Toward a unified view. *MIS Quarterly*, 27(3), 425–478.

[15] World Bank. (2023). *Financial Inclusion Overview*. https://www.worldbank.org/en/topic/financialinclusion/overview

[16] Zhou, T. (2011). Understanding mobile Internet continuance usage from the perspectives of UTAUT and flow. *Information Development*, 27(3), 207–218.

[17] NPCI (2023). *Annual Report*. National Payments Corporation of India.

Digital Disruption and Economic Evolution: The Transformative Role of Technology and Innovation in Finance

N. Subbu Krishna Sastry[1], P. Radhakrishnan[2] and S. Ayyappan[3]

[1]Faculty-School of Management, CMR University, Bangalore, India

[2]Associate Professor and Head in Commerce BS & BI, Sri Krishna Arts and Science College, Coimbatore, Tamil Nadu, India

[3]Professor, School of Management, CMR University, Bangalore, India

E-mail: [1]subbukrishna.s@cmr.edu.in; [2]oviansastry@gmail.com; [3]ayyappan.s@cmr.edu.in; [3]sapacet@gmail.com

ABSTRACT: *Technology and innovation have emerged as pivotal forces reshaping the global economic and financial landscape. This chapter explores the multi-dimensional paradigm shift driven by emerging technologies such as artificial intelligence, blockchain, fintech, big data, and quantum computing. It examines how these advancements are revolutionizing value creation, financial transactions, global economic models, market dynamics, and inclusive financial services. Drawing upon recent developments, global case studies, and forward-looking trends, this chapter critically evaluates how technological innovation is not only changing operational practices but also redefining foundational principles in economics and finance.*

Keywords: Artificial Intelligence, Buy Now Pay Later (BNPL), Central Bank Digital Currencies (CBDCs), Decentralized Autonomous Organizations (DAOs), Decentralized Finance (DeFi), Distributed Ledger Technology (DLT).

1. INTRODUCTION: A NEW AGE OF ECONOMIC TRANSFORMATION

The 21st century has witnessed an unprecedented acceleration in the pace of technological change. With the digital economy now overtaking traditional industrial structures, technology is no longer just a tool—it is a transformative force in economics and finance. Unlike previous industrial revolutions characterized by mechanization or electrification, the ongoing digital revolution involves cognitive automation, decentralization, and data-driven decision-making.

From decentralized finance (DeFi) disrupting banking to AI redefining credit scoring and economic forecasting, this shift is holistic. Governments, corporations, and individuals are simultaneously adapting to new norms, blurring the boundaries between consumers, producers, and regulators.

2. HISTORICAL CONTEXT: FROM INDUSTRIAL CAPITAL TO DIGITAL CAPITAL

2.1 The Industrial Economy

For much of modern history, economic value was tied to physical assets—factories, machinery, and labor. The financial system was built on centralized models of value exchange, where banks and governments regulated the flow of capital through physical money and manual systems.

2.2 The Information Economy

With the emergence of the internet and information technology, the late 20th century saw a shift toward knowledge-based economies. Data began to play a central role in shaping economic activities. However, it was still largely passive and not actionable at scale.

2.3 The Digital Economy

Today's economy is powered by real-time data, algorithms, artificial intelligence, and decentralized networks. Economic value now lies in digital assets, intellectual property, and network effects. This has given rise to new economic actors, such as cryptocurrency miners, data brokers, and algorithmic traders.

3. TECHNOLOGICAL DRIVERS OF PARADIGM SHIFT

3.1 Artificial Intelligence and Machine Learning

AI has transformed economic forecasting, behavioral analysis, and risk management. Machine learning models can now predict consumer behavior, optimize supply chains, and detect fraud with astonishing accuracy.

- **Recent Trends**: Generative AI like ChatGPT and Google Gemini are being embedded in financial analytics, portfolio advising, and customer service.
- **Impact**: Reduced operational costs, improved customer engagement, and real-time decision-making.

3.2 Blockchain and Distributed Ledger Technology (DLT)

Blockchain enables secure, immutable, and decentralized record-keeping. From cross-border payments to tokenized assets, it offers transparency, speed, and security.

- **Recent Trends**: Integration of blockchain into carbon credit trading, supply chain finance, and national identity systems.
- **Impact**: Trust without intermediaries, reduced fraud, global financial inclusion.

3.3 Fintech Ecosystem

Fintech startups are dismantling traditional banking models by offering personalized, mobile-first financial services.

- **Examples**: Neobanks like Chime, Revolut, and Niyo; investment platforms like Robinhood and Zerodha.
- **Impact**: Lower fees, financial literacy, democratized investing.

3.4 Big Data and Predictive Analytics

Data is the new currency. Economic modelling, credit assessments, and consumer targeting are now driven by real-time data from various sources including IoT, mobile apps, and sensors.

- **Recent Trends**: Use of alternative data (e.g., mobile usage, geolocation) for credit scoring in Africa and Asia.
- **Impact**: Broader access to credit, personalized financial products, real-time economic indicators.

3.5 Quantum Computing (Emerging Trend)

Still in its early stages, quantum computing promises to revolutionize portfolio optimization, cryptography, and complex economic modelling.

- **Impact Potential**: Rapid simulations of macroeconomic scenarios and optimization at a scale previously impossible.

4. REDEFINING ECONOMIC MODELS AND VALUE CREATION

4.1 Platform-Based Economies

Companies like Amazon, Alibaba, and Uber have shown how digital platforms create ecosystems that generate value through user participation rather than asset ownership.

- **Economic Shift**: From linear value chains to network-based models.
- **Case Insight**: Alibaba's integration of logistics, finance, and commerce reshapes supply and demand dynamics.

4.2 Gig Economy and Micro-Entrepreneurship

Platforms like Fiverr, Upwork, and Swiggy have enabled new forms of work, redefining labor markets and income streams.

- **Trend**: Freelancers and gig workers as primary earners, driving growth in digital payments and microloans.
- **Economic Impact**: Rise in informal yet digitally connected economic activity.

4.3 Tokenization of Assets

Assets like real estate, art, and even music royalties are being fractionalized and traded as digital tokens on blockchain platforms.

- **Benefits**: Liquidity, affordability, access for retail investors.
- **Regulatory Challenge**: Classification of tokens as securities.

5. FINANCIAL INNOVATION AND THE RISE OF DECENTRALIZED FINANCE (DEFI)

DeFi leverages blockchain to offer financial services without traditional intermediaries.

5.1 Core Components

- **Smart Contracts**: Self-executing agreements with predefined rules.
- **DEXs (Decentralized Exchanges)**: Platforms like Uniswap, PancakeSwap that facilitate peer-to-peer trading.
- **Stablecoins**: Digital assets pegged to fiat currencies to reduce volatility.

5.2 Advantages and Risks

- **Pros**: Financial inclusion, transparency, autonomy.
- **Risks**: Hacking, smart contract failures, lack of regulatory oversight.

5.3 Global Adoption Trends

- **Africa and Latin America**: High adoption of crypto wallets due to inflation and banking exclusion.
- **India and Southeast Asia**: Surge in DeFi usage despite regulatory ambiguity.

6. CENTRAL BANK DIGITAL CURRENCIES (CBDCS)

CBDCs represent the state's response to the crypto revolution. These digital forms of fiat currency are issued and regulated by central banks.

6.1 Current Implementations

- **China's Digital Yuan**: Integrated into mobile payment apps for nationwide pilot.
- **India's Digital Rupee**: Launched in wholesale and retail pilot programs.

- **Europe and U.S.**: Exploring programmable money with restrictions for specific use cases.

6.2 Policy and Ethical Implications

- **Surveillance Concerns**: Programmable money could enable excessive state control.
- **Financial Inclusion**: Digital wallets can reach unbanked populations without physical branches.

7. REIMAGINING FINANCE THROUGH EMBEDDED AND INVISIBLE SYSTEMS

7.1 Embedded Finance

This model allows non-financial businesses to offer financial services seamlessly.

- **Examples**: Buy Now Pay Later (BNPL) from Amazon or Flipkart; Insurance embedded in flight bookings.
- **Trend**: Every app becomes a bank.

7.2 Invisible Payments

AI, IoT, and wearables are making payments invisible—tap, voice, or face recognition.

- **Impact**: Convenience-driven consumer spending; new fraud risks.

8. ENVIRONMENTAL, SOCIAL, AND GOVERNANCE (ESG) AND SUSTAINABLE FINANCE

8.1 Green Technology Integration

Blockchain for carbon tracking, AI for ESG compliance, and green fintech platforms are merging sustainability with profitability.

8.2 Trends in Sustainable Investing

- **Global Shift**: Over $40 trillion in assets under management now aligned with ESG principles (as of 2024).
- **Fintech Role**: Robo-advisors offering ESG portfolios based on user values.

9. POLICY, REGULATION, AND GOVERNANCE IN A TECH-DRIVEN WORLD

9.1 Regulatory Sandbox Models

Countries like Singapore, UK, and India have adopted sandbox models to test fintech innovations under controlled environments.

9.2 Cross-Border Challenges

- **Data Sovereignty**: Who owns the data in international transactions?
- **Digital Taxation**: Addressing revenues generated in one country by companies based in another.

9.3 Need for Techno-Legal Synergy

Effective governance now requires interdisciplinary expertise—law, tech, finance, and ethics.

10. CHALLENGES AND ETHICAL CONSIDERATIONS

- **Cybersecurity Threats**: Rise in ransomware, data theft, and DeFi exploits.
- **Digital Divide**: Unequal access to digital tools and literacy.
- **Algorithmic Bias**: AI systems can perpetuate discrimination if not properly designed and audited.
- **Job Displacement**: Automation impacting clerical, analytical, and even executive roles.

11. CASE STUDIES

11.1 India: UPI and Aadhaar Ecosystem

- UPI processed over 14 billion transactions monthly in early 2025.
- Aadhaar-linked bank accounts expanded financial inclusion, especially for rural populations.

11.2 Nigeria: Rise of Mobile Money

Platforms like Paga and Flutterwave enable financial access in a country with over 40% unbanked population.

11.3 Estonia: E-Residency and Digital Governance

Estonia's fully digital public services offer a model for integrating technology into governance and finance.

12. FUTURE OUTLOOK: THE NEXT WAVE

12.1 Web3 and DAO Economies

Web3 shifts ownership and control from platforms to users via decentralized autonomous organizations (DAOs).

12.2 AI-Augmented Economists

Economic forecasting tools powered by AI will surpass current capabilities, providing real-time global economic insights.

12.3 Quantum Finance

Though nascent, quantum algorithms may disrupt risk modeling, arbitrage, and cryptography.

12.4 Digital Twin Economies

Simulated economic environments using real-world data for policy testing and urban planning.

13. CONCLUSION: A CALL FOR BALANCED INNOVATION

The role of technology and innovation in economics and finance is not just additive—it is transformative. It redefines how we understand value, risk, trust, and equity. Yet, with great power comes the responsibility to ensure inclusiveness, fairness, and security. Policymakers, technologists, and economists must collaborate to foster a digital economy that is resilient, ethical, and sustainable.

REFERENCES

[1] World Economic Forum (2024). The Future of Financial Infrastructure.

[2] BIS (2024). CBDC Tracker and Use Cases Report.

[3] IMF (2024). AI and the Transformation of Financial Markets.

[4] OECD (2023). Digital Disruption in Finance.

[5] Reserve Bank of India (2024). Digital Rupee Pilot Project Overview.

[6] Brynjolfsson, E. and McAfee, A. (2020). The Machine, the Platform, the Crowd.

[7] Tapscott, D. and Tapscott, A. (2016). Blockchain Revolution.

[8] Statista (2025). Global Fintech Adoption Rate.

[9] McKinsey & Company (2024). Fintech and the Future of Money.

[10] UNDP (2024). Financial Inclusion and Sustainable Development Goals.

Investing Made Easy: The Impact of Technology on Stock Market Participation

S. Ayyappan[1], Y. Shivashankarachar[2] and Mayan K. Sreerudran[3]

[1]Professor School of Management Studies, CMR University, Bangalore, Karnataka, India

[2]Scholar, School of Management Studies, CMR University, Bangalore, Karnataka.

[3]Ph.D Research Scholar, School of Management, CMR University, Bangalore, India

E-mail: [1]ayyappan.s@cmr.edu.in; [1]sapacet@gmail.com; [2]shivashankarachar.y@cmr.edu.in; [2]shivu1finance@gmail.com; [3]mayan.sreerudran@cmr.edu.in

ABSTRACT: *In recent years, technology has profoundly transformed the financial landscape, particularly in the realm of stock market investing. From mobile trading apps to robo-advisors and AI-powered analytics, modern technological innovations have democratized access to financial markets and simplified investment processes. This paper examines the impact of these technological advancements on stock market participation, exploring how they have reduced barriers to entry, increased market transparency, and empowered a new generation of retail investors.*

Keywords: AI-Powered Analytics, Artificial Intelligence (AI), Decentralized Finance (DeFi), Leverage Educational Resources, Virtual Reality (VR).

1. INTRODUCTION

Investing in the stock market was once considered the domain of financial elites and institutional investors. Complex procedures, high brokerage fees, and limited access to financial information often deterred the average individual from participating in stock market activities. However, the advent of technology has revolutionized this dynamic. The integration of digital platforms, artificial intelligence, big data analytics, and mobile applications has made investing more accessible, user-friendly, and efficient for the common investor. This article delves into how technology has reshaped stock market participation and what this means for the future of personal finance.

2. EVOLUTION OF STOCK MARKET TECHNOLOGY

The stock market has a rich history dating back centuries, but its most significant technological strides have occurred over the past few decades. From the introduction of electronic trading systems in the 1970s to the proliferation of online brokerage firms in the 1990s, each technological leap has incrementally lowered the barriers for investors.

The 21st century ushered in mobile trading applications, algorithmic trading, and robo-advisory services, transforming how individuals invest. These innovations have allowed investors to manage their portfolios in real-time, access a wealth of financial data, and execute trades with a few taps on a smartphone.

3. KEY TECHNOLOGICAL INNOVATIONS IN STOCK MARKET INVESTING

3.1 Mobile Trading Applications

Mobile trading apps like Robinhood, Zerodha, Groww, and E*TRADE have become immensely popular due to their intuitive interfaces, low or zero commission fees, and the ability to trade anytime, anywhere. These apps have demystified investing for beginners and provided tools like price alerts, stock screeners, and educational content.

3.2 Robo-Advisors

Robo-advisors are digital platforms that provide automated, algorithm-driven financial planning services with minimal human supervision. Platforms like Betterment, Wealthfront, and India's ETMONEY use algorithms to create personalized investment portfolios based on an individual's risk tolerance and financial goals.

3.3 AI and Big Data Analytics

Artificial Intelligence (AI) and big data analytics have enabled sophisticated market predictions and personalized investment strategies. These technologies process vast amounts of market data, news, and financial reports in real-time to offer actionable insights and portfolio recommendations.

3.4 Social Trading Platforms

Social trading platforms allow investors to mimic the trades of experienced investors. Applications like eToro and StockTwits combine social networking with investing, enabling knowledge sharing and collaborative investment strategies.

4. IMPACT ON STOCK MARKET PARTICIPATION

4.1 Increased Retail Investor Involvement

The ease of use and accessibility of modern trading platforms have attracted a new demographic of retail investors, particularly millennials and Gen Z.

Lower costs, user-friendly interfaces, and the gamification of investing have contributed to this surge.

4.2 Enhanced Market Transparency

Technology has increased the availability and accessibility of financial information. Real-time stock quotes, news updates, and detailed analytics are now at every investor's fingertips, enabling more informed decision-making.

4.3 Financial Inclusion

Previously marginalized groups, including individuals in rural and remote areas, now have access to stock markets through mobile internet and affordable smartphones. This has broadened the investor base and promoted financial inclusion.

4.4 Behavioral Changes in Investing

Technology has influenced investor behavior by promoting short-term trading and speculative investing. The instant nature of trading apps and the influence of social media trends can lead to impulsive investment decisions.

5. CHALLENGES AND RISKS

5.1 Cybersecurity Concerns

As more financial transactions occur online, the risk of cyberattacks and data breaches has increased. Investors must be vigilant about the security of their personal and financial information.

5.2 Market Volatility and Speculation

The gamification of trading and the ease of speculative investments can contribute to market volatility. Events like the GameStop short squeeze highlight how retail investor activism, fueled by technology, can disrupt financial markets.

5.3 Information Overload

While access to information is beneficial, the sheer volume of data can overwhelm investors, leading to analysis paralysis or reliance on unverified sources.

6. CASE STUDIES

6.1 Robinhood and the Democratization of Trading

Robinhood's commission-free trading model revolutionized the brokerage industry, compelling traditional firms to eliminate trading fees. Its role in events like the GameStop saga illustrates both the potential and pitfalls of tech-driven investing.

6.2 Zerodha's Impact in India

Zerodha, India's largest stockbroker by active clients, transformed stock market participation by offering a user-friendly platform with minimal charges. It has played a pivotal role in increasing retail investor participation in India.

7. FUTURE TRENDS IN TECH-DRIVEN INVESTING

7.1 Integration of Blockchain and Cryptocurrencies

Blockchain technology and digital assets are increasingly being integrated into investment portfolios. Decentralized finance (DeFi) platforms may further democratize access to financial services.

7.2 AI-Powered Personalized Portfolios

Future investment platforms will offer even more personalized services using AI and machine learning, tailoring portfolios to individual preferences, risk tolerances, and ethical considerations.

7.3 Virtual Reality (VR) Trading Environments

VR could redefine trading experiences by creating immersive, interactive investment environments, enabling investors to visualize market data in innovative ways.

8. ROLE OF FINANCIAL EDUCATION IN THE TECH-DRIVEN INVESTING ERA

As technology simplifies access to the stock market, the importance of financial literacy has grown. While intuitive platforms make trading easier, a foundational understanding of financial concepts remains critical to prevent poor investment decisions and financial losses.

8.1 Importance of Investor Awareness Programs

Many regulatory bodies and financial institutions now offer free webinars, online tutorials, and investor awareness campaigns. Organizations like SEBI in India conduct financial literacy programs, particularly targeting rural and semi-urban populations to encourage responsible investing.

8.2 Educational Features in Trading Apps

Modern investment platforms often integrate educational modules within their applications. These include video tutorials, FAQs, glossaries, and risk assessment tools designed to guide users before making investment decisions.

9. IMPACT OF SOCIAL MEDIA ON STOCK MARKET TRENDS

Social media has emerged as a powerful influence on stock market trends. Platforms like Twitter, Reddit, and YouTube provide forums where investment strategies, market analysis, and stock recommendations are shared widely, often swaying market sentiments.

9.1 The Rise of Influencer Investing

Financial influencers or 'finfluencers' have gained popularity, especially among young investors. While they democratize financial advice, concerns persist about misinformation and unregulated advice affecting novice investors.

9.2 Viral Market Movements

Events like the GameStop saga demonstrated how online communities can collectively influence stock prices. Such instances underline the need for regulatory oversight and investor caution in interpreting social media-driven market trends.

10. REGULATORY FRAMEWORK AND TECHNOLOGY-DRIVEN MARKETS

The rapid growth of tech-based investing platforms necessitates updated regulatory frameworks. Governments and financial authorities must balance fostering innovation with protecting investors and maintaining market integrity.

10.1 SEBI's Initiatives in India

SEBI has introduced several measures to regulate algorithmic trading, safeguard digital transactions, and enhance cybersecurity protocols for trading platforms.

10.2 Global Regulatory Responses

Globally, regulatory bodies like the U.S. SEC and UK's FCA have increased oversight of digital brokers and robo-advisors, ensuring compliance with investor protection norms.

11. ENVIRONMENTAL, SOCIAL, AND GOVERNANCE (ESG) INVESTING IN THE DIGITAL AGE

Technology has also popularized ESG investing, where investors consider a company's environmental, social, and governance practices alongside financial performance.

11.1 ESG Filters and Tools

Many trading platforms now offer ESG score filters, enabling investors to select companies aligned with their ethical and sustainability values.

11.2 Impact on Corporate Practices

The rising demand for ESG-compliant investments has encouraged companies to adopt transparent, sustainable business practices, knowing their market valuation may depend on ESG ratings.

12. PSYCHOLOGICAL EFFECTS OF TECHNOLOGY ON INVESTOR BEHAVIOR

12.1 Instant Gratification and Trading Addiction

The convenience of mobile trading apps has increased instances of frequent trading and speculative behavior. The dopamine-driven nature of instant portfolio updates and real-time gains or losses can lead to addictive patterns.

12.2 Mitigating Behavioral Biases

Some advanced platforms incorporate behavioral nudges—notifications and pop-ups reminding users about diversification, long-term goals, or risks involved in speculative trades.

13. CONCLUSION AND KEY RECOMMENDATIONS

13.1 Conclusion

The rapid advancement of technology has significantly transformed the landscape of stock market participation. Digital platforms, mobile trading apps, robo-advisors, and AI-driven analytics have democratized access to financial markets, enabling a broader and more diverse group of investors to participate. Particularly, younger generations and retail investors have increasingly leveraged these tools for real-time market insights, portfolio management, and simplified trading experiences.

13.2 Key Recommendations

13.2.1 *For Investors*

- Leverage educational resources provided by digital platforms to improve financial literacy and informed decision-making.
- Adopt disciplined investing strategies and avoid impulse trading influenced by market hype or social media trends.
- Utilize risk management tools such as stop-loss orders and diversified portfolios available on digital platforms.

- Regularly review app and platform privacy settings to safeguard personal and financial data.

13.2.2 *For Financial Service Providers*

- Enhance user education modules and provide transparent, jargon-free content on investment products and market risks.
- Continuously invest in platform security and data protection to build investor trust.
- Incorporate personalized advisory services using AI while ensuring recommendations are ethically aligned and tailored to investor profiles.
- Offer simulation tools or virtual trading platforms for new investors to practice without financial risk.

13.2.3 *For Policymakers and Regulators*

- Develop updated regulatory frameworks addressing fintech innovations, algorithmic trading, and social media-driven market movements.
- Implement investor protection mechanisms against fraud, misinformation, and unauthorized data usage.
- Support initiatives that bridge the digital divide ensuring equal access to investment opportunities in rural and underserved areas.
- Promote financial literacy programs in collaboration with financial institutions and educational entities.

REFERENCES

[1] Investopedia (2025). Millennials and Gen Z Are Using AI to Improve Their Investing—Should You? Highlights the growing adoption of AI tools by younger investors for portfolio management and financial decision-making.

[2] Baveja, G.S. and Verma, A. (2024). Impact of Financial Literacy on Investment Decisions and Stock Market Participation Using Extreme Learning Machines. Analyzes how financial literacy influences investment behaviors, emphasizing the role of technology in enhancing investor education.

[3] Amundi Research Center (2023). Retail Investors' Behaviour in the Digital Age: How Digitalisation is Impacting Investment Decisions. Examines the effects of digital tools like mobile apps and robo-advisors on retail investor behavior and market participation.

[4] Economic Times (2025). The Rise of Retail Investors: Democratizing India's Financial Markets. Discusses factors contributing to increased retail participation in India, including technological advancements and simplified account opening processes.

[5] Investopedia (2023). Investopedia's 2023 Robo-Advisor Consumer Survey. Provides insights into user preferences and behaviors regarding robo-advisors, highlighting trends in digital investment platforms.

[6] MarketWatch (2024). Online Broker eToro Partners with X to Educate Investors, Cut Through Social-Media Misinformation. Details initiatives to combat misinformation and enhance investor education through collaborations between online brokers and social media platforms.

[7] Financial Times (2024). Deepfake 'Menace' Hurting Retail Investors, Warns Head of India's BSE Bourse. Highlights concerns over the use of deepfakes and fraudulent activities targeting retail investors in the digital age.

[8] ArXiv (2024). Application and Practice of AI Technology in Quantitative Investment. Explores the integration of AI in quantitative investment strategies and its implications for market participation.

[9] ArXiv (2024). Sentiment Trading with Large Language Models. Investigates the use of large language models for sentiment analysis in trading, demonstrating their impact on investment decisions.

[10] DematDive (2025). How Demat Accounts Are Transforming Retail Investment in 2025. Discusses the role of dematerialized accounts in facilitating retail investment and enhancing market accessibility.

[11] Deloitte (2023). The Future of Retail Brokerage. Analyzes emerging trends in retail investing and the evolving expectations of self-directed investors in the digital era.

[12] GlobeNewswire (2023). Global Stock Trading and Investing Applications Market Size, Share & Trends Analysis Report 2023–2030. Provides market analysis on the growth of stock trading and investing applications, reflecting increased digital participation.

[13] Business Research Insights (2025). Self-Directed Investors Market Size and Growth Report, 2033. Offers insights into the expanding market of self-directed investors and the technological tools facilitating this growth.

[14] Finance on Point (2024). The Future of Retail Investment Platforms: Trends and Insights. Examines the evolution of retail investment platforms and the integration of mobile applications in investment activities.

[15] EY (2024). How Investors Make Digital Assets Part of Their Lives. Explores the incorporation of digital assets into investment portfolios and the role of technology in this transition.

[16] Singh, S.K. (2024). Impact of Technology on Stock Market. Quest Journals. This study examines how technological advancements have transformed the Indian stock market, highlighting increased retail participation through online trading platforms and mobile applications. It also discusses challenges such as market inconsistencies arising from rapid technological adoption.

[17] Amundi ETF (2025). Decoding Digital Investment: Embracing the New Digital Norm. Based on a survey of over 11,000 retail investors across 25 countries, this report analyzes how digitalization influences investment decisions, emphasizing the growing reliance on digital tools among younger investors.

[18] Kotecha, N. (2025). Artificial Intelligence in the Stock Market: The Trends and Challenges Regarding AI-Driven Investments. Open Journal of Business and Management, 13, 709–734. This paper explores the role of AI

in enhancing market efficiency and investor decision-making, while also addressing the ethical and regulatory challenges associated with AI-driven investments.

[19] IOSCO (2025). Digital Engagement Practices (DEPs). This report discusses how digital engagement techniques, such as gamification and notifications, can improve retail investor participation and education, while also highlighting potential risks like overtrading and exposure to high-risk products.

[20] World Economic Forum (2025). 2024 Global Retail Investor Outlook. This report sheds light on the increasing participation of retail investors from traditionally underserved groups, including younger individuals and those from emerging markets, facilitated by technological advancements and digital platforms.

Navigating the Digital Frontier: A Literature Review on Business Digitalization

S. Ayyappan[1], G. Binu[2] and Ankitha Theres[3]

[1]Professor, School of Management, CMR University, Bangalore, India

[2]Assistance professor Dept of Commerce, Christ college of Science & Management. Malur, India

[3]Research Scholar School of Management - HRBR Campus, CMR University Bangalore, India

E-mail: [1]ayyappan.s@cmr.edu.in; [1]sapacet@gmail.com; [2]binug@christcollegemalur.com; [3]ankitha.theres@cmr.edu.in

ABSTRACT: *The rise of digital technology has compelled organizations to undergo significant changes or, at the very least, reassess their operational strategies. Many major corporations have poured significant financial resources into what is commonly referred to as "Digitalization." Digitalization, the integration of digital technologies into various aspects of life and business, has revolutionized industries across the globe, but even if Digitalization offers numerous benefits, including increased efficiency, innovation, and improved customer experiences, it also presents challenges such as security risks, the digital divide, technological dependency, and ethical considerations. The objective of our article is to present a literature review on digitalization and provide an overview of the notable constraints and obstacles associated with digitalization and its advancement. The literature review concerning digitalization was conducted through a systematic search across various research databases and platforms including but not limited to ScienceDirect, Google Scholar, and ACM Digital Library. Articles, research papers, books, and conference proceedings published between 2012 and 2024 were considered for inclusion in the review. Synthesizing and analyzing information from various publications and authors revealed a comprehensive understanding of the challenges and opportunities associated with digitalization. The results highlighted common themes such as security risks the digital divide, technological dependency, ethical considerations, and the demand for digital resources. Additionally, the review identified key strategies for addressing these challenges and leveraging digital technologies for positive societal impact.*

Keywords: Digitalization, Organizations, Integration, Customer Experiences, Challenges.

1. INTRODUCTION

In recent decades, the forces of globalization have intensified the need for businesses to adapt. This adaptation is essential not only for survival but also for thriving in competitive landscapes. Efficient adaptation requires businesses to seamlessly integrate digital processes and collaborative tools. Consequently, the significance of digital transformation has grown exponentially. Research underscores the necessity of incorporating digital transformation into existing business frameworks, as it encompasses more than just technological changes. It affects various facets of business operations (Elhamma, 2023). Successful business transformation hinges on the ability to both leverage existing resources and explore new possibilities to enhance organizational agility.

Digital technologies have the potential to disrupt the competitive landscape by reshaping traditional markets. The emergence of platforms has revolutionized existing market structures, leading to the advent of the sharing economy. These platforms facilitate the exchange of digital goods and services, blurring the lines between traditional market boundaries. In this virtual domain, competition transcends physical constraints, allowing for faster and more fluid information flows. As a result, the barriers to entry that once hindered new entrants become less significant in the face of digital innovation.

This article dives deep into the complex world of digitalization, examining its definitions, numerous advantages, and built-in limitations. With the global economy steadily moving towards digital integration, grasping the nuances of this trend becomes crucial for businesses striving to stay competitive in an increasingly interconnected world.

As businesses worldwide wrestle with the need to adapt and innovate, understanding the complexities of digitalization emerges as a vital strategic requirement. From streamlining operations to enhancing customer experiences, the potential rewards of digital transformation are extensive and alluring. Yet, amidst the promises of efficiency gains and expanded markets, there are challenges and constraints that require careful consideration by navigating through the intricacies of digitalization, this article aims to provide businesses with the insights needed to fully leverage its potential while mitigating inherent risks. In doing so, it aims to be a guiding light amidst the ever-changing landscape of the digital age, empowering enterprises to chart a path towards sustainable growth and resilience in this digital era. The literature review for this article was conducted through a comprehensive search strategy aimed at capturing relevant studies pertaining to digital transformation and its associated challenges and benefits. Relevant kinds of literature were obtained through academic databases such as Scopus, IEEE Xplore, and Google Scholar. The search encompassed a variety of keywords and phrases including digital transformation, business innovation, digitalization challenges, and among others. Studies were selected based on predefined inclusion criteria, which included relevance to the topic, publication in peer-reviewed journals, and recency of publication. Exclusion criteria comprised studies not available in English, duplicate publications, and those lacking empirical evidence or substantial theoretical contributions. A total of 64 studies were identified and included in the review process. The synthesis and analysis of findings were carried out by systematically categorizing and comparing insights from various publications and authors, allowing for a comprehensive understanding of the complexities and nuances surrounding digital transformation in business contexts.

This article will be structured as follows: Firstly, we will clarify the notion of digitalization through a literature review, then, we will present the components of the digitalization phenomenon, and finally, we will point out the main advantages and limits of the digitalization of businesses

2. DEFINITION AND COMPONENTS OF DIGITALIZATION

2.1 Digitalization's Definition

The digitalization of companies involves incorporating digital technologies and solutions across all facets of a business or organization (Elhamma and El-moumane, 2023). This evolution entails leveraging digital tools, technologies, and data to optimize business operations, boost efficiency, and align with the evolving digital landscape. It encompasses aspects like operations, communication, customer engagement, marketing, and the broader spectrum of business processes.

The industrial management literature defines digitalization as the phenomenon of intelligent connected machines that information and digital technologies power (Lenka *et al.* 2017).

Digitalization is defined as the use of digital technologies and of data in order to create revenue, improve business, replace/transform business processes, and create an environment for digital business, whereby digital information is at the core (Clerck, 2017).

Digitalization is the growing application of ICT across the economy "encompassing a range of digital technologies, concepts and trends such as artificial intelligence, the "Internet of Things" (IoT) and the "Fourth Industrial Revolution" (Morley *et al.,* 2018).

Digital transformation is the combined effects of several digital innovations bringing about novel actors (and actor constellations), structures, practices, values, and beliefs that change, threaten, replace, or complement existing rules of the game within organizations, ecosystems, industries, or fields (Hinings *et al.,* 2018).

Digitalization is the process of spreading a general-purpose technology. The last similar phenomenon was electrification. Digitalization of products and services shortens distances between people and things. It increases mobility.

It makes network effects decisive. It allows the use of specific data to such an extent that it permits the satisfaction of individual customer needs – be it consumers or businesses. It opens up ample opportunities for innovation, investment, and the creation of new businesses and jobs. Going forward it will be one of the main drivers of sustainable growth (Devereux and Vella, 2018).

The concept of "digital transformation" is derived from the broader notion of "digitalization", which refers to the utilization of digital technologies to drive business innovation and generate new sources of revenue and value (Kohtamäki *et al.,* 2019).

The term "digital transformation" encompasses much more than simply incorporating new technologies. It represents a fundamental shift in business models, encompassing a change in approach to internal and external processes. To fully realize the benefits of digitalization, companies must cultivate new skills, foster a supportive corporate culture, and adopt innovative organizational and operational models (Eller *et al*., 2020).

The advantages of digital transformation are substantial, encompassing heightened efficiency, speed, and quality of work, along with cost reductions, enhanced asset utilization, and overall business efficacy.

Digitalization offers tremendous opportunities for improving efficiency, speed, and quality of work, reducing costs, enhancing asset utilization, and optimizing the use of raw materials, labor, and other key aspects of business performance. It is a complex phenomenon that encompasses various levels, including digital entrepreneurship, digital strategies, digital processes, and digital education (Kraus *et al.,* 2019). furthermore, orchestrating a successful digitalization effort can be challenging, as it requires restructuring existing processes, realigning strategic goals, and adjusting organizational structures (Hinings *et al.,* 2018).

Digitalization is considered the set of changes that digital technology causes or influences in all aspects of human life (Benkaraache and Ghanouane, 2020)

The term "digitalization" goes beyond simply digitization (Apte and Nerlekar, 2020) although digitization typically refers to the straightforward conversion of analog information into digital form, the terms "digital transformation" and "digitalization" are often used interchangeably and encompass a wider array of political, commercial, and social issues. They refer to the integration of innovative digital technologies related to the Internet into a company's operations (Benkaraache and Ghanouane, 2020).

Research emphasizes that Digitalization should be included in the existing business perspectives, as this topic addresses much more than just technological shifts (Bouncken *et al.,* 2021).

The combination of various technologies, such as cloud technologies, sensors, big data, and 3D printing, enables the development of entirely new products and business models that incorporate digital services within physical products (Abou-foul *et al.,* 2021).

Several researchers from different disciplines have contributed to the evaluation of Digitalization and its opportunities and challenges (Burton-Jones *et al.,* 2020; Hai *et al.,* 2021). As digitalization reshapes industries, its impact extends beyond mere economic shifts to affect societies at large. Consequently, as the significance of digital transformation becomes increasingly evident, it also brings with it heightened expectations.

Digitalization is a process that affects all aspects of society and the economy, and there are several factors that contribute to its progress. Technological advancements, changes in consumer behavior, government policies and regulations, as well as increased access to the internet and the popularity of mobile devices, are all key factors in digitalization. Companies are also increasingly being driven to digitize to stay competitive, realize cost savings, and meet the demands of their customers (Ejbari and Bouali, 2022). Moreover, businesses must undertake a digital transformation project to ensure their survival in a constantly evolving world (Ejbari and Bouali, 2022). The digital freedom of access to products and information also risks leading to imitation and increased competition. As a result, companies are required to review their strategies to maintain their longevity and satisfy the changing expectations of their customers (Ejbari and Bouali, 2022).

Digital tools such as Social, Mobile, Analytics, and Cloud (SMAC) technologies are driving digitalization (Teubner and Stockinger, 2020), and offering opportunities to change the way in which firms work (Aström *et al.,* 2022). In accordance with (Chan *et al.,* 2022), Social networks provide market exposure for a company and foster connections with stakeholders. Mobile networks further link various actors within the business ecosystem and offer continuous access to learning and information from anywhere, anytime. Cloud technology enables accessibility, storage, and the exchange of pertinent information, along with workflow monitoring and remote collaboration.

Lastly, analytics aids in comprehending business and customer requirements, identifying opportunities and market trends, and delivering personalized services and communications. Digital technologies are therefore easily available to the firm and can improve its effectiveness in profitable ways (Chan *et al.,* 2022), provided their introduction is accompanied by innovative business models or transformations of the traditional model (Aström *et al.,* 2022). Nevertheless, an investigation must continue on the impact of new technologies on the decision-making process of the firm (Troise *et al.,* 2022) and consumer privacy (Quach *et al.,* 2022). In a recent study, Witschel *et al.* (2022) demonstrated that the innovation of the business model is an effective way of continuing to be competitive in the digital era. To do so, these authors defended the role that dynamic capabilities play in the innovation of the business model, as well as contextual factors, leadership, and business mentalities. Although, Wen *et al.* (2022) affirmed that manufacturing firms with greater viability are more adaptable to Digitalization and tend to implement differentiated competitive strategies, for which reason they concluded that the effect of incentivizing innovation is greater for firms of higher viability.

The antecedents of Digital transformation (digital orientation, digital intensity, and digital maturity) were also analyzed to understand their influence on the financial success of firms (Nasiri *et al.,* 2022). Khan and Javaid (2022) considered that the IoT was a critical component of Industry 4.0, which improved product manufacturing efficiency because it was done with fewer errors and costs. Somohano-Rodríguez *et al.* (2022) analyzing the role that enabling digital Industry 4.0 (I4.0) technologies played in SME innovations, found that strategic planning advanced I4.0 and that enabling Information and Communication digital technologies promoted innovation more intensely than enabling digital technologies for integration and advanced robotics. When transitioning processes from manual to digital, and with digitalization in place, machines become automated through the utilization of digital services such as Cloud computing, IoT, Big Data analytics, Database Analytics, Blockchain technology, and Smart machines. This integration allows machines to work in conjunction with humans, advancing automation while synchronizing with standardization. Advancements in robotics, artificial intelligence, and machine learning are ushering in a new era of automation, where machines can match or even surpass human performance across various domains. Automation offers businesses opportunities to enhance performance, quality, and speed while minimizing or eliminating errors. Additionally, it helps in reducing labor costs and fostering skill growth. In certain activities, the productivity and outcomes achieved through automation exceed human capabilities. Therefore, within the framework of this paper, we understand the concept of digitalization as a comprehensive change in processes using innovative digital technologies, guided by a specific digital strategy, and supported by qualified digital capabilities, aimed at creating value and increasing business performance. 2.2. Digitalization's components Digitalization represents a profoundly disruptive, ongoing, and intricate process. Organizations need to be agile and ready to surmount the challenges posed by this digital transformation swiftly to thrive in the contemporary market landscape (Morakanyane *et al.,* 2017). Digitalizing companies entails the transformation of conventional business processes, operations, and models through the incorporation of digital technologies. The table below summarizes the essential components of digitalization:

Table 1: The Essential Components of Digitalization

Components	***Definition***
Digital Strategy	Firms require a well-defined digital strategy that outlines their objectives, initatives and roadmap for digital transformations, aligned with overall business goals (Weill and Woener, 2018).
Data Analytics	Business intelligence: utilizing analytics tools to derive insights from data, aiding in data-driven decision making, understanding customer behavior, and enhancing operational efficiency.
Cloud computing	Leveraging cloud services for storage, computing power and software applications, offering scalability flexibility and cost effectiveness.
Internet of things (IOT)	Connecting physical devices to the internet for real time monitoring, predictive maintenance, and process automation across industries.
Digital customer experience	Enhancing interaction through digital channels including personalized marketing, self-service options and seamless omnichannel experiences (Weil and Woerner, 2018).
Automation and Robotics	Implementing automation technologies to streamline tasks, reduce errors, and boost productivity.
Artificial intelligence and machine learning	Integrating AI and ML algorithms for decision automation, personalized customer experiences, operational optimization, and data insights.
Cybersecurity	Deploying robust measures to safeguard digital assets, customer data and sensitive information from cyber threats.
Digital talent Development	Investing in recruiting and upskilling employees with digital expertise.
Collaboration tools and platforms	Utilizing digital tools for communication, teamwork, and knowledge sharing.
Regulatory compliance and Governance	Ensuring adherence to regulations and standards governing digital operations, data privacy and cybersecurity.

Digitalization is an ongoing process, requiring companies to continuously adapt their strategies to leverage emerging technologies and maintain competitiveness in the digital era.

3. ADVANTAGES AND LIMITS OF DIGITALIZATION

3.1. Advantages of Digitalization in Business

This article is poised to enrich our comprehension of the multifaceted benefits of digitalization in business, spanning from operational efficiency and customer experience to innovation, sustainability, and societal influence. Jacobides *et al.* (2018) delved into the ways digital platforms facilitate collaboration within ecosystems, driving value co-creation, competitive advantage, and sustained business growth. Gupta *et al.* (2019) examined how digital technologies, like artificial intelligence and big data analytics, empower personalized customer experiences, targeted marketing, and operational efficiency, bolstering business success. Chesbrough (2020) discussed open innovation in the digital age, stressing how digitalization encourages collaboration, knowledge sharing, and co-innovation among organizations, accelerating growth and market leadership. Moreover, Smith *et al.,* (2019) explored how digitalization enhances operational efficiency and cost reduction through automation and data-driven decision-making.

Additionally, Chen (2020) investigated how digitalization drives market expansion and internationalization for businesses via e-commerce platforms and digital marketing strategies. Furthermore, Gupta *et al.* (2020) analyzed how digitalization elevates customer experiences and loyalty through personalized interactions, targeted advertising, and seamless omnichannel engagement. Lee and Park (2020) highlighted the benefits of digitalization in supply chain management, emphasizing real-time tracking, inventory optimization, and demand forecasting enabled by IoT and AI technologies. Similarly, Wang and Li (2021) discussed the strategic advantages of digital transformation in fostering innovation and agility, enabling rapid adaptation to market changes and capitalization on emerging opportunities. In addition, Zhou *et al.* (2021) examined the environmental sustainability benefits of digitalization, including reduced paper consumption, minimized travel through remote collaboration tools, and optimized energy usage via smart building technologies. Moreover, Kim *et al.* (2021) investigated how digitalization enhances employee productivity and satisfaction through remote work capabilities, flexible scheduling, and digital training programs. Lastly, Kim *et al.* (2021) explored digitalization's advantages in risk management and compliance, showcasing how advanced analytics and AI systems bolster fraud detection, regulatory compliance, and cybersecurity. Furthermore, Li and Wang (2021) analyzed the societal impact of digitalization, emphasizing its role in bridging socioeconomic disparities, promoting digital inclusion, and fostering economic growth through digital skills development and entrepreneurship. We have previously highlighted the transformative impact of digitalization on the business landscape. Now, let us delve into specific advancements and their advantages.

Enhanced Operational Efficiency

Digital technologies streamline workflows, minimizing errors and boosting operational efficiency. This streamlined approach translates to cost savings, as operations are executed with greater precision.

Cloud-Based Data Storage

Cloud storage has become standard practice for businesses, offering secure data management. Major players like Microsoft and Google provide high-security cloud services, ensuring robust digital asset management.

Empowerment through Data Analysis

Digital technologies enable sophisticated data analysis tools like Google Analytics. These tools are indispensable for modern businesses, facilitating informed decision-making and driving growth.

3.2 Limits of Digitalization in Business

Digitalization represents a profoundly disruptive, ongoing, and intricate process. Organizations need to be agile and ready to surmount the challenges posed by this digital transformation swiftly to thrive in the contemporary market landscape (Morakanyane *et al.* 2017). Digital transformation heralds a paradigm shift, transcending mere technological upgrades to redefine the essence of business operations. Consequently, as organizations embark on this transformative journey, they must meticulously assess various dimensions, including stakeholder reactions, customer impacts, financial considerations, and strategic alignment. Through such endeavors, companies not only fortify their competitive edge but also chart a course toward future growth and expansion. However, navigating this transformation is fraught with multifaceted challenges. Analyses of workforce dynamics underscore concerns about heightened unemployment and exacerbated income disparities arising from technological advancements. These challenges are compounded by the risks associated with digitalization, spanning data breaches, cyber threats, and privacy infringements, which erode consumer trust and tarnish brand reputations. Moreover, discussions surrounding digitalization's limitations in ensuring equitable access reveal persistent disparities in internet connectivity and digital literacy, particularly among marginalized communities. Similarly, assessments of its impact on supply chain management unveil vulnerabilities to cyber threats, operational disruptions, and overreliance on digital platforms. Consequently, addressing these challenges necessitates a comprehensive approach that prioritizes responsible digital transformation.

The challenges of digitalization are multifaceted and warrant comprehensive examination. Chen *et al.* (2019) explored the impact on the workforce, highlighting the potential for increased unemployment and income inequality due to job displacement and automation. Moreover, Kopalle *et al.* (2021) delved into the risks associated with digitalization, including data breaches, cyberattacks, and privacy concerns, which undermine consumer trust and brand reputation. Furthermore, Zhang and Lu (2020) discussed the limitations in achieving equitable access to technology, especially in marginalized communities with limited internet connectivity and digital literacy. Lee and Park (2020) analyzed the downsides in supply chain management, such as increased vulnerability to cyber threats and disruptions from system failures. Additionally, Chen and Tian (2021) examined the challenges in organizational culture and change management, highlighting employee resistance and cultural barriers to integrating digital technologies. Moreover, Wang and Li (2021) explored the environmental impacts, such as increased energy consumption and electronic waste generation. Lastly, Kim *et al.* (2021) investigated the limits in customer relationships, including depersonalized interactions and concerns about data privacy. Additionally, Li and Zhang (2021) discussed regulatory challenges, including antitrust concerns and the need for ethical standards. Lastly, Kim *et al.* (2021) analyzed the social implications, including social isolation and the digital divide. One of the main drawbacks of undergoing digital transformation is the potential rise in complexity and fragmentation. For instance, as businesses transition away from traditional methods, they often embrace various new technologies, leading to a more intricate overall system. Moreover, the piecemeal adoption of these technologies can further fragment systems, with data fragmentation being a significant hurdle. Nevertheless, digital transformation offers an opportunity to tackle these issues by identifying disparate systems and fostering a more integrated approach to technology utilization. For instance, many companies leverage AI and automated data management to consolidate their technology stack and establish a more cohesive data architecture. Thus, while integrating new technology and managing data from diverse sources can introduce complexity, a primary advantage of digital transformation lies in centralizing and simplifying these systems. Another drawback is the lack of standardization across different industries. Due to the novelty of digital transformation, there are no universally accepted standards for its implementation. This absence of standardization complicates comparisons between solutions and vendors, making it challenging for businesses to determine the optimal approach. However, this lack of standardization also fosters creativity and flexibility in finding tailored solutions that suit individual business needs. Digital transformation is inherently adaptable, allowing businesses to tailor their approach based on factors such as size, digital maturity, and specific requirements. High costs are often perceived as a significant disadvantage of digital transformation. Investments in new hardware, software, and employee training can accumulate expenses. Additionally, reassessing existing processes and procedures incurs costs associated with evaluation and modification. However, digital transformation doesn't necessarily have to be prohibitively expensive. Incremental approaches enable conservative technology investments, yielding returns from early-stage innovations. By adopting a phased approach, businesses can identify opportunities to reduce costs, such as centralizing technology, automating processes, and migrating to cloud solutions. There is also a risk of failure associated with digital transformation due to the substantial changes it entails. Implementing new technologies or altering processes can lead to unexpected challenges and financial losses if initiatives fall short. Mitigating this risk involves understanding common failure points, preparing for challenges, and maintaining flexibility. Businesses should identify transformational needs, acquire necessary skills, test technologies before deployment, and promote a digital-first culture to minimize failure risks. Digital transformation can disrupt employees by requiring them to acquire new skills and adapt to changes in work processes. Furthermore, technological advancements may render some roles redundant, causing stress and anxiety. Transparent communication and providing opportunities for training and advancement can alleviate these concerns and foster a smoother transition for employees.

Loss of customer trust is another potential drawback of digital transformation. Changes to systems or processes may unsettle customers, leading them to seek alternatives. Maintaining trust requires transparent communication about transformation goals and benefits. By prioritizing customer needs, businesses can leverage technology and data management to enhance the overall customer experience. Finally, digital transformation increases the risk of data breaches and cyberattacks as businesses store and share more data electronically. Robust cybersecurity measures, including employee training and investment in security technologies, are essential to mitigate these risks. However, hasty cybersecurity investments without proper assessment can exacerbate issues such as complexity and costs.

4. CONCLUSION

In conclusion, the literature reviewed provides a multifaceted understanding of business digitalization, encompassing various definitions, boundaries, and advantages. Through this review, it becomes evident that digitalization is not merely a technological shift but a comprehensive transformation that reshapes organizational structures, processes, and strategies. One key finding is the diversity of definitions surrounding digitalization, reflecting its complex and evolving nature. While some scholars emphasize the adoption of digital technologies, others highlight broader organizational changes and cultural shifts. Despite these differences, a common thread emerges: digitalization entails leveraging technology to enhance efficiency, innovation, and competitiveness. Moreover, this review underscores the importance of recognizing the limits and challenges associated with digitalization. From concerns about data privacy and cybersecurity to the risk of job displacement, businesses must navigate various obstacles on their digital transformation journey.

Understanding these limitations is crucial for developing effective strategies and mitigating potential risks. In light of these findings, it is clear that business digitalization is not a one-size-fits-all endeavor. Instead, it requires careful consideration of organizational goals, resources, and capabilities.

Moving forward, further research is needed to address emerging trends and challenges in business digitalization. From the rise of artificial intelligence and machine learning to the growing importance of data ethics and governance, there are numerous avenues for future exploration. By staying abreast of these developments and fostering a culture of innovation, businesses can continue to thrive in an increasingly digital world. This article provides a clear understanding of Digitalization foundations in regard to the advancements achieved in the last few years: on the one hand, the developments achieved in the service industry are being made in combination with synergies between digital services and other new technologies, such as AI or IoT; on the manufacturing domain, companies are also pursuing new venues in finding competitive advantages by applying innovative digital practices on their industrial process (e.g. servitization strategies). Moreover, several authors have concluded that additional debate on the digitalization agenda is needed, to further develop a deeper understanding of how digital initiatives are changing existing business models.

- **Conflict of Interest:** The authors reported no conflict of interest.
- **Data Availability:** All data are included in the content of the paper.
- **Funding Statement:** The authors did not obtain any funding for this research.

REFERENCES

[1] Abou-Foul, M., Ruiz-Alba, J.L. and Soares, A. (2021). The impact of digitalization and servitization on the financial performance of a firm: An empirical analysis. *Production Planning & Control*, 32(12), 975–989.

[2] Abriane, A., Rachid, Z.I.K.Y. and Bahida, H. (2021). Les déterminants de l'adoption de la digitalisation par les entreprises: Revue de littérature. Revue Française d'Economie et de Gestion, 2(10).

[3] Apte, M. I. and Nerlekar, V. (2020) Literature Review on Study of Impact of Digitalization on Financial Performance of Urban Cooperative Banks.

[4] Arnold, C., Kiel, D. and Voigt, K.-I. (2016) "How the Industrial Internet of Things changes business models in different manufacturing industries", International Journal of Innovation Management, Vol. 20, No. 8, pp. 1640015-1-1640015-25.

[5] Aström, J., Reim, W. and Parida, V. (2022) Value creation and value capture for AI business model innovation: a three–phase process framework. Rev Manag Sci 16:2111–2133.

[6] Awan, U., Sroufe, R. and Shahbaz, M. (2021) Industry 4.0 and the circular economy: a literature review and recommendations for future research. Bus Strat Environ 30(4):2038–2060.

[7] Benkaraache, T. and Ghanouane, K. (2020) Modèle théorique d'évaluation de l'apport de la transformation digitale à la chaîne de valeur des entreprises. Revue Internationale des Sciences de Gestion, 3(2).

[8] Boitan, I.A. and Stefoni, S.E. (2022) Digitalization and the shadow economy; impact assessment and policy implications for EU countries. East. Eur Econ Early Access: Jul. 2022.

Navigating the Intersection of Entrepreneurship and Management by Understanding Evolving Practices and Strategic Dynamics

S. Ayyappan[1] and Saba Khan[2]

[1]Professor, School of Management, CMR University, Bengaluru, India

[2]PhD Research Scholar, School of Management, CMR University, Bengaluru, India

E-mail: [1]sapacet@gmail.com; [2]saba.khan@cmr.edu.in

ABSTRACT: *Modern institutions are now more concerned about the interplay between management and business, as are we. It is worth noting that these two functions are treated as so distinct from each other; the former deals with the efficient organization and control of affairs while the latter deals with innovation, opportunities, and risks. The relationship between these two stems is – or should be – vital for a business trying to develop in the modern world. Organizations should not just be channeling their efforts to the efficient achievement of the set goals, but they must also be flexible, innovative, and resourceful, which in most cases, requires a lot of entrepreneurial thinking.*

This research investigates the emerging trends, practices, and strategic changes regarding management's relations with business. The study analyzes secondary data, including case studies, industry reports, and scholarly works, to describe type contemporary management practices which rely on entrepreneurial strategies while examining the processes by which management structures build support for entrepreneurial initiatives and innovations.

Furthermore, the analysis pinpoints new developments that are redefining the linkage of management with entrepreneurship. Especially, agile management that is, management that focuses on constant change, iteration development, and responsiveness to change, and digital transformation, which enables the use of technology to change business models, is cutting across the two fields. These changes suggest a movement towards more flexible, collaborative and innovative approaches of doing things such that management functions are changing to respond to the need of an entrepreneurial culture.

One of the issues that has been contested is whether management should support entrepreneurship. There are many scholars and practicing managers who argue that there should be controlled management alongside free entrepreneurship. There is broad consensus amongst academic thinkers and entrepreneurs regarding the need to build entrepreneurship into the management structures to stimulate inventions and competitiveness. This paper seeks to address this issue through studying the changes in management as a result of entrepreneurship and the resultant strategic positioning of the organization.

In the end, this work deepens the understanding of the intersection between entrepreneurship and management and how this integration can be utilized for businesses to succeed in a more complex and volatile environment.

Keywords: Entrepreneurship, Management, Strategic Dynamics, Innovation, Environment.

1. INTRODUCTION

The intersection of entrepreneurship and management is a vital component of business success in the modern, competitive marketplace. Entrepreneurship involves identifying and capitalizing on new opportunities, while management focuses on optimizing resources, processes, and structures to achieve organizational goals. Both fields complement each other in various ways, particularly as businesses scale from startups to large corporations. Entrepreneurs must increasingly adopt management practices to grow their ventures, while managers are encouraged to think more entrepreneurially to foster innovation and adaptability.

The purpose of this paper is to explore the evolving relationship between entrepreneurship and management, particularly in the context of contemporary business challenges. The research aims to analyze the strategic dynamics that occur as entrepreneurs scale their ventures and as managers integrate entrepreneurial thinking into established organizational frameworks.

The need for effective management practices will not only complement entrepreneurial efforts but also improve for better business outcomes (Humairoh, H., & Annas, M. 2023). Entrepreneurship intersects with management when entrepreneurial initiatives are embedded within organizational processes, highlighting the importance of sound managerial practices to secure sustainable competitive advantages. This synergy boosts organizational competitiveness in a complex and ever-evolving business landscape, driving innovation and strategic growth. (Ionescu, V.C., & Grigore, A.M. 2016)

Entrepreneurship is crucial in management as it fosters innovation, enhances product quality, and adapts to environmental changes. It drives economic sustainability by promoting goal-oriented activities, ensuring effective resource utilization, and encouraging managerial abilities for successful business operations. (Ukachukwu Euguenia).

2. LITERATURE REVIEW

2.1 Entrepreneurship and Management the Definition

Entrepreneurship and management are distinct yet interconnected concepts essential for organizational success. Entrepreneurship involves the identification and exploitation of opportunities to create value, often characterized by innovation and risk-taking. In contrast, management focuses on the organization, planning, and coordination of resources to achieve specific goals. Understanding these definitions is crucial for fostering effective business practices.

Entrepreneurship is defined as the process of creating and managing a new business venture to capitalize on market opportunities. It encompasses activities such as: Corporate Entrepreneurship: Innovative activities within existing companies aimed at revitalizing growth and competitiveness Intrapreneurship: Employees acting as entrepreneurs within a larger organization, driving innovation and change (Raheem *et al.*, 2014).

Management refers to the systematic coordination of organizational resources to achieve defined objectives. Planning and Organizing: Establishing goals and determining the best course of action to achieve them (Roof & Presswood, 2004). Leadership: Guiding and inspiring teams to work towards common goals, which is often confused with management (Roof & Presswood, 2004) (Ionescu & Grigore, 2016).

2.2 Challenges in executing Management and Entrepreneurship

Traditional management practices may make it challenging to lead an entrepreneurial culture to execute innovation and adaptability. (Erić-Nielsen *et al.*, 2019).

Inflexible organization i.e., it can make decision making very tough when the organization has Rigid hierarchies in fast changing business environment. (Erić-Nielsen *et al.*, 2019). Identifies causes of managers' lack of action-taking.

It is an absolute challenge to the managers to explores paths and enhance personal action taking abilities. It is of great significance to understand between purposeful and non-purposeful action takers. With this the the managers can create context for purposeful action taking. (Bruch & Ghoshal, 2004).

2.3 Emerging Trends in Management and Entrepreneurship

The paper identifies emerging trends in digital innovation management, including the use of artificial intelligence, educating leaders and employees, digital knowledge management practices, and collaboration with innovation networks, alongside opportunities for sustainability, improved foreign aid, and platformization.

Trends in entrepreneurship: This paper introduces a new concept in the field known as entreprenology, which is evolving into two branches: applied entrepreneurship and theoretical entrepreneurship. These branches provide deeper insights into the academic exploration of entrepreneurial practices. Filion, L.J. (1998). The aim of the paper is to offer value to academics, policy-makers, and international stakeholders. It also seeks to capture the organizational design experiments being conducted at universities around the globe.

Agile Management: Agile methodologies are gaining traction in entrepreneurship and management due to their focus on flexibility, collaboration, and rapid adaptation to change. Both entrepreneurs and managers are embracing agile practices to encourage innovation and stay responsive to shifts in the market (Rigby, Sutherland, & Takeuchi, 2016).

Entrepreneurs are leading the way in building sustainable businesses, while managers are progressively incorporating social responsibility and sustainability into their corporate strategies to align with consumer demands and regulatory requirements (Elkington, 1997).

2.4 The Importance of Entrepreneurial Thinking in Management

The importance of entrepreneurial thinking in management is becoming more widely acknowledged as essential for driving innovation, gaining competitive advantage, and making effective decisions. This approach encourages managers to cultivate a mindset that welcomes risk, fosters creativity, and promotes proactive problem-solving, all of which can greatly improve organizational performance. This discussion will delve into the main elements of entrepreneurial thinking in management, focusing on its influence on innovation, competitive advantage, and the creation of an entrepreneurial culture. When business leaders show entrepreneurial behavior, it helps companies establish high-performance work systems and transmit knowledge which leads to better innovation outcomes (Aristana *et al.*, 2024).

Entrepreneurial thinking plays a middle position between entrepreneurial innovation and competitive advantage to show how firms use dynamic capabilities to benefit. (Alsafadi & Aljuhmani, 2023).

3. OBJECTIVES OF THE RESEARCH

Our study examines how business and entrepreneurship connect today. The study looks at how entrepreneurs use their principles in managing daily operations. This research is focusses to explore the main developments that influence how entrepreneurship and management work together. To discover what impact combining entrepreneurial thinking has on today's business management system. Investigate how entrepreneurial principles are incurporated into management practices.

- To analyze the intersection of entrepreneurship and management in contemporary business settings.
- To investigate how entrepreneurial principles are incorporated into management practices.
- To identify the key trends shaping the dynamics between entrepreneurship and management.
- To explore the strategic implications of blending entrepreneurial practices within management structures.

4. RESEARCH METHODOLOGY

This study examines the relationship between management and entrepreneurship employing secondary data. Academic literature, case studies, business reports, and industry publications are the source materials of the data. An extensive examination of the changing practices and strategic dynamics between the two fields is made possible by the collection of secondary data.

4.1 Data Collection Techniques

- Companies case studies
- Research Papers
- Google Scholar
- Business Magazines
- Industry reports

5. DATA ANALYSIS AND INTERPRETATION

Thematic Analysis: To find common trends and themes in the various ways that management practices are influenced by entrepreneurial thinking, the data will be looked at Organizational structures, innovation tactics, and leadership styles will be major areas of significance.

Company Name	*Integration of Leadership Management and Entrepreneur Strategies*	*Key Success Areas*
Spotify	Two core leadership development courses, management app program, leadership app program.	inclusive leadership, distributed team leadership and Crisis management.
Spotify	Leadership Circles program	Individual growth. Career growth
Boston Consultancy Group	Design for adoption methodology	Behavioral Science

Company Name	*Integration of Leadership Management and Entrepreneur Strategies*	*Key Success Areas*
Microsoft	Growth mindset. Model, Coach, Care.	Commitment to continuous learning and improvement in all the levels.
Cisco	Global leader and technical leader program, The Business leader program, The manager Assimilation program, The leadership fellows program.	Allow employees to practice with their entrepreneur skills by contributing to the organizational development.
Freeletics	Micro learning, People managers round table, Leadership On-Boarding.	Strong Supported management system.

Source: deel.com

5.1 Case Study Analysis

5.1.1 *Amazon Web Services (AWS)*

The development of cloud technological services offered by Amazon started as a project aimed at improving the company's infrastructural technology. Seeing a larger market gap, the company undertook this internal problem and turned it into a solution in form of AWS, one of the leaders in the cloud computing sector. The change highlights Amazon's devotion to intrapreneurship, where the company empowers internal staff to create solutions that evolve into full-fledged business units.

5.1.2 *Play Station by Sony*

Sony engineer Ken Kutaragi's own passion for enhancing the gaming experience prompted him to create a new sound chip for Nintendo. Seeing the potential, Sony backed Kutaragi's initiative, ultimately leading to the development of the PlayStation. This project not only cemented Sony's entry into the gaming market but also reinforced the company's encouragement of employee innovation.

5.1.3 *Post it Notes 3M*

The development of Post-it Notes is a prime example of intrapreneurship. 3M researcher Arthur Fry used a coworker's low-tack adhesive to develop a product that became a staple in offices across the globe. 3M's culture of permitting employees to try out new ideas on company time made this innovation possible.

5.1.4 *The Email Platform by Google*

Gmail was born thanks to the policy implemented by Google to have its employees spend 20% of their work hours on projects they are passionate about. One of the world's most-talked-about email services became a fine display of the idea of allowing their employees freedom for creativity to create a groundbreaking product.

5.1.5 *Infosys Technologies*

This step taken by Infosys to encourage its employees to think beyond their immediate task is termed zero-distance innovation and is aimed at creating an ongoing culture of improvement and innovation. The very fact that they incubated new ventures within the company creates an example of the way structured programs can foster intrapreneurship.

5.1.6 *Embodied within ITC's e-Choupal*

An undertaking by ITC to achieve direct farm-to-consumer contact through digital control showcases the intrapreneurship in a big enterprise. Unlike fostering the supply chain system in a complete manner, this program also helps improve the quality of life of farmers in a way of good access to the markets; hence it is a solid blend between business innovation and social responsibility.

5.2 Key Discussions

5.2.1 *Management of Entrepreneurial Approach Thinking*

A New Focus of Attention for All Managers in Various Industries. The pace of technological change and its contemporary jumble-and-dismantle accelerate entrepreneurial thinking to survive in an unrelenting cutthroat environment. It is a power that allows one to think outside the box, weigh the risks, and make real-time changes to make sure there is no loss of opportunity. Companies like Tesla have managed to blend entrepreneurial spirit and management methods to lead the way for innovation in electric vehicles while figuring out the troubles with scaling production and operational efficiency.

5.2.2 *The Strategic Integration of Entrepreneurship and Management*

Seeks to unite the visionary and creative aspects of entrepreneurship with the organized and processive-oriented structures of management. This union basically deals with creative thinking or innovation for achievement in organizations and stability for further growth of the entrepreneurship work. Management of Innovation: Companies such as Apple and Google have established systems within their organization to run the process of innovation.

These systems allow new approaches to risk-taking, support R&D work, and allow department collaboration to bring ideas to market. Management Agility: Agile management, pioneered in software development, is finding more and more applicability in other fields. This system empowers the managers to face change with speed, working in a continuous improvement and innovation-oriented culture.

5.2.3 *Key Challenges of Interlinking Entrepreneurship and Management*

Although beneficial, embedded with some do Ables is a tough road of merging the world of entrepreneurship with management. This issue pertains to the cultural disconnect between entrepreneurship-inherent unstructured risk-taking, and management-bound formal stability. The first is therefore invariably willing to take on risks and abstract itself from trying new ideas, while the second has its absolute respect for predictability and efficiency. An organizational culture where both entrepreneurship and management values are respected and synthesized is necessary to counteract this challenge. Leadership will thus play a pivotal role, supporting its members in the ability to accept both creativity and structure in achieving their objectives.

6. CONCLUSION

An integration of an entrepreneurial style of thinking into management practices is very noble for organizations that wish to thrive within the dynamic business environment of today. Combination creates scope for innovation, agility, and edge--capacities which help companies to be acclimatized to changes and gain competitiveness in a world of constant alteration and motion. Further, entrepreneurial thinking allows a manager to fuel a culture of creativity and proactivity in problem-solving and, thereby, base long-term enduring success. Through the variable changes in the business environment, the conjoining of entrepreneurship and management will remain at the fulcrum of organizational excellence.

FUTURE RESEARCH DIRECTIONS

Further studies can focus on how digital transformation affects the intersection of entrepreneurship and management, especially in sectors taking huge strides in technology. Besides, delving into the impact of organizational cultures on how entrepreneurial thinking is merged with management frameworks could also enlighten practitioners and scholars alike.

REFERENCES

[1] Entrepreneurship Implementation as Moderation in the Success of Small and Medium Enterprises (SMEs). *International Journal of Advanced Multidisciplinary*, *2*(1), 83–94.

[2] Entrepreneurship, Management and Leadership. An Organizational Perspective. *Revista De Management Comparat International*, *17*(5), 477.

[3] N. The Role of Entrepreneurship towards Economic Sustainability.

[4] Raheem, S., Oyelola, O.T. and Oresanya, O.T. (1993). Business Revolution through Corporate Entrepreneurship. *Risk*, 9.

[5] Is It Leadership or Management? *College and University*, *79*(4), 3.

[6] Entrepreneurship, Management and Leadership. An Organizational Perspective. *Revista De Management Comparat International*, *17*(5), 47.

[7] The Challenges of Managing the Entrepreneurial Organization. *Ekonomika*, *65*(2).

[8] Bruch, H. and Ghoshal, S. (2004). Management is the art of doing and getting done.

[9] From entrepreneurship to entreprenology: The emergence of a new discipline. *Journal of enterprising culture*, *6*(01), 1–23.

[10] Filion, L.J. (1998). From entrepreneurship to entreprenology: The emergence of a new discipline. *Journal of enterprising culture*, *6*(01), 1–23.

[11] Rigby, D.K., Sutherland, J. and Takeuchi, H. (2016). Master the process that's transforming management: Interaction. *Harvard business review*, *94*(7), 2.

[12] Aristana, I.N., Puspitawati, N.M.D., Salain, P.P.P., Koval, V., Konarivska, O. and Paniuk, T. (2024). Improving Innovative Work Behavior in Small and Medium Enterprises: Integrating Transformational Leadership, Knowledge Sharing, and Psychological Empowerment. *Societies*, *14*(11), 228.

[13] Alsafadi, Y. and Aljuhmani, H.Y. (2024). The influence of entrepreneurial innovations in building competitive advantage: the mediating role of entrepreneurial thinking. *Kybernetes*, *53*(11), 4051–4073.

[14] https://www.deel.com/blog/companies-with-best-leadership-development-programs

[15] https://aws.amazon.com/what-is-aws

[16] https://inspireip.com/sony-playstation-innovation-employee-ideas

[17] https://www.danaconnect.com/the-power-of-dedicated-innovation-time-unpacking-googles-20-time-policy

[18] https://www.infosys.com/insights/other-insights/innovation-challenge.html

Paradigm Shift in Economics and Finance—The Role of Technology, Innovation, and Financial Behavior

S. Ayyappan[1], Ankitha Theres[2],
Mayan K. Sreerudran[3] and M. Sakthivadivel[4]

[1]Professor, School of Management, CMR University, Bangalore, India
[2]School of Management – HRBR Campus, CMR University Bangalore, India
[3]Ph.D Research Scholar, School of Management, CMR University, Bangalore, India
[4]Assistant Professor, SS, Department of Computer Science (AIML & Cyber Security), Dr. Mahalingam College of Engineering & Technology, Pollachi, Tamil Nadu, India
E-mail: [1]ayyappan.s@cmr.edu.in; [1]sapacet@gmail.com; [2]ankitha.theres@cmr.edu.in; [3]mayan.sreerudran@cmr.edu.in; [4]sakthivadivelm@gmail.com

Chapter Overview: *This chapter explores the transformative impact of technology and innovation on modern economics and finance, focusing particularly on how these shifts are reshaping financial behavior. As we move deeper into the digital era, the traditional distinctions between micro- and macroeconomics are challenged, giving rise to mesoeconomic frameworks that examine sectoral, institutional, and network-level dynamics.*

Key Themes:

- **Technological Catalysts:** The chapter discusses the role of AI, big data, mobile platforms, and blockchain in redefining financial processes and services.
- **Behavioral Transformation:** Behavioral economics is now embedded in financial technology through nudging, gamification, and hyper-personalized services. Consumer trust is shifting from traditional institutions to algorithms and digital platforms.
- **Mesoeconomic Insight:** A middle-ground perspective that captures the interaction of networks, sectors, and innovation systems is introduced as essential for analyzing today's economy.
- **Human-Tech Hybrid Models:** The synthesis section proposes a new paradigm where human behavior is augmented by intelligent systems, raising critical questions around ethics, governance, and financial literacy.

The chapter includes tables and figures to provide empirical context:

- Technology-Behavior Impact Matrix
- Growth Metrics of FinTech and DeFi (2020–2024)
- Illustrative Diagram of the Digital Financial Ecosystem

1. INTRODUCTION

The global economy and financial systems are undergoing a transformative shift driven by rapid advances in technology and innovation. This new paradigm is reshaping traditional economic models, redefining the role of financial institutions, and significantly influencing individual and collective financial behavior. The emergence of digital platforms, artificial intelligence, decentralized finance, and new modes of social interaction are converging to form a new behavioral and institutional landscape. This chapter explores the profound impact of these technological developments on economics and finance, with a particular focus on their implications for financial behavior.

2. TECHNOLOGY AND INNOVATION: CATALYSTS OF CHANGE

2.1 Artificial Intelligence and Predictive Finance

AI is revolutionizing financial services by enabling more accurate risk assessments, automating trading strategies, and forecasting economic trends with greater precision. AI-driven robo-advisors, for example, offer real-time, personalized investment advice, allowing users to make informed decisions with minimal human intervention. Predictive analytics, powered by big data, help institutions and individuals anticipate market shifts and respond proactively.

AI's impact goes beyond mere automation. It's about enhancing cognitive capabilities in finance.

- **More Accurate Risk Assessments:** Traditional credit scoring relies on historical data. AI, particularly machine learning, can analyze vast, diverse datasets (e.g., social media activity, transaction patterns, even psychological indicators from text) to identify subtle risk signals that human analysts might miss. This leads to more granular and dynamic risk profiling, benefiting both lenders (reducing defaults) and borrowers (potentially enabling access to credit for those underserved by traditional models).
- **Automating Trading Strategies:** Algorithmic trading, powered by AI, executes trades at speeds and volumes impossible for humans. This includes high-frequency trading (HFT) that profits from minuscule price discrepancies, but also more complex strategies like arbitrage, statistical arbitrage, and even sentiment-driven trading (analyzing news and social media for market sentiment). The concern here is flash crashes and the potential for market manipulation or systemic risk if algorithms become overly interconnected.
- **Forecasting Economic Trends with Greater Precision:** AI models can process real-time economic indicators, satellite imagery (e.g., tracking factory output), anonymized mobile data (e.g., retail foot traffic), and

news feeds to generate more timely and accurate forecasts for GDP, inflation, employment, and market movements. This can help central banks in policymaking and businesses in strategic planning.

- **AI-driven Robo-advisors:** These platforms democratize investment advice. Beyond personalized recommendations, they can automatically rebalance portfolios, manage tax-loss harvesting, and provide goal-based planning. The "minimal human intervention" aspect is key, making financial planning accessible to a broader audience who might not have sufficient assets for traditional human advisors. The challenge lies in ensuring transparency of algorithms and addressing potential biases.
- **Predictive Analytics, Powered by Big Data:** This is the engine behind AI's capabilities. Big data encompasses not just volume but also velocity (real-time streaming data), variety (structured and unstructured data), and veracity (data quality). For institutions, this means identifying fraud patterns earlier, optimizing marketing campaigns, and personalizing product offerings. For individuals, it could mean proactive alerts about impending financial stress or personalized recommendations for debt consolidation.

2.2 Blockchain and Decentralized Finance (DeFi)

Blockchain technology underpins the rise of decentralized finance, a system where financial transactions occur peer-to-peer without intermediaries. Smart contracts execute agreements automatically, reducing transaction costs and increasing transparency. This decentralization challenges traditional financial institutions by redistributing trust to technology-based systems.

Blockchain is a foundational technology disrupting the very architecture of finance.

- **Peer-to-Peer Transactions Without Intermediaries:** This is the core revolutionary aspect. Instead of needing a bank to verify and settle a payment, blockchain allows direct value transfer. This bypasses the fees, delays, and censorship risks associated with traditional financial institutions.
- **Smart Contracts Execute Agreements Automatically:** These are self-executing contracts with the terms of the agreement directly written into lines of code. Once conditions are met (e.g., goods received, data confirmed), the contract automatically triggers payment or asset transfer. This has vast implications for insurance, supply chain finance, real estate, and legal agreements, reducing the need for escrow services, lawyers, and manual reconciliation.
- **Reducing Transaction Costs and Increasing Transparency:** By removing intermediaries and automating processes, transaction costs (e.g., cross-border payment fees, legal fees) can be significantly reduced.

Transparency comes from the immutable and publicly verifiable ledger of transactions, reducing fraud and increasing auditability.

- **Redistributing Trust to Technology-Based Systems:** This is a profound behavioral and institutional shift. Instead of trusting a centralized entity (like a bank or government) to hold and manage your assets, trust is placed in the cryptographic security and distributed consensus mechanisms of the blockchain. This concept of "trustless" systems is fundamental to the ethos of DeFi. Challenges include the complexity for mainstream adoption, regulatory uncertainty, and the potential for smart contract vulnerabilities.

1.3 Digital Transformation in Banking

Banks are embracing digital transformation to enhance customer experiences and operational efficiency. Mobile banking, contactless payments, and real-time fraud detection systems are now standard features. These innovations not only streamline services but also shape user expectations and behaviors.

Traditional banks are not being replaced overnight but are adapting rapidly to the digital imperative.

- **Enhance Customer Experiences and Operational Efficiency:** The move to digital is driven by consumer demand for convenience and instant gratification. Mobile apps offer 24/7 access to accounts, bill payments, and transfers. Contactless payments (NFC, QR codes) provide speed and convenience at the point of sale. Real-time fraud detection uses AI to identify anomalous transactions instantly, protecting both banks and customers.
- **Standard Features:** These innovations are no longer competitive advantages but essential for survival. Banks that fail to offer these features risk losing customers to FinTechs or more digitally advanced competitors.
- **Shape User Expectations and Behaviors:** The expectation of instant access and seamless transactions is now ingrained. Users expect personalized services and proactive alerts. This forces banks to move from being mere transaction processors to becoming integrated financial partners. It also impacts how frequently users interact with their finances, moving from periodic branch visits to daily app usage.

3. BEHAVIORAL IMPACTS OF TECHNOLOGICAL INNOVATION

3.1 Digital Nudging and Gamification

FinTech applications increasingly use behavioral economics principles to influence user decisions. Gamified savings apps, visual progress trackers, and micro-investing platforms like Acorns encourage positive financial habits. However, these same features can also promote impulsive behavior, particularly in trading apps that mimic gaming environments.

- **FinTech Applications Increasingly Use Behavioral Economics Principles:** "Nudging," as popularized by Thaler and Sunstein, involves subtle interventions to guide choices without restricting options. In finance, this means using default options, simplified information presentation, and timely reminders.
- **Gamified Savings Apps, Visual Progress Trackers:** These make saving feel less like a chore and more like a game. Seeing a progress bar fill up towards a savings goal provides positive reinforcement. Micro-investing platforms like Acorns round up spare change from purchases and invest it, making investing feel effortless and less intimidating. These foster positive financial habits by leveraging psychological principles like immediate gratification and goal-setting.
- **Can Also Promote Impulsive Behavior:** This is the crucial downside. Trading apps that mimic gaming environments (e.g., flashy animations, push notifications, leaderboards) can trigger dopamine responses, leading to excessive or impulsive trading, often driven by fear of missing out (FOMO) or a desire for quick gains, disregarding fundamental investment principles. This raises ethical concerns and regulatory challenges.

3.2 Big Data and Personalized Financial Ecosystems

Technologies now enable hyper-personalized financial experiences. Algorithms analyze spending habits, income patterns, and life goals to provide tailored advice and alerts. For instance, budgeting apps may suggest specific savings strategies or flag unusual spending in real-time, promoting financial discipline. The ability to create highly tailored financial experiences is a game-changer.

- **Hyper-Personalized Financial Experiences:** Beyond generic advice, algorithms can analyze individual spending habits, income fluctuations, debt levels, and even long-term aspirations (e.g., buying a house, retirement) to create a unique financial profile.
- **Tailored Advice and Alerts:** Budgeting apps can provide real-time feedback on spending categories ("You've spent 80% of your entertainment budget this month"). They can suggest specific savings strategies ("If you save $X per week, you'll reach your down payment goal by Y date"). Flagging unusual spending (e.g., a large transaction outside your usual patterns) can prevent fraud and highlight potential overspending, promoting financial discipline. This shifts finance from a reactive to a proactive experience.

3.3 Social Media and Collective Financial Behavior

Social platforms have become influential in shaping investment decisions. Online communities such as Reddit's r/WallStreetBets demonstrate how collective sentiment can drive market movements, sometimes contrary to fundamental analysis. This social investing trend highlights the emotional and cognitive dimensions of financial decision-making in the digital age. This is a well-structured and comprehensive overview of the impact of technology and innovation on financial behavior and the global financial system. Let's elaborate on each section, adding detail, context, and potential implications.

3.3.1 *Technology and Innovation: Catalysts of Change*

This section effectively sets the stage by highlighting the core technological drivers.

(A) *Artificial Intelligence and Predictive Finance*

AI's impact goes beyond mere automation. It's about enhancing cognitive capabilities in finance.

- **More Accurate Risk Assessments:** Traditional credit scoring relies on historical data. AI, particularly machine learning, can analyze vast, diverse datasets (e.g., social media activity, transaction patterns, even psychological indicators from text) to identify subtle risk signals that human analysts might miss. This leads to more granular and dynamic risk profiling, benefiting both lenders (reducing defaults) and borrowers (potentially enabling access to credit for those underserved by traditional models).
- **Automating Trading Strategies:** Algorithmic trading, powered by AI, executes trades at speeds and volumes impossible for humans. This includes high-frequency trading (HFT) that profits from minuscule price discrepancies, but also more complex strategies like arbitrage, statistical arbitrage, and even sentiment-driven trading (analyzing news and social media for market sentiment). The concern here is flash crashes and the potential for market manipulation or systemic risk if algorithms become overly interconnected.
- **Forecasting Economic Trends with Greater Precision:** AI models can process real-time economic indicators, satellite imagery (e.g., tracking factory output), anonymized mobile data (e.g., retail foot traffic), and news feeds to generate more timely and accurate forecasts for GDP, inflation, employment, and market movements. This can help central banks in policymaking and businesses in strategic planning.
- **AI-driven Robo-advisors:** These platforms democratize investment advice. Beyond personalized recommendations, they can automatically rebalance portfolios, manage tax-loss harvesting, and provide goal-based planning. The "minimal human intervention" aspect is key, making financial planning accessible to a broader audience who might not have sufficient assets for traditional human advisors. The challenge lies in ensuring transparency of algorithms and addressing potential biases.

- **Predictive Analytics, Powered by Big Data:** This is the engine behind AI's capabilities. Big data encompasses not just volume but also velocity (real-time streaming data), variety (structured and unstructured data), and veracity (data quality). For institutions, this means identifying fraud patterns earlier, optimizing marketing campaigns, and personalizing product offerings. For individuals, it could mean proactive alerts about impending financial stress or personalized recommendations for debt consolidation.

(B) *Blockchain and Decentralized Finance (DeFi)*

Blockchain is a foundational technology disrupting the very architecture of finance.

- **Peer-to-Peer Transactions Without Intermediaries:** This is the core revolutionary aspect. Instead of needing a bank to verify and settle a payment, blockchain allows direct value transfer. This bypasses the fees, delays, and censorship risks associated with traditional financial institutions.
- **Smart Contracts Execute Agreements Automatically:** These are self-executing contracts with the terms of the agreement directly written into lines of code. Once conditions are met (e.g., goods received, data confirmed), the contract automatically triggers payment or asset transfer. This has vast implications for insurance, supply chain finance, real estate, and legal agreements, reducing the need for escrow services, lawyers, and manual reconciliation.
- **Reducing Transaction Costs and Increasing Transparency:** By removing intermediaries and automating processes, transaction costs (e.g., cross-border payment fees, legal fees) can be significantly reduced. Transparency comes from the immutable and publicly verifiable ledger of transactions, reducing fraud and increasing auditability.
- **Redistributing Trust to Technology-Based Systems:** This is a profound behavioral and institutional shift. Instead of trusting a centralized entity (like a bank or government) to hold and manage your assets, trust is placed in the cryptographic security and distributed consensus mechanisms of the blockchain. This concept of "trustless" systems is fundamental to the ethos of DeFi. Challenges include the complexity for mainstream adoption, regulatory uncertainty, and the potential for smart contract vulnerabilities.

(C) *Digital Transformation in Banking*

Traditional banks are not being replaced overnight but are adapting rapidly to the digital imperative.

- **Enhance Customer Experiences and Operational Efficiency:** The move to digital is driven by consumer demand for convenience and instant gratification. Mobile apps offer 24/7 access to accounts, bill payments, and transfers. Contactless payments (NFC, QR codes) provide speed and convenience at the point of sale. Real-time fraud detection uses AI to identify anomalous transactions instantly, protecting both banks and customers.

- **Standard Features:** These innovations are no longer competitive advantages but essential for survival. Banks that fail to offer these features risk losing customers to FinTechs or more digitally advanced competitors.
- **Shape User Expectations and Behaviors:** The expectation of instant access and seamless transactions is now ingrained. Users expect personalized services and proactive alerts. This forces banks to move from being mere transaction processors to becoming integrated financial partners. It also impacts how frequently users interact with their finances, moving from periodic branch visits to daily app usage.

3.3.2 *Behavioral Impacts of Technological Innovation*

This section delves into the fascinating intersection of technology and human psychology in finance.

(A) *Digital Nudging and Gamification*

This highlights the application of behavioral economics to financial products.

- **FinTech Applications Increasingly Use Behavioral Economics Principles:** "Nudging," as popularized by Thaler and Sunstein, involves subtle interventions to guide choices without restricting options. In finance, this means using default options, simplified information presentation, and timely reminders.
- **Gamified Savings Apps, Visual Progress Trackers:** These make saving feel less like a chore and more like a game. Seeing a progress bar fill up towards a savings goal provides positive reinforcement. Micro-investing platforms like Acorns round up spare change from purchases and invest it, making investing feel effortless and less intimidating. These foster positive financial habits by leveraging psychological principles like immediate gratification and goal-setting.
- **Can also Promote Impulsive Behavior:** This is the crucial downside. Trading apps that mimic gaming environments (e.g., flashy animations, push notifications, leaderboards) can trigger dopamine responses, leading to excessive or impulsive trading, often driven by fear of missing out (FOMO) or a desire for quick gains, disregarding fundamental investment principles. This raises ethical concerns and regulatory challenges.

(B) *Big Data and Personalized Financial Ecosystems*

The ability to create highly tailored financial experiences is a game-changer.

- **Hyper-Personalized Financial Experiences:** Beyond generic advice, algorithms can analyze individual spending habits, income fluctuations, debt levels, and even long-term aspirations (e.g., buying a house, retirement) to create a unique financial profile.
- **Tailored Advice and Alerts:** Budgeting apps can provide real-time feedback on spending categories ("You've spent 80% of your entertainment budget this month"). They can suggest specific savings strategies ("If you save $X per week, you'll reach your down payment goal by Y date"). Flagging unusual spending (e.g., a large transaction outside your usual patterns) can prevent fraud and highlight potential overspending, promoting financial discipline. This shifts finance from a reactive to a proactive experience.

(C) *Social Media and Collective Financial Behavior*

Social media has amplified and accelerated the collective dimension of financial behavior.

- **Influential in Shaping Investment Decisions:** Information, both accurate and inaccurate, spreads rapidly. Online influencers and communities can significantly sway market sentiment.
- **Reddit's r/WallStreetBets and Collective Sentiment:** This is a prime example of how retail investors, coordinating on social platforms, can collectively drive market movements for specific stocks (e.g., GameStop, AMC), sometimes creating "short squeezes" that inflict massive losses on institutional short-sellers. This phenomenon highlights the power of collective action and the disconnect between traditional fundamental analysis and sentiment-driven trading.
- **Emotional and Cognitive Dimensions:** Social investing often taps into emotions like greed, fear, and FOMO. The validation received within online communities can reinforce biases and lead to herd behavior, where individuals follow the crowd even if it contradicts their own analysis. This complicates traditional economic models that assume rational decision-making.

3.4 Redefining Trust and Authority

In traditional finance, trust is placed in institutions and regulators. In the digital era, trust shifts toward algorithms and distributed networks. Blockchain-based systems provide verifiable transaction histories, reducing reliance on centralized oversight. This reallocation of trust fundamentally alters how individuals perceive and engage with financial systems. This is a fundamental paradigm shift in the underlying basis of financial systems.

- **Trust Shifts Toward Algorithms and Distributed Networks:** In a world where financial data is constantly flowing and decisions are automated, the integrity of the algorithms and the security of the underlying networks become paramount. People trust the code to execute as programmed.
- **Blockchain-Based Systems Provide Verifiable Transaction Histories:** The immutability and transparency of blockchain ledgers mean that every transaction is recorded and cannot be altered. This verifiable history reduces the need for a central authority to reconcile records or resolve disputes, as the truth is embedded in the network itself.
- **Reducing Reliance on Centralized Oversight:** This has profound implications for regulators. Instead of supervising a few large financial institutions, they may need to grapple with regulating decentralized autonomous organizations (DAOs) and a multitude of self-executing smart contracts.
- **Reallocation of Trust Fundamentally Alters Perception and Engagement:** For users, this means a shift from "Do I trust my bank?" to "Do I trust this protocol/algorithm?" This requires a different kind of financial literacy – understanding cryptographic security, smart contract risks, and decentralized governance models.

4. THE EMERGENCE OF MESOECONOMICS

Mesoeconomics bridges the gap between micro- and macroeconomic analysis by focusing on institutions, networks, and sectors. It is particularly useful for understanding how technology-driven changes propagate through economies. For example, examining how innovation clusters (like Silicon Valley) influence regional and national growth provides insights that neither micro nor macro lenses alone can offer. Mesoeconomics perspectives are essential in capturing the complexity of today's interconnected, tech-centric economic structures. This section introduces a crucial analytical framework for understanding the complex interactions.

Bridges the Gap Between Micro- and Macroeconomic Analysis:

- **Microeconomics:** Focuses on individual decision-makers (households, firms) and specific markets.
- **Macroeconomics:** Examines the economy as a whole (GDP, inflation, unemployment).
- **Mesoeconomics:** Focuses on an intermediate level – sectors, industries, institutions, networks, and regions. It recognizes that economic activity is not just an aggregate of individual actions, nor is it solely driven by broad national policies.
- **Understanding How Technology-Driven Changes Propagate:** Technology's impact is often not uniform. It spreads through specific

channels, affecting certain industries or regions more profoundly first, and then radiating outwards. Mesoeconomics helps trace these pathways.

- **Innovation Clusters (like Silicon Valley):** This is a perfect example. Silicon Valley is not just a collection of individual tech companies; it's an ecosystem of interconnected firms, venture capitalists, universities, talent pools, and supportive infrastructure. Mesoeconomics examines how this cluster generates innovation, attracts investment, and influences economic growth both regionally and nationally. It helps understand the multiplier effects and network externalities.
- **Capturing the Complexity of Today's Interconnected, Tech-Centric Economic Structures:** The global economy is a complex adaptive system. Mesoeconomics provides the lens to analyze the emergent properties and feedback loops within and between sectors and networks, which are crucial for policymaking in the digital age.

5. SYNTHESIS: A HUMAN-TECH HYBRID MODEL OF FINANCIAL BEHAVIOR

The confluence of technological innovation and behavioral economics suggests a new model of financial decision-making—one that is augmented by data and guided by intelligent systems. Consumers are no longer purely rational agents but are influenced by algorithmic recommendations, social dynamics, and continuous feedback loops. This hybrid model challenges existing regulatory frameworks and necessitates new approaches to financial literacy, ethics, and governance. This section summarizes the core argument and points to future challenges.

- **Confluence of Technological Innovation and Behavioral Economics:** The central theme is that human financial behavior is no longer solely driven by traditional economic rationality but is heavily influenced and augmented by technology.
- **Augmented by Data and Guided by Intelligent Systems:** Financial decisions are increasingly informed by personalized data insights and recommendations from AI. This means the "rational agent" assumption of classical economics is even less applicable.
- **Consumers Influenced by Algorithmic Recommendations, Social Dynamics, and Continuous Feedback Loops:** This is the heart of the "hybrid model."
    - **Algorithmic Recommendations:** Robo-advisors, personalized budgeting apps, and even online shopping recommendations spill over into financial choices.
    - **Social Dynamics:** The power of online communities, social proof, and viral trends on platforms like Reddit.

- **Continuous Feedback Loops:** Real-time updates, notifications, and visual trackers in apps provide immediate feedback, reinforcing certain behaviors (positive or negative).

- **Challenges Existing Regulatory Frameworks:** Traditional regulations were designed for a centralized, institution-led financial system. How do you regulate decentralized protocols, autonomous algorithms, or the spread of misinformation on social media that impacts markets?
- **Necessitates New Approaches to Financial Literacy, Ethics, and Governance:**
    - **Financial Literacy:** Needs to evolve beyond understanding traditional products to include digital security, algorithmic transparency, data privacy, and the risks of DeFi.
    - **Ethics:** Questions arise about algorithmic bias, predatory nudging, and the responsible use of personal financial data.
    - **Governance:** New models are needed for regulating decentralized systems and for ensuring accountability in AI-driven financial services.

6. TABLES AND FIGURES

Table 1: Impact of Technology on Financial Behavior

Technology	*Innovation Example*	*Behavioral Effect*
AI & Big Data	Robo-advisors, fraud detection	Delegated decision-making, improved risk awareness
Blockchain & DeFi	Smart contracts, tokenization	Trust in code, decentralization of authority
Mobile Apps	Digital wallets, micro-investing	Real-time engagement, instant feedback loops
Social Platforms	Reddit investing forums	Herd behavior, emotionally-driven trading
Gamification	Savings apps, visual trackers	Increased savings, potential overtrading

This table neatly categorizes the key technologies, provides concrete examples, and identifies their primary behavioral effects. It's an excellent summary of the paper's core arguments.

- **AI & Big Data:** Reinforces the shift towards automated decision-making and heightened awareness of risks, potentially reducing human cognitive load but also requiring trust in the technology.

- **Blockchain & DeFi:** Highlights the radical shift in where trust is placed – from institutions to code and decentralized systems.
- **Mobile Apps:** Emphasizes the real-time, always-on nature of modern finance and the power of immediate feedback.
- **Social Platforms:** Underscores the emotional and collective aspects, which can lead to both opportunities (democratization of information) and risks (herd behavior, irrational exuberance).
- **Gamification:** Captures the dual nature – positive habit formation vs. potential for impulsive, gambling-like behavior.

Figure 1: Digital Financial Ecosystem (illustrative only)

[Insert conceptual diagram showing consumers, data flows, financial tech platforms, regulators, and institutions interconnected]

Table 2: Growth Metrics of FinTech and DeFi (2020–2024)

Metric	*2020*	*2022*	*2024 (est.)*
Global FinTech investment ($B)	105	210	310
DeFi market cap ($B)	15	55	120
Users of mobile banking (B)	2.5	3.6	4.3
AI adoption in finance (%)	12%	35%	60%

- **Consumers:** At the center, interacting with various components.
- **Financial Tech Platforms (FinTechs, DeFi Protocols):** Showing the diverse range of digital services.
- **Traditional Financial Institutions (Banks, Asset Managers):** Highlighting their continued, albeit evolving, role.
- **Data Flows:** Emphasizing the continuous exchange of information between all entities.
- **Regulators:** Showing their oversight function, which is becoming increasingly complex.
- **Social Media:** Depicting its influence on consumer behavior and market dynamics.
- **AI/Analytics Engines:** Illustrating the processing of data to generate insights and automate decisions.

Table 2: Growth Metrics of FinTech and DeFi (2020–2024)

This table provides empirical evidence of the rapid adoption and growth of these technologies, reinforcing the idea of a "transformative shift."

- **Global FinTech Investment:** Shows the immense capital flowing into the sector, indicating investor confidence and the scale of innovation.

- **DeFi Market Cap:** Illustrates the explosive growth of decentralized finance, from a niche concept to a significant segment.
- **Users of Mobile Banking:** Demonstrates the widespread mainstream adoption of digital banking services.
- **AI Adoption in Finance:** Highlights the increasing integration of AI into financial operations and decision-making processes, moving from early experimentation to more widespread implementation.

7. CONCLUSION

The paradigm shift in economics and finance is not merely about technological adoption; it represents a fundamental transformation in how individuals, institutions, and systems interact. Technology and innovation are reshaping financial behavior, introducing new risks and opportunities, and demanding a rethinking of economic theory and policy. As we navigate this new era, an interdisciplinary approach that integrates economics, technology, psychology, and ethics will be essential to ensure inclusive, sustainable, and resilient financial ecosystems.

REFERENCES

[1] Arner, D.W., Barberis, J. and Buckley, R.P. (2017). Fintech and regtech: Impact on regulators and banks. *Journal of Banking Regulation,* 19(4), 1–14.

[2] Bains, P., Courtois, B. and Saher, M. (2021). The future of banking: A new digital paradigm. IMF Working Paper.

[3] Gai, K., Qiu, M. and Sun, X. (2018). A survey on FinTech. *Journal of Network and Computer Applications,* 103, 262–273.

[4] Kahneman, D. (2011). Thinking, Fast and Slow. Farrar, Straus and Giroux.

[5] Nakamoto, S. (2008). Bitcoin: A Peer-to-Peer Electronic Cash System.

[6] OECD (2020). Digital Disruption in Banking and its Impact on Competition. OECD Publishing.

[7] Susskind, R. and Susskind, D. (2015). The Future of the Professions: How Technology Will Transform the Work of Human Experts. Oxford University Press.

[8] Thaler, R.H. and Sunstein, C.R. (2008). Nudge: Improving Decisions About Health, Wealth, and Happiness. Yale University Press.

[9] World Bank (2022). The Global Findex Database 2021: Financial Inclusion, Digital Payments, and Resilience. World Bank Publications.

The Impact of Fintech on Financial Inclusion in Emerging Economies

Nisha Saurabh Kumari* and Sheenu Arora

Assistant Professor, TIAS

*E-mail: nishasaurabhr0303@gmail.com

ABSTRACT: *The advent of financial technology (fintech) has brought transformative changes to the global financial landscape, particularly in emerging economies. This study explores the role of fintech in enhancing financial inclusion by enabling wider access to banking, credit, insurance, and investment services for previously unbanked and underbanked populations. Through mobile banking, digital wallets, peer-to-peer lending platforms, and blockchain-based solutions, fintech has significantly reduced the barriers of traditional banking systems such as geographical constraints, high transaction costs, and stringent documentation requirements. The research analyzes case studies from select emerging economies to assess how fintech initiatives have contributed to economic empowerment, especially among marginalized groups. Furthermore, it investigates the regulatory challenges, technological limitations, and risks associated with fintech adoption. The study concludes by providing policy recommendations for promoting responsible fintech growth that supports inclusive and sustainable development.*

Keywords: Financial Inclusion, Fintech, Emerging Economies, Digital Banking, Peer-to-Peer Lending, Mobile Payments.

1. INTRODUCTION

In recent years, financial technology—commonly known as fintech—has emerged as a transformative force within the global financial landscape. Particularly in emerging economies, fintech is increasingly seen as a critical tool to foster financial inclusion, empower underserved populations, and stimulate economic growth. By leveraging digital innovation, fintech enables individuals and businesses to access financial services that were previously out of reach due to geographical, economic, or infrastructural barriers. The convergence of mobile technology, data analytics, blockchain, and artificial intelligence has significantly lowered the cost of providing financial services, creating new pathways for inclusion in regions where traditional banking systems have failed to penetrate (World Bank, 2022).

Financial inclusion, defined as the access to affordable and appropriate financial products and services for all individuals, especially the underserved and unbanked populations, is vital for poverty alleviation, economic resilience, and inclusive growth (Demirgüç-Kunt *et al.*, 2018). Despite global progress, a substantial portion of the population in emerging economies remains financially excluded. For instance, according to the Global Findex Database (2021), approximately 1.4 billion adults worldwide remain unbanked, with a significant majority residing in low- and middle-income countries. Traditional financial institutions have struggled to extend their reach due to high operational costs, regulatory complexities, and the absence of formal identification or credit history among marginalized populations. This has created a gap that fintech companies are increasingly filling through innovative digital solutions.

The evolution of fintech has brought about significant changes in the way financial services are delivered. Mobile money platforms like M-Pesa in Kenya, digital lending platforms such as Tala and Branch, and crowdfunding and peer-to-peer (P2P) lending systems have demonstrated the potential of fintech to broaden access to credit, savings, insurance, and payments. These services are particularly valuable in rural or semi-urban areas where formal financial infrastructure is sparse or non-existent. Through the use of mobile devices and internet connectivity, fintech applications can deliver financial services to remote populations, thus mitigating the costs and limitations of traditional brick-and-mortar banking.

Emerging economies present a unique context for fintech innovation due to the confluence of several factors: rapid mobile phone penetration, youthful and tech-savvy populations, unmet demand for financial services, and increasing regulatory openness. According to the GSM Association (2021), mobile penetration in sub-Saharan Africa reached over 46%, and mobile internet usage continues to rise sharply in South Asia and Latin America. This technological leapfrogging has enabled fintech companies to bypass traditional infrastructure and directly connect with users, providing them with tools for digital payments, savings, credit scoring, and financial management.

Moreover, fintech has enabled the democratization of credit through the use of alternative data, such as mobile phone usage, utility bill payments, and social media behavior, to assess creditworthiness. This is particularly important in emerging economies, where large segments of the population lack formal credit histories or collateral. By adopting data-driven lending models, fintech platforms can offer microloans to small businesses and individuals who are otherwise excluded from formal banking systems. Such financial access not only enhances individual economic participation but also contributes to entrepreneurship and local economic development (Ozili, 2018).

Furthermore, fintech contributes to gender inclusion by providing women with direct and private access to financial resources. Studies have shown that women are more likely to be financially excluded due to cultural norms, lack of documentation, and limited mobility. However, with mobile money and digital wallets, women can save, borrow, and transact independently, thereby gaining economic agency and enhancing household welfare. A notable example is in Bangladesh, where mobile financial services have enabled rural women to participate in the financial ecosystem without needing to travel to bank branches (GSMA, 2020).

However, while the impact of fintech on financial inclusion is promising, it is not without challenges. Issues such as digital literacy, cybersecurity, data privacy, and regulatory uncertainty can hinder the widespread adoption and trust in fintech services. In many emerging economies, digital divides persist due to limited access to smartphones or internet connectivity, which may further marginalize vulnerable populations. Moreover, the use of personal data for credit assessments raises ethical and legal concerns, especially in regions with weak data protection laws. Thus, the role of governments and regulators becomes crucial in ensuring that fintech growth is inclusive, transparent, and sustainable.

To address these concerns, several countries have implemented regulatory sandboxes, which allow fintech companies to test innovations under the supervision of regulatory bodies. Such initiatives aim to strike a balance between innovation and consumer protection. Additionally, international organizations such as the World Bank, the International Monetary Fund (IMF), and the United Nations are working with local governments to design policies that encourage fintech-driven inclusion while safeguarding users' rights and financial stability.

It is also important to consider the broader economic implications of fintech-led inclusion. By formalizing the informal economy through digital financial services, governments can enhance tax collection, reduce corruption, and improve service delivery. Financially included individuals are more likely to save, invest, and withstand economic shocks, thereby contributing to national development goals and the United Nations Sustainable Development Goals (SDGs), particularly SDG 1 (No Poverty), SDG 5 (Gender Equality), and SDG 8 (Decent Work and Economic Growth).

Despite these developments, there is a need for more empirical research to understand the nuanced impact of fintech on various demographic segments across different emerging markets. The diversity of economic structures, regulatory environments, and cultural attitudes toward technology implies that the success of fintech solutions is highly context-dependent. For instance, while mobile money has flourished in East Africa, similar models have faced resistance or slower uptake in parts of South Asia or Latin America due to differences in financial behavior, infrastructure, and trust in digital systems.

In conclusion, fintech represents a powerful vehicle for promoting financial inclusion in emerging economies. By leveraging technology to overcome traditional barriers, it offers scalable, efficient, and inclusive financial solutions to underserved populations. However, for fintech to realize its full potential, a supportive ecosystem is required—one that includes robust digital infrastructure, inclusive regulatory frameworks, consumer education, and cross-sector collaboration. As emerging economies continue to navigate the digital financial revolution, understanding the impact of fintech on financial inclusion will be critical in shaping equitable and resilient financial systems for the future.

2. REVIEW OF LITERATURE

The rapid advancement of financial technology (fintech) has attracted significant scholarly attention regarding its potential to enhance financial inclusion, particularly in **emerging economies**. Literature across economics, development studies, and finance converges on the idea

that fintech plays a transformative role in bridging financial access gaps for underserved populations. However, findings also highlight key challenges and contextual dependencies that influence fintech's effectiveness in promoting inclusive financial ecosystems.

One of the most cited success stories in fintech-driven inclusion is **M-Pesa in Kenya**, which has significantly expanded access to financial services, especially among the rural and low-income population. Jack and Suri (2014) found that the adoption of M-Pesa led to a measurable reduction in poverty, with approximately 2% of Kenyan households lifted above the poverty line. The platform enabled users to store money, send and receive remittances, and access microloans, demonstrating fintech's potential to replace traditional banking infrastructure.

In the Indian context, **Aadhaar-enabled payment systems and the Unified Payments Interface (UPI)** have revolutionized digital financial inclusion. According to the Reserve Bank of India (2020), these systems have facilitated real-time transactions and increased the accessibility of financial services even in previously unbanked regions. Sengupta and Aubuchon (2008) argue that combining digital identity with mobile banking significantly lowers the cost of service delivery and increases trust in formal financial systems.

From a global perspective, the World Bank's Global Findex Database (2022) provides evidence that digital financial services have become a crucial tool for inclusion, especially following the COVID-19 pandemic. Mobile money accounts, in particular, have grown rapidly in Sub-Saharan Africa, Latin America, and South Asia, allowing users to access a range of services without needing traditional bank branches. The rise in **agent banking** and **digital wallets** is especially relevant in countries with large informal sectors and limited banking infrastructure.

Scholars also emphasize the role of **alternative credit scoring** in promoting inclusion. Many fintech firms use non-traditional data, such as mobile usage patterns and social media behavior, to assess creditworthiness, thus extending credit to individuals without formal credit histories (Bazarbash

& Beaton, 2020). This innovation has enabled platforms like Tala and Branch to provide microloans to underserved populations in countries like Kenya, the Philippines, and India.

However, not all literature is optimistic. Some scholars point to the **digital divide**, particularly along gender and rural-urban lines. GSMA (2021) reports that women in low- and middle- income countries are significantly less likely to use mobile internet, which can limit their access to fintech services. Additionally, issues such as **cybersecurity**, **data privacy**, and **consumer protection** remain under-researched in the context of emerging markets. Arner, Barberis, and Buckley (2015) stress the need for regulatory frameworks that balance innovation with risk mitigation.

In conclusion, the literature supports the idea that fintech has significantly improved financial inclusion in emerging economies by offering scalable, accessible, and affordable financial solutions. However, the extent of its impact depends on complementary factors such as digital infrastructure, regulatory support, and inclusive product design. Further research is needed to evaluate long-term outcomes and the resilience of fintech-driven financial inclusion.

3. CONCEPTUAL FRAMEWORK

3.1 Introduction

The conceptual framework serves as the theoretical and analytical structure that outlines the relationship between **Fintech (independent variable)** and **Financial Inclusion (dependent variable)** in the context of **emerging economies**. It identifies the key constructs, explains their interactions, and supports hypothesis development or research questions for empirical study.

3.2 Key Constructs

3.2.1 *Independent Variable: Fintech Development*

Fintech refers to the application of technological innovations in financial services. In this study, fintech is operationalized through the following components:

- Mobile Money Services (e.g., M-Pesa, Paytm)
- Digital Payment Platforms (e.g., UPI, Alipay)
- Digital Lending Platforms (e.g., Tala, Branch)
- Insurtech and Digital Insurance Access
- Crowdfunding and P2P Lending
- Blockchain and Cryptocurrency Solutions

3.2.2 *Dependent Variable: Financial Inclusion*

Financial inclusion is the process by which individuals and businesses have access to useful and affordable financial products and services that meet their needs. Key dimensions include:

- Access to Financial Services (e.g., bank accounts, mobile wallets)
- Usage of Financial Services (e.g., regular saving, digital payments)
- Quality of Financial Services (e.g., transparency, reliability)
- Affordability and Convenience

3.2.3 *Moderating/Control Variables*

These influence the strength or direction of the relationship:

- Digital Literacy and Financial Awareness
- Regulatory Environment
- Internet and Mobile Penetration
- Income Level and Employment Status
- Gender and Rural–Urban Divide
- Trust in Digital Systems

Fintech Services

```
        |
        |----- > Mobile Money
        |----- > Digital Lending
        |----- > Digital Payments
        |----- > Insurtech
        |----- > Blockchain/Crypto
        |
        v
```

Improved Financial Inclusion

```
        |----- > Greater Access
        |----- > Increased Usage
        |----- > Better Affordability
        |----- > Higher Quality
        |
      [Influenced/Moderated by:]
        |----- > Digital Literacy
        |----- > Regulation
        |----- > Internet/Mobile Penetration
        |----- > Socio-demographics
```

3.4 Theoretical Underpinning

This framework is grounded in:

- **Technology Acceptance Model (TAM)** – explains how perceived ease of use and perceived usefulness influence technology adoption.
- **Diffusion of Innovation Theory (Rogers, 2003)** – explains how, why, and at what rate new ideas and technology spread.
- **Financial Intermediation Theory** – highlights the role of intermediaries (like banks and now fintech firms) in mobilizing funds and reducing information asymmetry.

3.5 Hypothesized Relationships

- **H1:** Fintech services positively impact financial access in emerging economies.
- **H2:** Fintech innovations lead to increased usage of financial services.
- **H3:** The relationship between fintech and financial inclusion is moderated by digital literacy and infrastructure.
- **H4:** Regulatory environment strengthens or weakens fintech's impact on inclusion.

3.6 Visual Diagram (Suggested Layout)

You can present the conceptual framework diagrammatically like this: Fintech Services (IV)

```
        /       |       \        \

Mobile Money  Lending  Payments  Blockchain
        \       |       /        /

         \      v      /

         ---> Financial Inclusion (DV) <---
         |     (Access, Usage, Quality) |
         |                              |

Moderating Variables:        Control Variables:
 -  Digital Literacy          - Gender
 -  Infrastructure            - Income Level
 -  Regulation                - Geography
```

3.7 Application

This framework can guide:

- Empirical data collection (e.g., survey design based on fintech usage and financial access)
- Case studies in different emerging economies
- Policy analysis regarding digital finance strategies

4. DISCUSSION AND THEORETICAL IMPLICATIONS

4.1 Discussion

The emergence of Fintech—defined as the application of innovative technologies in the delivery of financial services—has revolutionized traditional banking systems, especially in regions where access to financial services was previously limited or non-existent. In emerging economies, where a significant portion of the population remains unbanked or underbanked, Fintech presents a viable solution for bridging the financial inclusion gap.

Digital payment platforms, mobile wallets, peer-to-peer lending services, and digital-only banks have substantially lowered entry barriers by offering cost-effective, convenient, and accessible financial services. Mobile money services such as M-Pesa in Kenya, Paytm in India, and bKash in Bangladesh have demonstrated the power of Fintech in reaching rural and low-income populations, many of whom had no prior formal banking relationship.

Moreover, Fintech solutions often leverage technologies such as artificial intelligence, blockchain, and biometric verification to provide secure and tailored financial products. This enables financial institutions to serve previously excluded groups such as micro-entrepreneurs, women, and informal sector workers—demographics often overlooked by traditional banks due to lack of collateral or formal credit history.

Despite these advancements, challenges remain. Digital literacy, cyber security threats, infrastructure limitations, and inconsistent regulatory environments pose significant obstacles to widespread adoption. Additionally, trust in digital financial platforms remains a critical factor, particularly in areas where consumer awareness and protection are minimal.

4.2 Theoretical Implications

This study draws upon the **Diffusion of Innovation Theory** (Rogers, 1962) to explain how Fintech solutions are adopted across various segments of emerging markets. According to this theory, the adoption of innovation follows a pattern influenced by relative advantage, compatibility, complexity, trialability, and observability. In the context of Fintech, mobile banking and digital payment systems are often perceived as having a relative advantage in terms of speed, cost, and convenience.

Furthermore, the **Technology Acceptance Model (TAM)** supports the idea that perceived usefulness and perceived ease of use significantly affect the willingness of individuals to adopt Fintech platforms. These models suggest that for financial inclusion to advance, Fintech services must not only be available but must also be perceived as trustworthy, user-friendly, and beneficial.

The **Capability Approach** (Sen, 1999) also underpins this discussion. Financial inclusion is not only about access but about enabling individuals to utilize financial services to improve their well-being. Fintech, in this light, acts as a facilitator of economic capability by providing tools for saving, investing, and securing livelihoods.

Collectively, these theoretical insights underscore the importance of a multidimensional approach to Fintech-driven financial inclusion. Governments, private players, and civil society must collaborate to ensure that innovation is inclusive, responsible, and empowering for the underserved segments of society.

REFERENCES

[1] Arner, D.W., Barberis, J. and Buckley, R.P. (2015). The evolution of fintech: A new post-crisis paradigm? *Georgetown Journal of International Law*, 47(4), 1271–1319.

[2] Bazarbash, M. and Beaton, K. (2020). Financial inclusion: What have we learned so far?
International Monetary Fund. https://www.imf.org

[3] Demirgüç-Kunt, A., Klapper, L., Singer, D. and Ansar, S. (2022). The Global Findex Database 2021: Financial inclusion, digital payments, and resilience in the age of COVID-19. World Bank.

[4] GSMA (2021). The Mobile Gender Gap Report 2021. https://www.gsma.com/mobilefordevelopment/resources/mobile-gender-gap-report-2021/

[5] Jack, W. and Suri, T. (2014). Risk sharing and transactions costs: Evidence from Kenya's mobile money revolution. *American Economic Review*, 104(1), 183–223. https://doi.org/10.1257/aer.104.1.183

[6] Ozili, P.K. (2018). Impact of digital finance on financial inclusion and stability. *Borsa Istanbul Review*, 18(4), 329–340. https://doi.org/10.1016/j.bir.2017.12.003

[7] Sahay, R., Čihák, M., N'Diaye, P., Barajas, A. and Mitra, S. (2015). Financial inclusion: Can it meet multiple macroeconomic goals? IMF Staff Discussion Note SDN/15/17.

[8] Ghosh, S. (2016). How has mobile banking affected financial inclusion in India? Applied Economics Letters, 23(16), 1141–1145. https://doi.org/10.1080/13504851.2016.1139672

[9] World Bank (2022). Fintech and the future of finance: Emerging trends and regulatory challenges. https://www.worldbank.org

[10] Chuen, D.L.K. and Teo, E.G.S. (2015). Emergence of FinTech and the LASIC principles. *Journal of Financial Perspectives,* 3(3), 24–36.

[11] Zins, A. and Weill, L. (2016). The determinants of financial inclusion in Africa. Review of Development Finance, 6(1), 46–57. https://doi.org/10.1016/j.rdf.2016.05.001

[12] Beck, T. and Brown, M. (2011). Which households use banks? Evidence from the transition economies. *Economics of Transition*, 19(1), 143–177. https://doi.org/10.1111/j.1468-0351.2010.00367.x

[13] Suri, T. and Jack, W. (2016). The long-run poverty and gender impacts of mobile money. Science, 354(6317), 1288–1292. https://doi.org/10.1126/science.aah5309

[14] Gabor, D. and Brooks, S. (2017). The digital revolution in financial inclusion: International development in the fintech era. *New Political Economy*, 22(4), 423–436. https://doi.org/10.1080/13563467.2017.1259298

[15] Pazarbasioglu, C., Mora, A.G., Uttamchandani, M., Natarajan, H., Feyen, E. and Saal, M. (2020). Digital financial services. World Bank. https://doi.org/10.1596/33432

[16] Manyika, J., Lund, S., Singer, M., White, O. and Berry, C. (2016). Digital finance for all: Powering inclusive growth in emerging economies. McKinsey Global Institute.

[17] AFI (Alliance for Financial Inclusion). (2021). FinTech for financial inclusion: A framework for digital financial transformation. https://www.afi-global.org

[18] Pradhan, R.P., Arvin, M.B., Hall, J.H. and Nair, M. (2017). Financial depth, internet penetration and economic growth nexus: Evidence from 71 countries. *Applied Economics Letters*, 24(3), 153–156. https://doi.org/10.1080/13504851.2016.1168922

[19] Wang, Y., Han, J. and Beynon, M.J. (2020). Fintech development and financial inclusion: A comparative study of China and India. *China Economic Review*, 62, 101454. https://doi.org/10.1016/j.chieco.2020.101454

[20] Singh, A. and Roy, D. (2021). Fintech and financial inclusion: Evidence from India. *Journal of Public Affairs*, 21(3), e2254. https://doi.org/10.1002/pa.2254

[21] Kim, Y., Park, Y.J. and Choi, J. (2016). The adoption of mobile payment services for "fintech". *International Journal of Applied Engineering Research,* 11(2), 1058–1061.

[22] Chen, L. (2016). From fintech to finlife: The case of fintech development in China. *China Economic Journal*, 9(3), 225–239. https://doi.org/10.1080/17538963.2016.1215057

[23] Rahman, M.M. and Abdullah, M.A. (2021). Does fintech foster financial inclusion? Evidence from Bangladesh. *Asian Journal of Economics and Banking*, 5(2), 125–138.

[24] Evans, D. S. and Pirchio, A. (2015). An empirical examination of why mobile money schemes ignite in some developing countries but flounder in

most. University of Chicago Coase-Sandor Institute for Law & Economics Research Paper, (753).

[25] Kapoor, S. and Ravi, S. (2021). Digital financial inclusion in India: A review of policy and practice. *South Asia Economic Journal,* 22(1), 42–64. https://doi.org/10.1177/1391561421997125

The Platform Economy: Innovation, Inequality, and the Future of Work

M. Vijayakumar and C. Thiyaneswaran

Associate Professor in Commerce BS & BI, Sri Krishna Arts and Science College, Coimbatore, Tamilnadu, India

ABSTRACT: *The platform economy has emerged as a transformative force in the 21st century, reshaping business models, employment structures, and economic interactions. This article explores the evolution of digital platforms and their influence on innovation and labor markets. While platforms offer opportunities for efficiency and growth, they also exacerbate income inequality and labor precarity. The study outlines the conceptual framework of platform capitalism, reviews relevant literature, and sets specific objectives. It discusses the necessity of innovation, the significance of this shift, and its broad implications for society. Limitations and challenges are acknowledged, along with recommendations for sustainable technological progress. Ultimately, the article calls for balanced development that fosters innovation without compromising worker welfare.*

Keywords: AI Systems, Digital Platforms, Platform Capitalism, Platform Economy.

1. INTRODUCTION

The rise of digital platforms such as Uber, Airbnb, Amazon, and TaskRabbit marks a paradigm shift in economic organization and labor dynamics. These platforms act as intermediaries, connecting consumers with service providers through algorithm-driven marketplaces. As they scale rapidly, they disrupt traditional business models and introduce novel forms of economic exchange. This transformation has led to increased flexibility, lower transaction costs, and global reach.

However, this shift is not without consequences. The platform economy often circumvents existing labor laws, contributing to job insecurity and weakening labor rights. Workers in the gig economy face unstable income, lack of benefits, and limited bargaining power. This duality—of innovation and inequality—requires a critical analysis of the current trajectory and the development of policies that ensure equitable and inclusive growth.

2. CONCEPTUAL BACKGROUND

The platform economy refers to a digital-based business model that leverages data and network effects to create value by facilitating exchanges between different user groups. These platforms thrive by acting as intermediaries and utilizing technology to scale rapidly, often monopolizing market segments. Platform capitalism, as theorized by Nick Srnicek (2016), emphasizes data as the new asset class, shifting focus from production to extraction and control of information.

This model has redefined the employer-employee relationship. Rather than hiring workers directly, platforms classify them as independent contractors, bypassing traditional labor obligations. The use of algorithmic management and performance monitoring further transforms labor relations, creating a workforce that is controlled but not officially employed. These developments challenge existing legal, economic, and ethical frameworks.

3. REVIEW OF LITERATURE

Srnicek, N. (2017). *Platform capitalism.* Polity Press. Srnicek explores the rise of platform-based business models and their economic and social implications. He classifies platforms into types (e.g., advertising, cloud, industrial) and argues that platforms concentrate power and data, leading to monopolistic practices and the exploitation of gig workers. His work provides a foundational framework for understanding innovation and inequality in the platform economy.

Kenney, M., & Zysman, J. (2016). This article discusses how platforms are reshaping industries by lowering transaction costs and enabling new forms of value creation. It highlights the tension between innovation and worker precarity, emphasizing that platform-based work often lacks traditional labor protections. The authors call for updated regulatory frameworks to address these shifts.

Schor, J. B., & Vallas, S. P. (2021). Schor and Vallas critically examine the promises and outcomes of the sharing (platform) economy. They argue that while platforms often claim to empower users and foster innovation, in practice, they frequently reproduce or exacerbate social inequalities. Their review helps contextualize the broader socioeconomic consequences of platform-based labor.

Van Doorn, N. (2017). Van Doorn investigates how platforms like Uber and TaskRabbit reproduce structural inequalities through gendered and racialized labor practices. Her analysis focuses on how marginalized groups are disproportionately represented in low-wage, flexible service work, offering critical insight into inequality within the platform economy.

De Stefano, V. (2016). De Stefano examines the legal and labor implications of gig and on-demand work. He critiques the erosion of traditional employment protections and suggests that current labor laws are ill-suited for the realities of platform-based work. His work contributes to the debate on how to regulate innovation while protecting vulnerable workers.

4. OBJECTIVES OF THE STUDY

1. To analyze the impact of platform-based innovation on traditional employment models.
2. To explore the relationship between digital platforms and income inequality.
3. To assess the challenges faced by gig workers in the platform economy.
4. To recommend policy and technological solutions for inclusive growth.

5. IMPORTANCE OF THE STUDY

This study is essential for understanding the complex interplay between innovation, labor, and inequality in the modern digital economy. Policymakers, business leaders, and labor unions must comprehend how platforms operate to ensure fair competition and equitable labor practices. By identifying gaps in current models, the study offers insights into sustainable and humane economic development.

Furthermore, the study contributes to academic discourse by framing the platform economy within the broader context of capitalism and technological change. It builds a foundation for future research and practical interventions aimed at aligning innovation with social justice.

6. LIMITATIONS OF THE STUDY

1. The study primarily uses secondary data and literature, limiting real-time empirical validation.
2. Rapid technological evolution may outdate some of the findings quickly.
3. The focus is largely on developed economies, limiting applicability to the Global South.
4. The analysis does not include sector-specific variations in platform labor dynamics.

7. NEED FOR INNOVATION

Technological innovation must prioritize ethical considerations and worker empowerment. As algorithmic management becomes widespread, there is a pressing need for transparent and accountable AI systems. These systems should enable fair evaluations, avoid discriminatory practices, and provide recourse mechanisms for workers.

Second, innovation should support decentralized and cooperative models. Platforms need not follow monopolistic paths; technologies like blockchain can enable distributed governance and ownership structures. Such innovations can reduce inequality and foster community wealth.

Finally, innovation must be inclusive, addressing the digital divide. Access to digital tools, literacy, and infrastructure is crucial for marginalized groups to benefit from the platform economy. Governments and private entities should collaborate to ensure digital participation for all.

8. SUGGESTIONS

1. Enforce regulations that classify gig workers with appropriate labor protections.
2. Promote platform cooperatives through financial incentives and supportive legal frameworks.
3. Develop open-source platform technologies to democratize access and innovation.
4. Encourage transparency in algorithmic decision-making through policy mandates.
5. Bridge the digital divide with public investments in infrastructure and digital literacy.
6. Introduce portable benefits systems for platform workers to ensure income security.
7. Foster multi-stakeholder dialogue among platforms, governments, and labor groups.

9. CONCLUSION

The platform economy represents a profound transformation in how work and value creation are organized. While it has driven unprecedented innovation and consumer convenience, it has also introduced new forms of inequality and labor insecurity. The dual nature of platforms—as drivers of progress and sources of precarity—must be addressed through thoughtful innovation and policy.

For the platform economy to evolve sustainably, stakeholders must embrace inclusive and ethical frameworks. By integrating technological innovation with social protections and participatory governance, society can harness the benefits of digital platforms while minimizing their downsides.

REFERENCES

[1] Srnicek, N. (2016). *Platform capitalism*. Polity Press.

[2] Kenney, M. and Zysman, J. (2016). The rise of the platform economy. *Issues in Science and Technology*, 32(3), 61–69.

[3] De Stefano, V. (2016). The rise of the "just-in-time workforce". *Comparative Labor Law & Policy Journal*, 37(3), 471–504.

[4] Scholz, T. (2016). *Platform cooperativism*. Rosa Luxemburg Stiftung.

[5] Sundararajan, A. (2016). *The sharing economy: The end of employment and the rise of crowd-based capitalism*. MIT Press.

[6] Ravenelle, A.J. (2019). *Hustle and gig: Struggling and surviving in the sharing economy*. University of California Press.

[7] Van Doorn, N. (2017). Platform labor: On the gendered and racialized exploitation of low-income service work in the 'on-demand' economy. *Information, Communication & Society*, 20(6), 898–914.

[8] Codagnone, C., Abadie, F. and Biagi, F. (2016). The future of work in the 'sharing economy'. *JRC Science for Policy Report*.

[9] Berg, J., *et al*. (2018). Digital labour platforms and the future of work: Towards decent work in the online world. *International Labour Organization*.

The Rise of FinTech and Digital-First Finance

M. Sakthivadivel[1], Ankitha Theres[2] and S. Ayyappan[3]

[1]Assistant Professor, SS, Department of Computer Science (AIML & Cyber Security), Dr. Mahalingam College of Engineering & Technology, Pollachi, Tamil Nadu, India

[2]Research Scholar, School of Management –3142

HRBR Campus, CMR University Bangalore, India

[3]Professor School of Management, CMR University, Bangalore, India

E-mail: [1]sakthivadivelm@gmail.com; [2]ankitha.theres@cmr.edu.in; [3]ayyappan.s@cmr.edu.in; [3]sapacet@gmail.com

Chapter Overview: *This chapter delivers a comprehensive study of how financial technology (FinTech) is fundamentally reshaping global financial systems. It begins by tracing the evolution of digital-first financial services, from the advent of* ***neobanks*** *and the widespread adoption of* ***digital wallets*** *to the seamless integration of* ***embedded finance*** *and the propagation of* ***platform-based financial services****. The core argument is that FinTech startups are not merely innovating on the periphery; they are radically redefining how financial services are designed, delivered, and consumed, challenging established paradigms and consumer expectations.*

A central theme of the chapter is the fascinating paradox of numerous money-losing Fin Techs garnering billions of investment. The chapter will take a case-based approach and is supported with valuable insights such as those from Harvard Business Review. It will explore the underlying systems that explain why so many of these organizations are able to obtain significant capital and rapidly developing influence on the financial landscape, even though they are typically unable to deliver traditional growth metrics – profits – during the early stages of their development. The chapter will help clarify the logic behind investor confidence in these organizations en masse, focusing on their scale, disruptive potential, and long-term value prop.

Keywords: COVID-19 Pandemic, Customer Acquisition Cost (CAC), Harvard Business Review (HBR), Lifetime Value (LTV), Near Field Communication (NFC), Unified Payments Interface (UPI), User Experience (UX).

1. INTRODUCTION: THE FINTECH REVOLUTION

The financial industry is undergoing a profound and irreversible transformation—a FinTech Revolution. This is no longer a new development but the start of a permanent, fundamental, and monumental transformation in how financial services operate throughout the world. The chapter will start out emphasizing that the digitization of finance is a permanent part of our future.

A key point of discussion will be the acceleration of financial digitization after the COVID-19 Pandemic. The pandemic served as a dramatically strong impetus to move toward the full adoption of digital channels for transactions, payments, and finance interactions, thereby accelerating a process that was already occurring. This digitalisation accelerates the trend and exposed the weakness of traditional financial institutions. The introduction will explain in clear terms why traditional banks are vulnerable to disruptors that are digital equals—their legacy technology, inflexible business models, and ultimately, unwillingness and slowness to innovate compared to nimble FinTech startups.

2. THE RISE OF DIGITAL-FIRST FINANCE

The following section will outline in full detail the principal tenets of digital-first finance that are the drivers of this change.

2.1 Neobanks: The New Age of Banking

Neobanks are fundamentally different from large and traditional banks. This chapter will define these characteristics:

- Digital and mobile-first banks with no physical branches at all. They are able to operate with much lower costs, and virtually all services are provided through mobile apps that are usually simple to use.
- **Full service:** Neobanks do not only provide standard account access, but they often offer innovative loan products, competitive rates for foreign exchange and customizable and competitive savings products.
- **Some of the neobanks will be highlighted in this chapter:** This chapter will provide insight into the details of a number of leading neobanks in the world, such as Revolut, Chime and N26. One of the attractions of neobanks is their variety of business model's and customer propositions.
- **How neobanks are competitive:** A discussion of what makes neobanks "competitive", such as speed of delivery, user experience (UX), designed through intuitive digital interfaces, and low-cost operational structure that leads to lower fees for consumers.

2.2 Digital Wallets: The Gateway to a Cashless Economy

Digital wallets have become ubiquitous, fundamentally altering transaction habits. Digital wallets have become ubiquitous, fundamentally altering how individuals and businesses conduct financial transactions. Their widespread adoption is reshaping payment habits by moving away from cash and physical cards toward contactless, mobile-first experiences.

(a) *Mechanism: How Digital Wallets Enable Seamless Contactless Transactions*

At their core, digital wallets facilitate contactless payments by securely storing users' payment information on mobile devices. Using technologies such as Near Field Communication (NFC), QR codes, or app-to-app transfers, users can complete transactions simply by tapping their phone or scanning a code—eliminating the need to carry cash or cards. This mechanism not only speeds up payments but also enhances hygiene and convenience, especially in a post-pandemic world.

(b) *Global Parallels: India's UPI System as a Model for Real-Time Payments*

One of the most remarkable success stories in digital wallets is India's Unified Payments Interface (UPI) system. Launched in 2016, UPI is an open, interoperable real-time payment system that enables instant fund transfers between any two bank accounts via mobile devices. UPI's architecture promotes interoperability among different digital wallets and banks, making it a globally recognized benchmark for efficient and inclusive digital payments.

India's UPI system shares parallels with international ecosystems such as China's Alipay and WeChat Pay, which have similarly transformed their domestic markets by integrating payments, social networking, and financial services into one platform. These examples demonstrate how digital wallets can catalyze cashless economies at scale.

(c) *Key Examples: Market Leaders Driving Adoption*

Platforms like Google Pay, Paytm, and Apple Pay have played pivotal roles in expanding digital wallet usage worldwide. Google Pay leverages UPI in India and NFC in other countries to offer seamless payments. Paytm, originally a mobile recharge service, evolved into a full-fledged digital wallet with wide merchant acceptance, especially in India's tier-2 and tier-3 cities. Apple Pay, with its strong focus on security and privacy, has driven contactless payments in developed markets globally.

Each platform differentiates itself through unique features such as rewards programs, bill payments, peer-to-peer transfers, and integration with other financial products—fueling rapid user growth and market penetration.

(d) *Impact: Advancing Financial Inclusion and Transactional Efficiency*

The rise of digital wallets has been instrumental in advancing financial inclusion by providing affordable and accessible financial services to previously unbanked and underbanked populations. By lowering the barriers to entry, these platforms enable more people to participate in the formal economy, enhancing economic opportunities.

Additionally, digital wallets significantly improve transactional speed and convenience, benefiting both consumers and businesses. Instantaneous payments reduce waiting times, improve cash flow for merchants, and foster a more dynamic economic environment.

2.3 Embedded Finance: Invisible Banking Inside Everyday Apps

Embedded finance marks a revolutionary shift in how financial services are delivered by integrating them directly into non-financial platforms and applications. This seamless embedding transforms everyday apps into multifunctional hubs where users access financial products without ever leaving their familiar digital environment.

Definition

Embedded finance refers to the integration of financial services—such as payments, lending, insurance, or investments—directly within non-financial platforms. Instead of visiting banks or fintech apps separately, users experience these services as a natural part of their journey on e-commerce sites, ride-hailing apps, or marketplaces. This approach makes financial transactions frictionless and contextually relevant.

Illustrative Examples

- **Amazon Pay Later:** This service offers instant credit to customers at checkout, enabling purchases without upfront payments. By embedding credit options directly into the Amazon shopping experience, it reduces friction and encourages higher conversion rates.
- **Ola Money:** Within the Ola ride-hailing app, users can make seamless payments and access micro-lending services. This integration enhances convenience, allowing riders to manage transportation and finances within a single app.
- **Shopify Capital:** Shopify provides merchants with fast, embedded lending options to help grow their businesses. By assessing sales data in real-time, Shopify offers credit precisely when merchants need working capital, boosting business continuity.

Benefits

- **Contextual Lending:** Embedded finance allows platforms to offer credit and other financial services at the exact moment users require them, increasing relevance and uptake.
- **Real-Time Underwriting:** Leveraging user data and behavior within the platform, lenders can perform rapid, automated risk assessments, enabling instant approvals and reducing operational costs.

- **Enhanced Ecosystem Monetization:** Platform providers benefit from new revenue streams by embedding financial products, deepening customer engagement, and increasing overall platform value.

3. HOW FINTECH STARTUPS CHALLENGE LEGACY INSTITUTIONS

This section will articulate the strategic advantages FinTechs possess over established banks. The financial services landscape is witnessing a profound transformation as FinTech companies outpace legacy banks in innovation, agility, and customer engagement. This section articulates the key strategic advantages FinTechs possess over traditional financial institutions and how incumbent banks are responding to this disruption.

3.1 Legacy Banks' Barriers

Traditional banks face several inherent challenges that hinder their ability to innovate rapidly:

- **Outdated IT Infrastructure:** Many banks operate on legacy systems that are costly to maintain, difficult to upgrade, and incompatible with modern digital technologies. This limits their ability to launch new products quickly and integrate seamlessly with emerging platforms.
- **Slow Product Development Cycles:** Bureaucratic structures and multiple layers of approval lead to prolonged development timelines, making banks less responsive to changing customer needs and market trends.
- **Complex Regulatory Frameworks:** Navigating stringent regulatory requirements demands significant resources and can slow down innovation. Compliance often results in risk-averse behavior, limiting experimentation with novel financial products.

3.2 FinTech Advantage

In contrast, FinTechs leverage several strengths to gain competitive edges:

- **Agile Product Development:** With lean organizational structures and a technology-first mindset, FinTechs rapidly iterate and deploy new offerings. This flexibility enables them to quickly adapt to user feedback and market dynamics.
- **Real-Time Analytics and Feedback Loops:** FinTechs harness big data and machine learning to analyze customer behavior continuously. This empowers them to personalize services, optimize user experience, and proactively address pain points.
- **Targeted Niche Markets:** Instead of competing with banks on broad, traditional services, many FinTechs focus on underserved segments such as freelancers, small and medium-sized enterprises (SMEs), and younger

demographics. Tailored solutions resonate better with these groups, driving higher engagement and loyalty.

3.3 Emergence of Banking-as-a-Service (BaaS) and Open Banking Ecosystems

The rise of **Banking-as-a-Service (BaaS)** platforms has lowered barriers for non-bank companies to offer financial products by providing turnkey banking infrastructure through APIs. This enables retailers, tech firms, and startups to embed banking services within their own offerings without building from scratch.

Simultaneously, **open banking frameworks**—mandated in regions like the EU and UK—encourage secure data sharing between banks and third-party providers. This fosters collaboration, accelerates innovation, and expands customer choice by enabling FinTechs to build on existing banking infrastructure.

3.4 Strategic Response of Traditional Banks

Recognizing the threat and opportunity posed by FinTechs, many incumbent banks are adapting through several strategic approaches:

- **Acquisitions:** Banks acquire promising FinTech startups to integrate innovative technologies and talent directly into their operations.
- **Partnerships:** Collaborations with FinTech firms allow banks to quickly access cutting-edge capabilities, improving product offerings and customer experience.
- **Internal Innovation Labs:** Establishing dedicated teams and labs focused on digital transformation helps banks experiment with new technologies and business models within a controlled environment.

Together, these dynamics are reshaping the financial ecosystem, where agility, customer-centric innovation, and collaborative frameworks define the future of banking.

4. WHY MANY FINTECHS REMAIN UNPROFITABLE—AND STILL THRIVE

This critical section addresses the core paradox highlighted in the chapter overview, drawing extensively on insights from the Harvard Business Review (HBR) article, *"Why Are Companies That Lose Money Still So Successful?"* FinTech firms, despite reporting losses, continue to thrive and reshape financial services. Understanding this phenomenon requires unpacking their strategic focus on growth, scalability, investor expectations, and network dynamics.

4.1 Growth Over Profits

- **Customer Acquisition Prioritized for Long-Term Market Dominance:** FinTechs often adopt a "grow at all costs" mentality, prioritizing rapid customer acquisition above immediate profitability. The rationale is simple: capturing a large user base early establishes strong network effects and market presence that become formidable competitive advantages. Profitability is viewed as a secondary goal to be achieved once dominant scale is secured.
- **Market Share Now, Profits Later: The "Land Grab" Strategy:** Aggressive investments in marketing, user incentives, and partnerships characterize the "land grab" approach. FinTechs focus on winning market share swiftly, even at the cost of short-term losses, with the expectation that monetization will follow naturally once their platform becomes the go-to choice for customers.

4.2 Scalability and Marginal Cost Advantages

- **Software-Driven Services Have Near-Zero Cost Per Additional User:** Unlike traditional businesses, digital platforms benefit from near-zero marginal costs. After the initial investment in developing technology and infrastructure, the cost to serve each new customer is negligible, enabling rapid scaling without proportional cost increases.
- **Economies of Scale Manifest Later in the Lifecycle:** While early stages demand heavy spending on product development and customer acquisition, economies of scale kick in as the user base grows. At large scale, FinTechs can operate with significantly lower average costs, unlocking substantial profit margins that were impossible at smaller scales.

4.3 Investor Perspective: Betting on Lifetime Value (LTV)

- **High Retention and Engagement Data Justify Early Losses:** Investors look beyond immediate profits to key metrics such as user retention, engagement rates, and transaction growth. These indicators signal the potential for sustained future revenues, making early losses acceptable in light of anticipated long-term returns.
- **Valuations Often Based on Projected LTV vs. CAC Ratios:** Investor valuations heavily factor in the lifetime value (LTV) of a customer relative to the customer acquisition cost (CAC). A high LTV/CAC ratio suggests that the initial investment in acquiring a customer will pay off many times over, justifying substantial upfront spending and tolerating losses in early years.

4.4 Network Effects and Ecosystem Value

- **FinTech Platforms Become More Valuable as Users Increase:** Network effects create a powerful feedback loop: as more users join the platform, its value increases exponentially for all participants. This creates a defensible market position that is difficult for competitors to penetrate.
- **Cross-Product Monetization: Lending, Insurance, Wealth Advisory:** Once a large and engaged user base is established, FinTechs can introduce additional high-margin financial products. By leveraging customer data and trust, they can expand into lending, insurance, wealth management, and other services, increasing revenue per user and deepening ecosystem stickiness.

5. CHALLENGES AND CRITICISMS

Despite their rapid growth and disruptive potential, FinTech companies face a spectrum of structural and ethical challenges that cast uncertainty over their long-term sustainability and societal impact.

- **Profitability Concerns:** The "growth over profit" model—central to many FinTechs—raises pressing questions about sustainability. While investors have tolerated early-stage losses in anticipation of future scale-driven profits, prolonged unprofitability is increasingly scrutinized. The key issue is how long these firms can operate at a loss before the market demands financial discipline. Economic downturns and shifts in investor sentiment may accelerate the need for a clear path to breakeven and sustainable operations.
- **Regulatory Grey Zones:** FinTechs often operate in domains where existing laws are either outdated or absent. Novel offerings such as Buy Now Pay Later (BNPL), decentralized finance (DeFi), and crypto-lending do not fit neatly into traditional regulatory categories. Moreover, the use of AI and algorithmic models in credit scoring and financial decision-making raises ethical concerns around fairness, transparency, and accountability. Regulatory uncertainty not only exposes consumers to risk but also creates operational ambiguity for startups navigating compliance expectations.
- **Trust and Compliance:** With great digital capability comes great responsibility. FinTechs collect vast troves of personal and financial data, making them prime targets for cyberattacks. Ensuring data privacy, safeguarding against algorithmic bias—particularly in lending decisions—and building resilient cybersecurity frameworks are no longer optional but essential for maintaining public trust. The long-term viability of FinTech depends not just on innovation, but on the ability to uphold ethical standards and regulatory integrity.

6. STRATEGIC IMPLICATIONS FOR POLICYMAKERS AND INCUMBENTS

This section will consider the broader implications of the FinTech revolution. The FinTech revolution extends beyond the private sector—it is reshaping how governments regulate, how financial institutions operate, and how citizens interact with money.

- **Balancing Innovation with Systemic Stability:** Regulators worldwide face the challenge of fostering financial innovation without compromising consumer protection or macroeconomic stability. Proactive approaches such as regulatory sandboxes, dynamic compliance frameworks, and technology-neutral regulations are emerging as best practices. Striking this balance is critical to nurturing responsible innovation while minimizing systemic risk.
- **Digital Literacy and Financial Inclusion as National Imperatives:** Digital financial tools are only as inclusive as the populations that can access and use them. Enhancing digital literacy—particularly among low-income, rural, and elderly populations—is essential for equitable participation in the evolving financial ecosystem. Financial inclusion must be integrated into national digital development strategies to ensure that FinTech does not exacerbate existing inequalities.
- **India's Public Digital Infrastructure as a Global Model:** India presents a globally relevant case study in proactive FinTech enablement:
    - **IndiaStack** provides foundational digital layers including Aadhaar (identity), eSign (authentication), and DigiLocker (document storage).
    - **Unified Payments Interface (UPI)** enables real-time, interoperable payments with unprecedented ease and scale.
    - **Account Aggregator Framework** empowers individuals to control and share their financial data securely for credit, insurance, and investment purposes.
    - India's approach demonstrates how digital public goods, open standards, and enabling regulations can democratize finance and catalyze innovation at scale. Other nations are now studying and replicating aspects of this model.

7. CONCLUSION: FINTECH AS A PERMANENT FORCE IN FINANCIAL EVOLUTION

FinTech is not merely changing the way financial services look—it is redefining the infrastructure, assumptions, and relationships that underpin the entire financial system.

The shift underway is profound: the next generation of financial services will be **invisible** (embedded within apps and platforms), **intelligent** (powered by real-time analytics and AI), and **inclusive** (designed for broad accessibility and impact). FinTech is increasingly becoming the default interface for a wide range of financial activities, from credit and payments to insurance and wealth management.

For traditional financial institutions, the message is clear: **evolve or risk obsolescence**. This means embracing:

- **Agility** in product innovation and digital operations,
- **Collaboration** with FinTechs through partnerships and investments, and
- **Open architectures** that support interoperability, customer-centric design, and data portability.

FinTech is no longer a disruptor on the margins. It is the new core of financial services. The institutions that recognize this and respond with bold, strategic transformation will shape the future of finance—not be left behind by it.

REFERENCES

[1] Harvard Business Review (2023). *Why Are Companies That Lose Money Still So Successful?* (This will be a direct reference for the case insight discussed).

[2] BIS Papers No. 126. *Fintech and the Transformation of the Financial Landscape.* (A key source for understanding the broader systemic impact and policy considerations).

[3] World Bank (2022). *The Global Findex Database: Financial Inclusion Post-COVID.* (Provides crucial data and analysis on the impact of digital finance on financial inclusion).

Towards a Holistic Healthcare Curriculum: Embedding Ayurveda, Yoga, and AYUSH Systems in Medical Education

S. Ayyappan[1] and Mayan K. Sreerudran[2]

[1]Professor, School of Management, CMR University, Bangalore, India

[2]Ph.D Research Scholar, School of Management, CMR University, Bangalore, India

E-mail: [1]ayyappan.s@cmr.edu.in; [1]sapacet@gmail.com; [2]mayan.sreerudran@cmr.edu.in

ABSTRACT: *Healthcare education is undergoing a paradigm shift, necessitating an integrative approach that aligns with India's pluralistic medical landscape. The National Education Policy (NEP) 2020 emphasizes the need for a holistic curriculum that bridges modern and traditional medical systems. This paper explores the integration of Ayurveda, Yoga, and other AYUSH disciplines into conventional medical education, ensuring that future healthcare professionals possess a well-rounded understanding of diverse healing practices. Given the rising global interest in integrative healthcare, embedding AYUSH systems into mainstream medical training can enhance patient-centered care, strengthen preventive healthcare, and promote community-based health solutions. This study examines the potential benefits, challenges, and structural modifications required for implementing such a curriculum. A well-designed integrative curriculum can equip medical graduates with the necessary skills to leverage complementary therapies, improve cross-disciplinary collaboration, and enhance primary and secondary healthcare delivery. Furthermore, the inclusion of Ayurveda and Yoga in modern medical training can help address prevalent lifestyle disorders, promote wellness-oriented healthcare, and foster a preventive approach rather than a reactive one. This paper also evaluates existing models of integrative healthcare education worldwide, identifying best practices that could be adapted to the Indian context. Policy recommendations will be proposed to overcome barriers such as regulatory challenges, curriculum restructuring, and faculty training. The study concludes that a holistic healthcare curriculum incorporating AYUSH systems can transform medical education, align with public health needs, and contribute to a more inclusive and sustainable healthcare ecosystem.*

Keywords: Integrative Healthcare Education, Ayurveda and Yoga in Medical Training, Holistic Curriculum Design, Preventive and Community Healthcare, NEP 2020 and AYUSH Integration.

1. INTRODUCTION

Healthcare education is evolving rapidly to address the growing complexity of health challenges and the increasing demand for integrative treatment approaches. In India, where diverse medical traditions coexist, there is a pressing need to bridge the gap between conventional allopathic medicine and traditional healing systems such as Ayurveda, Yoga, Unani, Siddha, and Homeopathy (AYUSH). Despite their historical significance and continued relevance in Indian healthcare, AYUSH disciplines have largely remained on the periphery of mainstream medical education.

The National Education Policy (NEP) 2020 advocates for a more holistic and interdisciplinary approach to education, emphasizing the importance of integrating traditional and modern knowledge systems. As global interest in integrative medicine grows, incorporating Ayurveda, Yoga, and other AYUSH modalities into medical curricula can enhance patient-centered care, strengthen preventive healthcare strategies, and foster a more inclusive healthcare ecosystem. This shift is particularly relevant in addressing lifestyle-related disorders, which require a broader therapeutic perspective beyond conventional biomedical interventions.

However, embedding AYUSH into medical education presents both opportunities and challenges. While integrative training can equip future healthcare professionals with a diverse skill set and encourage cross-disciplinary collaboration, it also requires significant curriculum restructuring, regulatory support, and faculty training. Drawing insights from global models of integrative healthcare education, this paper explores strategies for successfully embedding AYUSH principles into modern medical training in India. By identifying best practices and proposing policy recommendations, it aims to pave the way for a healthcare education system that is both comprehensive and culturally rooted, ultimately contributing to a more sustainable and patient-centric healthcare framework.

2. REVIEW OF LITERATURE

The integration of Ayurveda, Yoga, and other AYUSH systems into modern medical education has been a subject of extensive scholarly discussion over the past decade. Several researchers have explored the benefits, challenges, and policy implications of such an integrative approach, emphasizing its potential to create a more holistic, preventive, and patient-centric healthcare system.

Rawat *et al.* (2024) provided a comprehensive review of emerging techniques in trace elemental analysis for medicinal plants and food-based extracts, highlighting how machine learning and data analytics can enhance the scientific validation of Ayurveda. Their study emphasized the need for rigorous analytical methods to establish Ayurveda's credibility in modern medicine. Similarly, Naveen and Saxena (2024) discussed the importance of integrating AYUSH principles into preventive medicine, particularly in addressing lifestyle-related disorders. Their paper advocated for the inclusion of Yoga and Ayurveda in medical curricula to enhance preventive healthcare strategies and improve overall patient well-being. Concerns regarding the safety and efficacy of AYUSH therapies were explored by Nesari (2024), who conducted a literature review focusing on the safety of Ayurvedic herbs. The study underscored the importance of adopting an evidence-based approach to traditional medicine to ensure patient safety and regulatory compliance. In a related discussion, Patel and Roy (2023) examined how AYUSH practices have been successfully integrated into community healthcare models, particularly in rural areas. Their research highlighted case studies where Ayurveda and Yoga were used effectively in primary healthcare settings, demonstrating their accessibility and affordability in addressing public health challenges. Another critical aspect of AYUSH integration is the collaboration between allopathic and traditional medical practitioners. Srivastava and Jain (2023) analyzed the challenges and opportunities in cross-disciplinary collaboration, identifying key barriers such as differing treatment philosophies, regulatory constraints, and the lack of standardized integration frameworks. Their study suggested strategies for improving interdisciplinary cooperation, including joint training programs and shared research initiatives. Meanwhile, Kumar and Mehta (2023) explored policy frameworks governing AYUSH education in India, particularly in light of the National Education Policy (NEP) 2020. Their findings indicated that while the NEP promotes an interdisciplinary approach, significant policy revisions are needed to facilitate seamless integration within medical education. Sahu and Kumar (2023) focused on the role of Yoga in modern medical education, reviewing various case studies that illustrated its benefits for medical students. Their research demonstrated how incorporating Yoga into medical training can enhance mental health, stress management, and overall well-being among healthcare professionals. Similarly, Dwivedi and Prakash (2022) emphasized the need for increased funding and research in AYUSH disciplines. Their review proposed a roadmap for strengthening research methodologies, highlighting the importance of clinical trials and scientific validation to ensure credibility and acceptance within mainstream medicine. Madhavan and Nair (2022) explored the potential of AYUSH in preventive healthcare, analyzing how Ayurvedic principles and Yoga-based interventions can reduce the burden of chronic diseases such as diabetes and hypertension. Their findings supported the argument that an integrative approach to medicine, focusing on prevention rather than cure, could significantly improve public health outcomes. In a similar vein, Sharma and Singh (2022) reviewed the role of Ayurvedic interventions in chronic disease management, specifically in treating metabolic disorders. Their study provided evidence that combining Ayurveda with conventional treatments can enhance patient recovery and long-term health benefits. Subramanian and Iyer (2021) conducted a systematic review on AYUSH and evidence-based practice, identifying major gaps in clinical research and the need for standardized protocols. They argued that despite AYUSH's historical significance, its integration into modern medicine requires more rigorous scientific validation. This point was further elaborated by Rao and Iyer (2021), who compared the Indian AYUSH model with similar integrative approaches in China (Traditional Chinese Medicine) and Western countries (Complementary and Alternative Medicine). Their analysis provided insights into best practices that could be adapted to India's medical education system. Saxena and Ghosh (2019) examined the role of Ayurveda in mental health, highlighting its potential in treating disorders such as anxiety and depression. Their review suggested that Ayurvedic therapies, including herbal treatments and meditation, could complement psychiatric care, offering a holistic approach to mental well-being. Nanda and Gupta (2020) extended this discussion by reviewing how traditional medicine has been integrated into medical education worldwide. They identified key lessons from countries that have successfully incorporated alternative medicine into their healthcare systems, emphasizing the importance of curriculum restructuring and interdisciplinary training. Shetty and Rao (2020) addressed the challenges facing AYUSH research in India, particularly in terms of funding, regulatory approval, and academic support. Their study called for increased investment in scientific studies to establish the efficacy of AYUSH therapies. Similarly, Gupta and Sharma (2020) reviewed epidemiological studies demonstrating Ayurveda's role in preventing non-communicable diseases. Their findings highlighted how traditional medicine can play a crucial role in reducing disease incidence through dietary and lifestyle interventions. Joshi and Saxena (2016) explored public perceptions of integrative medicine, conducting survey-based research to assess attitudes toward AYUSH therapies. Their findings indicated that while there is growing acceptance of integrative medicine, misconceptions and skepticism persist due to a lack of awareness and standardized clinical guidelines. Chauhan and Sharma (2015) analyzed the complementary role of Yoga and Ayurveda in modern healthcare, presenting case studies where integrative treatments resulted in improved patient outcomes. Singh and Gupta (2014) provided a comparative analysis of global medical education models that successfully integrate traditional and modern medicine. Their review outlined recommendations for India, emphasizing the need for collaborative research, policy support, and curriculum enhancements. Finally, Natarajan and Rao (2013) made a strong case for the systematic inclusion of AYUSH in modern healthcare education, discussing its historical significance and potential policy implications. Their study provided foundational arguments for why integrative medicine should be embraced in India's medical education system.

3. BRIEF OVERVIEW OF AYURVEDA, YOGA, UNANI, SIDDHA, AND HOMEOPATHY

India has a long-standing tradition of holistic healing through its AYUSH systems—Ayurveda, Yoga & Naturopathy, Unani, Siddha, and Homeopathy—each of which offers a unique approach to health and wellness. Ayurveda, one of the world's oldest medical systems, is rooted in the concept of balance among three fundamental energies or doshas: Vata, Pitta, and Kapha. Ayurvedic treatments emphasize personalized healthcare through herbal medicines, dietary adjustments, detoxification therapies such as Panchakarma, and lifestyle modifications. Ayurveda plays a crucial role in preventive healthcare, promoting wellness and longevity through daily regimens (Dinacharya) and seasonal routines (Ritucharya).

Yoga and Naturopathy focus on the integration of body, mind, and spirit. Yoga, recognized by the World Health Organization (WHO), includes asanas (postures), pranayama (breathing techniques), and meditation, offering scientifically proven benefits in managing stress, cardiovascular health, and mental well-being. Naturopathy, often linked with Yoga, employs natural healing methods such as diet therapy, hydrotherapy, fasting, and acupuncture to promote self-healing.

Unani medicine, rooted in the Greco-Arabic medical tradition, is based on the four humors theory (blood, phlegm, yellow bile, and black bile). It offers treatments through herbal formulations, regimental therapies like Hijama (cupping therapy), diet therapy, and lifestyle modifications. Unani medicine has been widely used for managing arthritis, gastrointestinal disorders, metabolic syndromes, and skin conditions.

Siddha medicine, one of the oldest systems, is primarily practiced in Tamil Nadu, India. It integrates alchemy, pulse diagnosis (Nadi Pariksha), detoxification, herbal and mineral-based formulations, and yogic practices to restore balance in the body. Siddha medicine is particularly effective in treating chronic inflammatory disorders, metabolic syndromes, and age-related ailments.

Homeopathy, developed in the 18th century by Samuel Hahnemann, follows the principle of "like cures like", wherein highly diluted substances stimulate the body's natural healing response. Homeopathy has gained widespread global recognition, particularly for its role in treating allergies, autoimmune diseases, chronic pain, and mental health disorders. It is now practiced in over 80 countries, with increasing patient acceptance due to its non-invasive approach.

4 SCIENTIFIC BASIS AND EVIDENCE SUPPORTING AYUSH PRACTICES

Though traditionally based on empirical knowledge and centuries of practice, modern scientific research has increasingly validated the efficacy of AYUSH therapies. Several clinical studies have demonstrated that Ayurvedic formulations, such as Ashwagandha, Guduchi, and Turmeric, offer significant therapeutic benefits, particularly in managing conditions like diabetes, inflammation, and stress-related disorders. Panchakarma detoxification therapies have been found to improve gut health, metabolic functions, and immune response.

Yoga has been extensively studied in randomized controlled trials (RCTs), with evidence supporting its role in reducing hypertension, anxiety, depression, and cardiovascular risks. Studies have shown that regular Yoga practice helps regulate blood pressure, improve pulmonary function, and enhance neuroplasticity, making it an effective intervention for chronic disease management.

Unani medicine's herbal formulations and regimental therapies have demonstrated anti-inflammatory, anti-diabetic, and gastroprotective properties. Clinical trials have evaluated the effectiveness of Unani formulations in managing obesity, arthritis, and liver disorders. Similarly, Siddha medicine, with its polyherbal formulations and detoxification methods, has been recognized for its potential in managing metabolic disorders, neurodegenerative conditions, and chronic inflammation.

While Homeopathy remains a subject of debate due to its high dilution principles, research suggests that ultra-diluted homeopathic medicines may have immunomodulatory effects, psychosomatic benefits, and applications in chronic pain management. The Ministry of AYUSH, in collaboration with research bodies such as ICMR and CSIR, has been actively involved in conducting scientific validation studies to establish evidence-based applications of AYUSH therapies.

5. ROLE OF AYUSH IN ADDRESSING LIFESTYLE DISORDERS AND PREVENTIVE HEALTHCARE

In the modern healthcare landscape, lifestyle-related diseases such as diabetes, hypertension, cardiovascular diseases, obesity, and mental health disorders have become major public health concerns. Conventional allopathic medicine primarily focuses on disease management, whereas AYUSH systems emphasize preventive and holistic care. Ayurveda, for instance, offers guidelines for daily routines (Dinacharya) and seasonal regimens (Ritucharya), which help in maintaining optimal health and disease prevention. Herbal formulations like Triphala, Brahmi, and Neem are commonly used for detoxification, digestion, and immune system support.

Yoga and Naturopathy contribute significantly to mental well-being and stress management. Yoga practices such as meditation, breathing exercises (pranayama), and mindfulness techniques have been scientifically proven to reduce cortisol levels (stress hormone), enhance cognitive function, and improve emotional resilience. These interventions are particularly effective in managing anxiety, depression, and psychosomatic disorders.

Unani and Siddha medicine offer dietary and lifestyle recommendations tailored to an individual's body constitution (Mizaj in Unani and Mukkuttram in Siddha) to maintain balance and prevent disease onset. Homeopathy, with its focus on individualized treatment, plays a role in strengthening immunity and addressing chronic conditions without causing side effects.

The integration of AYUSH into mainstream healthcare can significantly enhance preventive medicine, reduce dependency on long-term pharmacological treatments, and promote wellness-oriented healthcare models. Countries like China, Germany, and the USA have already adopted integrative healthcare approaches, incorporating traditional medicine into public health systems. Recognizing its potential, the WHO has emphasized the importance of traditional medicine, leading to collaborative research efforts on Ayurveda and Yoga in countries like Japan, South Korea, and the United Kingdom.

In conclusion, AYUSH systems offer a comprehensive, preventive, and sustainable approach to healthcare. Their integration into modern medical education can equip future healthcare professionals with a broader therapeutic perspective, enabling cross-disciplinary collaboration and patient-centered care. With growing global recognition and scientific validation, the role of AYUSH in public health is set to expand, contributing to a more inclusive and holistic healthcare system.

6. GLOBAL RECOGNITION AND INTEGRATION OF TRADITIONAL MEDICINE

Traditional medicine, including Ayurveda, Yoga, Unani, Siddha, and Homeopathy (AYUSH), has gained increasing recognition worldwide as healthcare systems shift toward integrative and holistic approaches. The World Health Organization (WHO) has played a crucial role in promoting the incorporation of traditional and complementary medicine (TCM) into modern healthcare frameworks. The WHO Traditional Medicine Strategy 2014–2023 emphasizes the importance of evidence-based research, policy development, and education to ensure the safe and effective use of traditional healing systems. A significant milestone in this direction was the establishment of the WHO Global Centre for Traditional Medicine (GCTM) in Jamnagar, India, which aims to advance scientific validation and research in Ayurveda, Yoga, and other traditional therapies. Additionally, the WHO has included traditional medicine diagnoses in the International Classification of Diseases

(ICD-11), enabling better documentation and integration of these practices in global health systems.

The adoption of Ayurveda and Yoga has been particularly strong in Western countries, where they are recognized for their effectiveness in managing chronic diseases, mental health issues, and preventive healthcare. In the United States, the National Center for Complementary and Integrative Health (NCCIH) funds research on traditional medicine, while Ayurvedic treatments and Yoga are increasingly incorporated into wellness programs and hospital settings. Germany has embraced Ayurveda as part of its wellness tourism industry, with specialized Panchakarma centers offering therapeutic detoxification treatments. In the United Kingdom, Yoga and mindfulness-based interventions are recognized within the National Health Service (NHS) for managing stress, anxiety, and chronic pain. China, which has successfully integrated Traditional Chinese Medicine (TCM) into its national healthcare system, has been collaborating with India to explore synergies between TCM and Ayurveda. Similarly, Australia and Canada have incorporated traditional medicine courses into their medical education systems, while Ayurvedic and Homeopathic practitioners operate under regulated frameworks.

Beyond Ayurveda and Yoga, other AYUSH disciplines have also gained international acceptance. Unani medicine is widely practiced in Middle Eastern countries, particularly in Saudi Arabia, the UAE, and Iran, where it is used to treat metabolic disorders, joint pain, and respiratory diseases. Siddha medicine, while primarily confined to Tamil Nadu, India, is gaining recognition in Sri Lanka, Malaysia, and Singapore, with ongoing research on its herbal formulations for chronic inflammatory conditions. Homeopathy, originally developed in Europe, remains a mainstream complementary therapy in France, Germany, Brazil, Mexico, and the United Kingdom. In France, nearly 40% of doctors prescribe homeopathic medicines, and in Germany, homeopathy is covered by insurance plans, reflecting its widespread acceptance.

Despite growing global interest, the integration of AYUSH into mainstream healthcare systems faces several challenges. Differences in regulatory frameworks, the need for stronger scientific validation, and skepticism among allopathic practitioners have slowed the adoption of traditional medicine in some regions. However, ongoing research, policy support, and international collaborations are paving the way for greater recognition and acceptance of AYUSH practices. As global healthcare shifts toward more preventive and personalized medicine, traditional healing systems are expected to play a vital role in shaping the future of holistic and integrative healthcare.

7. THE NEED FOR AN INTEGRATIVE HEALTHCARE CURRICULUM

The current medical education system remains predominantly allopathic-centric, focusing on biomedical approaches to disease management while often neglecting holistic and preventive healthcare perspectives. This approach has led to an overemphasis on pharmacological treatments and surgical interventions, sometimes overlooking the role of lifestyle, nutrition, and traditional healing practices in maintaining overall health. Despite advancements in modern medicine, there remains a gap in addressing chronic diseases, mental health issues, and lifestyle disorders through preventive and patient-centered approaches. Medical students trained exclusively in allopathy may lack exposure to the benefits of traditional medicine systems such as Ayurveda, Yoga, Unani, Siddha, and Homeopathy (AYUSH), limiting their ability to offer integrative healthcare solutions to patients who seek alternative options.

In recent years, there has been a significant increase in patient preference for complementary and alternative medicine (CAM). People across the globe are turning to Ayurveda, Yoga, acupuncture, herbal medicine, and homeopathy for chronic disease management, mental well-being, and preventive healthcare. The World Health Organization (WHO) estimates that nearly 80% of the global population relies on traditional medicine for primary healthcare needs. In countries like India, China, Germany, the United States, and Australia, integrative healthcare models that combine modern and traditional medicine are gaining traction. Patients are increasingly looking for holistic treatment plans that not only alleviate symptoms but also address the root causes of disease through lifestyle modifications, stress management, and natural healing therapies. Given this shift, it is essential for medical education to evolve, equipping future healthcare professionals with knowledge of both biomedical and traditional healing systems to provide more comprehensive care.

Integrative medicine has the potential to enhance holistic patient care by combining the strengths of both modern and traditional medicine. While allopathy excels in acute care, emergency interventions, and advanced surgical techniques, AYUSH systems emphasize preventive healthcare, individualized treatments, and mind-body wellness. By incorporating principles of Ayurveda, Yoga, and Unani medicine into conventional medical education, healthcare professionals can adopt a multi-disciplinary approach that focuses on long-term health outcomes rather than merely treating symptoms. This integration can be particularly beneficial in addressing lifestyle disorders such as diabetes, hypertension, obesity, and stress-related illnesses, where a combination of dietary recommendations, yoga therapy, and herbal treatments can complement conventional pharmacological interventions.

Aligning medical education with the WHO's Traditional Medicine Strategy is a crucial step toward standardizing and integrating traditional medicine systems within global healthcare frameworks. The WHO advocates for evidence-based validation, policy development, and capacity-building to enhance the credibility and acceptance of traditional medicine. The establishment of the WHO Global Centre for Traditional Medicine (GCTM) in India reflects the growing international recognition of Ayurveda, Yoga, and other AYUSH disciplines. Integrating these systems into medical curricula can ensure that future doctors are well-equipped to offer diverse treatment options, engage in cross-disciplinary collaborations, and improve patient-centered healthcare delivery. By embracing an integrative healthcare curriculum, medical education can become more inclusive, sustainable, and aligned with the evolving healthcare needs of society.

8. GLOBAL MODELS OF INTEGRATIVE HEALTHCARE EDUCATION

Several countries have successfully integrated traditional and modern medicine into their healthcare education systems, setting valuable precedents for India. China is a leading example, where Traditional Chinese Medicine (TCM) is fully integrated into the national healthcare system. Chinese medical universities offer dual-degree programs in TCM and allopathic medicine, ensuring that students are well-versed in both disciplines. Germany has also incorporated traditional medicine into medical education, with homeopathy, naturopathy, and phytotherapy (herbal medicine) being part of physician training programs. The country has established dedicated research centers and regulatory frameworks that validate traditional therapies through clinical trials, making integrative healthcare more scientifically robust. Similarly, in the United States, institutions like the National Center for Complementary and Integrative Health (NCCIH) support research and education in integrative medicine, and medical schools increasingly offer electives on Ayurveda, acupuncture, and herbal medicine as part of holistic health programs.

The success of these countries highlights several best practices that can be adapted to improve integrative healthcare education. One of the key strategies is the inclusion of traditional medicine as a formal part of medical curricula rather than treating it as an alternative or supplementary discipline. Many universities worldwide have developed cross-disciplinary programs where students learn about both modern and traditional medicine, fostering collaboration between allopathic and alternative medicine practitioners. Another essential practice is the emphasis on research and evidence-based validation, ensuring that traditional therapies are incorporated into mainstream medicine based on scientific merit. Governments and academic institutions have also invested in specialized training centers, interdisciplinary research initiatives, and global partnerships to advance integrative healthcare education.

India, with its rich heritage in Ayurveda, Yoga, Unani, Siddha, and Homeopathy (AYUSH), can learn valuable lessons from these global models to enhance curriculum development and implementation. One crucial step is to introduce structured AYUSH courses within medical education, enabling students to gain a foundational understanding of traditional medicine alongside their allopathic training. Additionally, interdisciplinary research collaborations between AYUSH institutions and modern medical universities can strengthen the scientific validation of traditional therapies, enhancing their credibility in mainstream medicine. Developing integrative healthcare centers within medical colleges, where students can gain hands-on experience with AYUSH treatments, will also be instrumental. Lastly, aligning India's medical education reforms with the WHO's Traditional Medicine Strategy will help establish globally recognized standards for AYUSH integration, ensuring that future healthcare professionals are equipped to provide comprehensive, patient-centered, and culturally relevant medical care.

9. CHALLENGES IN INTEGRATING AYUSH INTO MEDICAL EDUCATION

Despite the growing recognition of traditional medicine and the benefits of integrative healthcare, several challenges hinder the seamless integration of AYUSH into medical education. One of the most significant barriers is regulatory and policy-related hurdles. The medical education system in India is heavily regulated, with distinct governing bodies for allopathic (National Medical Commission – NMC) and AYUSH (Central Council of Indian Medicine – CCIM, now under the National Commission for Indian System of Medicine – NCISM) disciplines. These parallel regulatory structures create bureaucratic obstacles in curriculum modification, making it difficult to develop a unified or complementary medical education framework. Furthermore, differences in accreditation, licensing, and practice guidelines between allopathy and AYUSH systems lead to policy conflicts, hindering cross-disciplinary education and collaboration.

Another major challenge is curriculum overload, as medical students already undergo an extensive and demanding academic workload. Integrating AYUSH into modern medical curricula would require careful restructuring to ensure that students receive adequate training in traditional medicine without compromising their allopathic education. The challenge lies in identifying core AYUSH concepts that can complement allopathic learning while avoiding excessive coursework. A well-balanced curriculum should prioritize evidence-based AYUSH practices, focusing on areas where traditional medicine has demonstrated strong efficacy, such as preventive healthcare, lifestyle management, and chronic disease treatment.

Additionally, faculty training and availability of skilled educators remain critical challenges. Most medical colleges have faculty members trained exclusively in either allopathy or AYUSH, with very few possessing expertise in both systems. The lack of qualified professionals who can teach integrative medicine creates a knowledge gap, making interdisciplinary education difficult to implement. Training programs for medical educators must be introduced to bridge this divide, enabling faculty members to understand and teach the scientific foundations of both modern and traditional medicine.

Lastly, interdisciplinary resistance and skepticism from allopathic practitioners pose a significant challenge. Many allopathic doctors question the scientific credibility of AYUSH due to the lack of large-scale clinical trials and standardized methodologies in some traditional practices. Overcoming this skepticism requires greater investment in research, clinical validation, and collaborative studies between AYUSH and allopathic institutions. Encouraging medical students to engage in evidence-based integrative healthcare research, fostering dialogues between allopathic and AYUSH practitioners, and promoting case studies showcasing the benefits of integrative medicine can help build trust and acceptance among the medical community. Addressing these challenges through policy reforms, curriculum restructuring, faculty development, and interdisciplinary collaboration is essential to successfully integrating AYUSH into medical education and creating a more holistic, patient-centered healthcare system.

10. PROPOSED FRAMEWORK FOR INTEGRATING AYUSH INTO MEDICAL CURRICULUM

To successfully integrate AYUSH (Ayurveda, Yoga & Naturopathy, Unani, Siddha, and Homeopathy) into modern medical education, a structured framework is essential. This framework should focus on a balanced and evidence-based approach, ensuring that students gain a comprehensive understanding of both allopathic and traditional medicine. The key elements of this framework include curriculum restructuring, collaborative learning, clinical exposure, and research-driven validation.

10.1 Curriculum Restructuring: Core and Elective Modules for AYUSH Education

A well-designed curriculum restructuring is necessary to incorporate AYUSH without overburdening medical students. One approach is to introduce core modules that provide a basic understanding of traditional medicine to all medical students, while elective modules allow students interested in AYUSH-based therapies to pursue specialized training. For example, core modules could cover fundamental principles of Ayurveda, Yoga, and Unani medicine, along with their applications in preventive healthcare and chronic disease management. Elective courses could delve deeper into herbal pharmacology, Panchakarma therapy, Yoga therapy, Siddha detoxification techniques, and Homeopathic principles. By offering AYUSH education in a structured and modular way, students can gain insights into traditional medicine without compromising their allopathic training.

10.2 Collaborative Learning: Promoting Cross-Disciplinary Exchange Between Allopathic and AYUSH Practitioners

To bridge the gap between allopathic and AYUSH practitioners, collaborative learning platforms should be introduced. This could include interdisciplinary workshops, joint lectures, case study discussions, and integrated treatment planning sessions where students and faculty from both medical streams can exchange knowledge and clinical experiences. For example, case studies of chronic diseases such as diabetes, arthritis, and mental health disorders can be analyzed from both allopathic and AYUSH perspectives, allowing students to explore integrative treatment approaches. Medical institutions should also encourage joint conferences and collaborative projects between AYUSH and allopathic research centers to promote dialogue and interdisciplinary collaboration. This approach will reduce skepticism, enhance mutual respect, and ensure that future healthcare professionals are well-equipped to integrate diverse treatment modalities for patient care.

10.3 Clinical Exposure: Hands-on Training in AYUSH Hospitals and Wellness Centers

Practical experience is crucial in medical education, and clinical exposure to AYUSH practices should be an integral part of the curriculum. Medical students should undergo mandatory rotational postings in AYUSH hospitals, wellness centers, and integrated healthcare clinics, where they can observe and participate in traditional treatments. For example, students can gain hands-on experience in Ayurvedic Panchakarma therapy, Siddha detoxification, Unani regimental therapies (Hijama, massage, and diet therapy), and Yoga-based interventions. These clinical rotations should also include exposure to herbal medicine formulations, pulse diagnosis (Nadi Pariksha in Ayurveda and Unani), and homeopathic patient management. Providing real-world exposure will help students understand the clinical applications of AYUSH and enable them to recommend integrative therapies with greater confidence and scientific awareness.

10.4 Research & Evidence-Based Practice: Encouraging Studies Validating AYUSH Therapies

One of the most critical aspects of integrating AYUSH into medical education is strengthening research and evidence-based practice. AYUSH disciplines have been criticized for lacking large-scale clinical trials and standardized research methodologies. To address this, medical institutions should invest in interdisciplinary research projects that validate traditional medicine through scientific studies, randomized controlled trials (RCTs), and meta-analyses. Encouraging students to participate in AYUSH-based research projects, publish in peer-reviewed journals, and engage in collaborative studies between AYUSH and modern medical researchers will enhance the credibility of traditional therapies. Universities and research centers should also focus on developing standardized treatment protocols for AYUSH therapies, ensuring that they meet global medical and pharmacological standards. Establishing AYUSH research chairs, funding grants, and postgraduate training programs in integrative medicine will further promote innovation and credibility in the field.

11. POLICY RECOMMENDATIONS AND ROADMAP FOR IMPLEMENTATION

To successfully integrate Ayurveda, Yoga, and other AYUSH disciplines into mainstream medical education, policy revisions must align with the National Education Policy (NEP) 2020. A structured curriculum that incorporates traditional healing systems alongside modern medical training should be developed, ensuring a well-rounded, evidence-based approach to healthcare education. Faculty development is crucial in this transition, requiring specialized training programs and collaborative efforts between AYUSH institutions and conventional medical colleges. Institutional partnerships, both nationally and internationally, can facilitate knowledge exchange and best practices for integrative healthcare education. Additionally, public awareness campaigns should be launched to promote the benefits of holistic medicine, addressing skepticism and encouraging acceptance among healthcare professionals and patients alike. Strengthening research funding for AYUSH and fostering cross-disciplinary projects will further validate traditional medicine practices through scientific inquiry, ultimately building credibility and enhancing their integration into modern medical frameworks.

12. CONCLUSION

The integration of AYUSH systems into medical education has the potential to transform India's healthcare landscape by promoting a more holistic, preventive, and patient-centric approach. This study highlights key benefits such as improved interdisciplinary collaboration, better management of lifestyle disorders, and enhanced community healthcare delivery. However, successful implementation requires strategic policy reforms, faculty training, public engagement, and increased research investment. Moving forward, the focus should be on developing standardized curricula, ensuring rigorous evaluation of integrative education models, and assessing their impact on patient outcomes. By embracing a holistic healthcare curriculum, India can establish a sustainable, inclusive, and globally relevant medical education system that bridges traditional and modern medicine, ultimately improving overall public health outcomes.

REFERENCES

[1] Bhattacharya, S. and Das, A. (2017). Ayurveda and modern medicine integration: Challenges and opportunities. *Journal of Integrative Medicine,* 15(2), 82–89.

[2] Chauhan, A. and Sharma, P. (2015). Yoga and Ayurveda in integrative healthcare: A review. *Journal of Ayurveda and Integrative Medicine,* 6(3), 176–182.

[3] Chaturvedi, S. and Tiwari, P. (2018). The role of AYUSH in primary healthcare: A policy perspective. *Indian Journal of Public Health,* 62(4), 297–303.

[4] Dasgupta, R. and Kumar, P. (2021). Integrating AYUSH with allopathy: Evidence-based perspectives. *Journal of Evidence-Based Complementary & Alternative Medicine,* 26(1), 12–18.

[5] Dwivedi, K. and Prakash, S. (2022). Strengthening AYUSH research: A roadmap for integrative healthcare. *Journal of Ayurveda and Integrative Medicine,* 13(2), 88–95.

[6] Gautam, G. and Singh, R. (2014). The impact of Ayurveda on global healthcare systems. *Complementary Therapies in Clinical Practice,* 20(4), 315–322.

[7] Ghosh, A. and Pandey, M. (2019). Yoga-based medical education: Bridging traditional and modern medicine. *Indian Journal of Physiology and Pharmacology*, 63(2), 112–119.

[8] Gupta, B. and Sharma, A. (2020). Ayurveda's role in modern disease prevention. *Journal of Ethnopharmacology,* 249, 112429.

[9] Joshi, R. and Saxena, V. (2016). Public perception of integrative medicine: A survey-based analysis. *BMC Complementary Medicine and Therapies,* 16, 243.

[10] Kumar, P. and Mehta, R. (2023). Policy frameworks for AYUSH education in India. *Health Policy and Planning,* 38(1), 54–62.

[11] Madhavan, A. and Nair, R. (2022). AYUSH and preventive healthcare: A new paradigm. *Indian Journal of Preventive Medicine,* 14(3), 201–208.

[12] Mahajan, S. and Singh, K. (2018). Efficacy of integrative medicine in chronic disease management. *Journal of Integrative and Complementary Medicine,* 24(2), 89–98.

[13] Mishra, S. and Saxena, P. (2021). Bridging allopathy and Ayurveda: An educational perspective. *International Journal of Ayurveda Research,* 12(1), 44–50.

[14] Nanda, R. and Gupta, S. (2020). Traditional medicine in medical education: A review. *Journal of Complementary and Integrative Medicine,* 17(4), 79–85. https://doi.org/10.1515/jcim-2019–0186

[15] Natarajan, R. and Rao, S. (2013). Integrative medicine: A case for AYUSH inclusion in modern healthcare. *Journal of Clinical Medicine,* 2(3), 213–219.

[16] Naveen, K. H. and Saxena, V. (2024). Strengthening AYUSH integration with preventive medicine. *Indian Journal of Community Medicine*, 49(2).

[17] Nesari, T. M. (2024). Safety concerns on AYUSH herbs: A call for a robust evidence-based approach. *Journal of Ayurveda Case Reports*, 7(3).

[18] Patel, A. and Roy, P. (2015). Community healthcare models integrating AYUSH. *International Journal of Public Health*, 60(1), 47–53.

[19] Prasad, R. and Kumar, S. (2017). The role of Ayurveda in personalized medicine. *Journal of Personalized Medicine,* 7(4), 32–39.

[20] Rao, M. and Iyer, G. (2021). Evidence-based integrative healthcare: A critical review. *Journal of Evidence-Based Medicine,* 14(2), 78–84.

[21] Rawat, H., Bhat, S. A. and Singh, R. (2024). Emerging techniques for the trace elemental analysis of plants and food-based extracts: A comprehensive review. *Talanta Open,* 19, 102414.

[22] Roy, P. and Nair, V. (2016). AYUSH and rural health programs in India. *Journal of Rural Health,* 32(2), 105–112.

[23] Sahu, A. and Kumar, D. (2023). Role of Yoga in modern medical education: A case study. *Journal of Integrative Medicine,* 21(1), 12–18.

[24] Saxena, M. and Ghosh, T. (2019). Ayurveda and mental health: Bridging the gap. *Indian Journal of Psychiatry,* 61(4), 327–335.

[25] Sharma, R. and Singh, D. (2022). Integrative approaches to chronic disease management. *Journal of Alternative and Complementary Medicine,* 28(3), 134–141.

[26] Shetty, P. and Rao, K. (2020). AYUSH research in India: Challenges and future directions. *Journal of Research in Ayurvedic Sciences*, 34(2), 45–52.

[27] Singh, A. and Gupta, R. (2014). Integrative medicine education: Lessons from global models. *Medical Education,* 48(5), 467–474.

[28] Singh, R. and Mishra, P. (2018). The future of AYUSH in India's medical education system. *Journal of Education and Health Promotion*, 7(1), 112.

[29] Srivastava, R. and Jain, P. (2023). Cross-disciplinary collaboration in healthcare: Integrating AYUSH and allopathy. *Healthcare Policy and Management*, 9(3), 75–83.

[30] Subramanian, S. and Iyer, P. (2021). AYUSH and evidence-based practice: A systematic review. *Journal of Clinical Research in Integrative Medicine,* 14(2), 98–105.

[31] Thakur, R. and Desai, M. (2015). AYUSH and palliative care: A new approach. *Palliative Medicine,* 29(3), 250–257.

[32] Tiwari, A. and Sharma, P. (2017). Ayurveda in non-communicable disease management. *Indian Journal of Endocrinology and Metabolism,* 21(4), 558–564.

[33] Varma, P. and Nair, S. (2022). Public perception and acceptance of AYUSH. *Journal of Health Education Research & Development,* 10(2), 45–54.

[34] Yadav, S. and Mishra, R. (2018). Bridging Ayurveda and biomedicine: A policy analysis. *Journal of Health Policy*, 28(1), 22–30.

[35] Zaveri, D. and Patel, R. (2016). Integrative medical education: Indian perspectives. *Journal of Health Sciences,* 35(2), 89–97.

A Comparative Study of Insider Threat Detection Frameworks

Anurag Singh[1], Manish Kumar[2] and Rajesh Kumar Upadhyay[3]

[1]Research Scholar & Assistant Professor, COER University, Roorkee, India

[2]Professor & Registrar, COER University, Roorkee, India

[3]Professor & Dean, COER University, Roorkee, India

E-mail: [1]anuragmaddi@gmail.com; [2]drmanishkumar76@gmail.com; [3]upadhya.rajesh@gmail.com

ABSTRACT: *Insider threats remain one of the most challenging and damaging cybersecurity issues for organizations across sectors. These threats are perpetrated by individuals with authorized access who misuses their privileges, either maliciously or unintentionally. Insider threats pose significant risks to organizations, leading to data breaches, financial losses, and reputational damage. Various frameworks have been developed to detect and mitigate insider threats, each with distinct methodologies, strengths, and limitations. This paper conducts a comparative analysis of prominent insider threat detection frameworks, evaluating their effectiveness, scalability, and applicability across different organizational contexts. The study examines frameworks such as the CERT Insider Threat Framework, MITRE ATT&CK for Insider Threats, and machine learning-based approaches. Findings suggest that no single framework is universally optimal; instead, a hybrid approach combining behavioral analytics, access control, and anomaly detection yields the best results. The paper concludes with recommendations for organizations to enhance their insider threat detection capabilities. A wide range of frameworks have been developed to detect and mitigate insider threats, each with unique mechanisms, data sources, and detection strategies. This paper conducts a comparative study of notable insider threat detection frameworks, evaluating their methodologies, strengths, weaknesses, and practical applications. We highlight key elements such as behavioral analysis, machine learning integration, psychological profiling, and real-time detection capabilities. The study concludes by proposing directions for a hybrid, adaptive framework to address the evolving nature of insider threats.*

Keywords: Anomaly Detection, Behavioral Analytics, Cybersecurity, Detection Frameworks, Insider Threat.

1. INTRODUCTION

The cybersecurity landscape is increasingly threatened by insiders—individuals within organizations who, intentionally or accidentally, compromise security. According to the **Ponemon Institute (2022)**, insider threats have surged by 44% over the last two years, with average incident costs exceeding $15 million. Traditional security systems, which emphasize perimeter defenses, often fail to detect anomalies originating from trusted users. This gap has led to the emergence of specialized insider threat detection frameworks. This study compares leading insider threat detection frameworks, assessing their methodologies, detection accuracy, and implementation challenges. The goal is to assist organizations in selecting or developing an effective insider threat mitigation strategy. This research aims to analyze and compare these frameworks systematically, focusing on architecture, methodology, data sources, and real-world performance.

2. LITERATURE REVIEW

Insider threat detection frameworks have evolved significantly, yet challenges remain in balancing accuracy, scalability, and interpretability. Legg *et al.* (2017) emphasize behavior-based anomaly detection using machine learning, demonstrating its effectiveness in identifying deviations from normal user activity, while Nurse *et al.* (2014) argue for integrating psychological and organizational factors to reduce false positives. Homoliak *et al.* (2019) compare rule-based and hybrid models, finding that combining user activity monitoring (UAM) with role-based access control (RBAC) improves detection rates in dynamic environments. Mayhew *et al.* (2015) highlight limitations in real-time analysis, noting that many frameworks struggle with scalability due to computational overhead. Recent advancements in deep learning, such as Liu *et al.'s* (2021) use of recurrent neural networks (RNNs), show promise in sequential pattern analysis but face challenges in explainability. Despite progress, gaps persist in standardized evaluation metrics and cross-domain applicability, underscoring the need for a unified, adaptive framework that addresses both technical and behavioral indicators of insider threats. Multiple approaches to insider threat detection have emerged over the past two decades. The frameworks typically fall into three categories:

- **Rule-Based Frameworks**: These use predefined rules and access policies to identify unauthorized behavior (Greitzer & Frincke, 2010).
- **Behavioral-Based Frameworks**: Leveraging user behavior analytics (UBA), these systems detect deviations from normal behavior (Eberle & Holder, 2009).
- **Machine Learning-Based Frameworks**: Employing supervised or unsupervised models, these systems can learn and adapt to user behavior patterns (Tuor *et al.*, 2017).

Some frameworks also include psychological indicators, physical access data, and sentiment analysis from communications.

3. METHODOLOGY

This study uses a qualitative comparative methodology. We analyzed ten prominent frameworks from academic and industry literature. Key dimensions for comparison include:

- Detection Technique
- Data Sources
- Real-time Capability
- Adaptability
- Explain ability
- Implementation Cost

Data was synthesized from peer-reviewed journals, white papers, and cybersecurity consortium reports.

4. COMPARATIVE ANALYSIS OF SELECTED FRAMEWORKS

Framework	*Detection Technique*	*Data Sources*	*Real-Time*	*Pros*	*Cons*
CERT Insider Threat Model	Behavioral + Rule-Based	HR data, Logs	No	Comprehensive profiling	Lacks real-time detection
MITRE Shield	Behavior Monitoring	System and network logs	Partial	Open-source, adaptable	Requires integration
Greitzer Human-Centric Model	Psychological + Behavioral	Surveys, Access logs	No	Incorporates psychometrics	High privacy concerns
User Behavior Analytics (UBA)	Statistical + Anomaly Detection	Access patterns	Yes	Works in real-time	High false positives
DeepLog	Deep Learning	System logs	Yes	Self-learning	Complex implementation
TWOS Framework	Text + Workflow + Observation	Email/chat + workflow	No	Linguistic and activity insights	Delayed detection
PALANTIR Framework	ML-based	Behavioral, contextual data	Yes	High accuracy	Data-intensive
CANARY Framework	Decoy-based	File system	Yes	Effective deception	Limited coverage
SEASTAR	Behavioral + Situational Awareness	Physical + digital logs	Partial	Integrated view	Complex to manage
Hybrid ACT-R Model	Cognitive modeling + ML	Behavioral + cognitive cues	No	Simulates decision-making	Theoretical, less applied

5. FINDINGS AND DISCUSSION

The comparative analysis reveals that no single framework is universally optimal. Some are strong in psychological profiling but weak in scalability. Others excel in real-time detection but suffer from high false positives. Key findings include:

- **Data Diversity Improves Accuracy**: Frameworks using multi-source data (e.g., SEASTAR, PALANTIR) show better threat detection rates.
- **Behavioral Modeling is Crucial**: Insider threats often manifest in subtle behavioral changes before actual breaches.
- **Explainability is a Major Gap**: Deep learning models such as DeepLog offer high accuracy but limited explainability.
- **Psychological Metrics Are Underutilized**: Though powerful, only a few models incorporate psychometric indicators due to ethical and privacy issues.

6. PROPOSED HYBRID FRAMEWORK

We propose a hybrid framework that combines:

- Behavioral Monitoring (UBA + Log Analysis)
- Psychological Risk Assessment (via anonymous surveys)
- Machine Learning with Explain ability (e.g., SHAP or LIME)
- Real-Time Alerts and Adaptive Policies

This layered approach aims to reduce false positives, respect privacy, and offer actionable insights.

7. CONCLUSION

Insider threats are complex and multifaceted, requiring equally sophisticated detection strategies. While many frameworks address parts of the problem, integrating their strengths offers a promising direction. Organizations should adopt a multi-layered insider threat detection strategy, integrating behavioral analytics, access controls, and continuous monitoring. Future research should focus on reducing false positives in machine learning models and improving real-time detection. Future research should focus on the ethical use of psychological data, improving explain ability of AI-based systems, and fostering interdisciplinary collaboration.

REFERENCES

[1] Eberle, W. and Holder, L. (2009). Insider threat detection using graph-based approaches. *Cybersecurity and Information Security*, 1(3), 5–14.

[2] Greitzer, F.L. and Frincke, D.A. (2010). Combining traditional cyber security audit data with psychosocial data: Towards predictive modeling

for insider threat mitigation. *Insider Threats in Cyber Security*, 85–113. Springer.

[3] Tuor, A., Kaplan, S., Hutchinson, B., Nichols, N. and Robinson, S. (2017). Deep learning for unsupervised insider threat detection in structured cybersecurity data streams. *AAAI Workshops*, WS-17-01.

[4] Glasser, J. and Lindauer, B. (2013). Bridging the gap: A pragmatic approach to generating insider threat data. *IEEE Security and Privacy Workshops*, 98–104.

[5] Salem, M.B., Hershkop, S. and Stolfo, S.J. (2008). A survey of insider attack detection research. *Insider Attack and Cyber Security*, 69–90. Springer.

[6] Liu, A., Coman, E. and Dorneich, M.C. (2020). Using ACT-R to model insider threat decision-making. *Cognitive Systems Research*, 64, 120–133.

[7] MITRE Corporation. (2021). *Shield: Knowledge base of active defense techniques*. Retrieved from https://shield.mitre.org

[8] Bishop, M. and Gates, C. (2008). Defining the insider threat. *Proceedings of the 4th Annual Cyber Security and Information Intelligence Research Workshop*, 1–3.

[9] Legg, P.A., Buckley, O., Goldsmith, M. and Creese, S. (2015). Automated insider threat detection system using user and role-based profile assessment. *IEEE Systems Journal*, 11(2), 1–10.

[10] Hanley, M. and Montelibano, J. (2011). *Insider threat control: Using centrality measures to detect insider threats*. CERT Coordination Center. Retrieved from

[11] Homoliak, I., Toffalini, F., Guarnizo, J., Elovici, Y. and Ochoa, M. (2019). Insight into insiders and IT: A survey of insider threat taxonomies, analysis, modeling, and countermeasures. *ACM Computing Surveys, 52*(2), 1–40.

[12 Legg, P.A., Buckley, O., Goldsmith, M. and Creese, S. (2017). Automated insider threat detection using user and role-based profile assessment. *IEEE Security & Privacy, 15*(1), 40-47. https://doi.org/10.1109/MSP.2017.2

[13] Liu, Y., Zhang, X. and Wang, L. (2021). Deep learning for insider threat detection: A systematic review. *Computers & Security, 102*, 102-122.

[14] Mayhew, M., Atighetchi, M., Adler, A. and Greenstadt, R. (2015). Use of machine learning in big data analytics for insider threat detection. *IEEE Security & Privacy Workshops, 15*(3), 1–6.

[15] Nurse, J.R., Buckley, O., Legg, P.A., Goldsmith, M., Creese, S., Wright, G.R. and Whitty, M. (2014). Understanding insider threat: A framework for characterising attacks. *IEEE Security & Privacy Workshops, 12*(4), 214–228.

Author Index

Applauds

Dear Vice-Chancellor Prof. Raghavendra Sir

We have attended many Conferences and Seminars. The Present Conference is one of the well organised academic event. We take with us sweet memories about the Conference which we will cherish for long time to come. We congratulate you and your young, dynamic and active team led by Prof. B.B. Tiwari for successfully organising the Conference under your guidance. We pray God to give you strength to organise many more such International events to serve the Society and make India one of Super Power by 2047.

With best wishes

S. Indrakant,
Visiting Professor,
Centre for Economics and Social Studies,
Begumpet, Hyderabad-500016

Thanks Prof Tiwari for your kind hospitality. I returned to Delhi after a useful trip to Bengaluru. Best wishes and kind regards, sincerely yours,

Prof. Prem Vrat
Pro-Chancellor,
The NorthCap University, Gurugram
Chairman, BoG, IIT (ISM) Dhanbad

Dear Tiwarisahab,

A very good morning as I reach my home in Ahmedabad after an exhilarating experience at the CMRU international conference. Having participated in many conferences and a few in foreign country as well, I have to say this was an extremely pleasant experience. In all departments and functionalities your teams performed A-Star. Congratulations to you and your team for putting up such a great show—a benchmark difficult to reach is thus established.

Best regards Hemant

Hemant Trivedi
Director CVMU-MBA
VVNagar Anand

Dear Prof. Tiwari

Congratulations for organising the conference successfully. You attracted many scholars and had many good papers. Arrangements were superb. I have attended many conferences and seminars. This is one of the best conferences. We cherish sweet memories about the conference for long time to come. Your school has lot of potentiality. You have capacity to organise many more international events. Congratulations to you and your young and dynamic members like Balaji, Ranjit, Eshwar Reddy, Ravi Kumar, Shareef, Nilesh and many others. Convey our Regards to your VC Prof. Raghavendra Sir.

Once congratulations to all of you.

Prof. S. Indrakant
Visiting Professor,
Centre for Economics and Social Studies,
Begumpet, Hyderabad-500016

SOCIAL-MEDIA

raghavendra hadadi · 1st
VC CMR University, Bangalore, Former VC Chandigarh ...
6h ·

CMR University SOEC School successfully conducted International Conference on Economics, Finance Management and Technology Conference on 5th and 6th April 2024. The smooth running of conference with more than 200 papers selected for presentations from all over India and abroad is an indicator of success. . The excellent remarks from the Guest and Delegates are testimony to the team work of CMRU SOEC under the Directorship of Dr BB Tiwari. I appreciate the team along with others of CMR University for fantastic coordination and hard work. We are indebted to the Sponsors of the conference. Dignitaries include Prof. Premvrat and Padmasree Prahlada Rao Eminent Scientist with many others leading sessions and tracks. The picture with Padmasree Prahlada Rao during concluding ceremony is also shared.

NEWS PAPER COVERAGE

CITY READ

CMR University's international conference concludes

The School of Economics and Commerce at CMR University, Bengaluru, conducted an international conference on 'Recent Advances In The Field Of Economics, Finance, Management & Technology (ICREFMT-2024)'. Held over two days, at the university's OMBR Campus, this event gathered renowned personalities from various sectors, enriching the discussions with insights and experiences. The conference showcased the expertise of over 244 delegates from India and abroad, with more than 150 full-length research papers submitted by paper presenters from both national and international spheres, participating in the event both online and offline.

ಸಿಎಂಆರ್ ವಿಶ್ವವಿದ್ಯಾಲಯದ ವತಿಯಿಂದ ನಡೆದ ಅಂತಾರಾಷ್ಟ್ರೀಯ ಸಮ್ಮೇಳನದಲ್ಲಿ ಐಐಟಿ ಧನ್‌ಬಾದ್‌ನ ಆಡಳಿತ ಮಂಡಳಿ ಅಧ್ಯಕ್ಷ ಪ್ರೇಮ್‌ವ್ರತ್ ಸಮ್ಮೇಳನದ ಸ್ಮರಣ ಸಂಚಿಕೆ ಬಿಡುಗಡೆ ಮಾಡಿದರು. ನಿವೃತ್ತ ಐಪಿಎಸ್ ಅಧಿಕಾರಿ ಡಾ.ಕೆ.ಸಿ ರಾಮಮೂರ್ತಿ, ಕುಲಾಧಿಪತಿ ಡಾ.ಸಬಿತಾ ರಾಮಮೂರ್ತಿ, ಉಪಕುಲಪತಿ ಡಾ.ಎಚ್.ಬಿ.ರಾಘವೇಂದ್ರ, ಕುಲಸಚಿವ ಡಾ.ಪ್ರವೀಣ್ ಇದ್ದರು.

ತಂತ್ರಜ್ಞಾನ ಆಧರಿತ ಸಮ್ಮೇಳನಗಳು ದೇಶದ ಪ್ರಗತಿಗೆ ಪೂರಕ

ಬೆಂಗಳೂರು, ಏ.7- ಅರ್ಥಶಾಸ್ತ್ರ ಹಣಕಾಸು ನಿರ್ವಹಣೆ ಮತ್ತು ತಂತ್ರಜ್ಞಾನ ವಿಷಯಾಧಾರಿತ ಅಂತಾರಾಷ್ಟ್ರೀಯ ಸಮ್ಮೇಳನಗಳು ದೇಶದ ಪ್ರಗತಿಯನ್ನು ಅವಲೋಕಿಸುತ್ತವೆ ಎಂದು ಗುರುಗ್ರಾಮ್‌ನ ಐಐಟಿ ಧನ್‌ಬಾದ್ ಆಡಳಿತ ಮಂಡಳಿ ಅಧ್ಯಕ್ಷ ಪ್ರೊ.ಪ್ರೇಮ್ ವ್ರತ್ ಹೇಳಿದರು.

ನಗರದ ಓಎಂಬಿಆರ್ ಲೇಔಟ್‌ನಲ್ಲಿನ ಸಿಎಂಆರ್ ವಿಶ್ವವಿದ್ಯಾಲಯ ಸಭಾಂಗಣದಲ್ಲಿ ಸ್ಕೂಲ್ ಆಫ್ ಎಕನಾಮಿಕ್ಸ್ ಮತ್ತು ಕಾಮರ್ಸ್ ವಿಭಾಗಗಳು ಆಯೋಜಿಸಿದ್ದ ಅರ್ಥಶಾಸ್ತ್ರ ಹಣಕಾಸು, ನಿರ್ವಹಣೆ ಮತ್ತು ತಂತ್ರಜ್ಞಾನ ಕ್ಷೇತ್ರದಲ್ಲಿ ಇತ್ತೀಚಿನ ಪ್ರಗತಿಗಳು ಕುರಿತ ಅಂತಾರಾಷ್ಟ್ರೀಯ ಸಮ್ಮೇಳನದಲ್ಲಿ ಅವರು ಮಾತನಾಡಿದರು.

ಚರ್ಚಿತ ವಿಷಯಗಳು ಇಲ್ಲಿ ಪಾಲ್ಗೊಂಡಿರುವ ಆರ್ಥಿಕ ತಜ್ಞರು, ಉದ್ಯಮಿಗಳು, ಸಂಶೋಧಕರು, ವಿದ್ಯಾರ್ಥಿಗಳು, ಪ್ರಾಧ್ಯಾಪಕರುಗಳಿಗೆ ಉತ್ತಮ ವೇದಿಕೆಯಾಗುತ್ತವೆ. ಭಾರತ ಸರ್ಕಾರದ ಮಹತ್ವಾಕಾಂಕ್ಷೆಯ ವಿಕಸಿತ ಭಾರತ ಸಂಪೂರ್ಣ ಸಾಕಾರಗೊಳ್ಳುವ ನಿಟ್ಟಿನಲ್ಲಿ ಇಂತಹ ವಿಷಯಾಧಾರಿತ ಅಂತಾರಾಷ್ಟ್ರೀಯ ಸಮ್ಮೇಳನಗಳು ವಿಶ್ವವಿದ್ಯಾಲಯ ಮಟ್ಟದಲ್ಲಿ ಜರುಗಬೇಕು, ಹೆಚ್ಚು ಹೆಚ್ಚು ಸಂಶೋಧನಾ ಪ್ರಬಂಧಗಳು ಮಂಡನೆಯಾಗಬೇಕು ಎಂದು ಅಭಿಪ್ರಾಯಪಟ್ಟರು.

ಆನ್‌ಲೈನ್ ಮತ್ತು ಆಫ್‌ಲೈನ್ ಎರಡು ಹಂತದಲ್ಲಿ ಆಯೋಜಿಸಿದ್ದ ಈ ಅಂತಾರಾಷ್ಟ್ರೀಯ ಸಮ್ಮೇಳನದಲ್ಲಿ ದೇಶ-ವಿದೇಶಗಳ 244ಕ್ಕೂ ಹೆಚ್ಚು ಪರಿಣಿತರು, ಉದ್ಯಮಿಗಳು, ಸಂಶೋಧಕರು, ವಿದ್ಯಾರ್ಥಿಗಳು, ಪ್ರಾಧ್ಯಾಪಕರು ಭಾಗವಹಿಸಿದ್ದರು. 150ಕ್ಕೂ ಹೆಚ್ಚು ಮೌಲ್ಯಾಧಾರಿತ ಸಂಶೋಧನಾ ಪ್ರಬಂಧಗಳು ಮಂಡನೆಯಾದವು.

ಗುರುಗ್ರಾಮ್‌ನ ಸ್ಟಾರೆಕ್ಸ್ ವಿಶ್ವವಿದ್ಯಾಲಯದ ಮಾಜಿ ಉಪಕುಲಪತಿ ಪ್ರೊ.ಎಂ.ಎಂ. ಗೋಯೆಲ್, ಅಲಹಾಬಾದ್ ವಿಶ್ವವಿದ್ಯಾಲಯದ ವಾಣಿಜ್ಯ ವಿಭಾಗದ ಮಾಜಿ ಡೀನ್ ಪ್ರೊ.ಪ್ರಹ್ಲಾದ್ ಕುಮಾರ್, ಮಾಜಿ ರಾಜ್ಯಸಭಾ ಸದಸ್ಯ, ಸಿಎಂಆರ್ ಸಮೂಹ ಶಿಕ್ಷಣ ಸಂಸ್ಥೆಗಳ ಅಧ್ಯಕ್ಷರಾದ ಡಾ.ಕೆ.ಸಿ.ರಾಮಮೂರ್ತಿ, ಸಿಎಂಆರ್ ವಿಶ್ವ ವಿದ್ಯಾಲಯದ ಕುಲಾಧಿಪತಿ ಡಾ.ಸಬಿತಾ ರಾಮಮೂರ್ತಿ, ಉಪಕುಲಪತಿ ಡಾ.ಎಚ್.ಬಿ.ರಾಘವೇಂದ್ರ, ಕುಲಸಚಿವ ಡಾ.ಪ್ರವೀಣ್ ಆರ್., ಸ್ಕೂಲ್ ಆಫ್ ಎಕನಾಮಿಕ್ಸ್ ಮತ್ತು ಕಾಮರ್ಸ್ ನಿರ್ದೇಶಕ ಡಾ.ಬಿ.ಬಿ.ತಿವಾರಿ ಮತ್ತಿತರರು ಉಪಸ್ಥಿತರಿದ್ದರು.

2 ದಿನಗಳ ಅಂತರಾಷ್ಟ್ರೀಯ ಸಮ್ಮೇಳನ

ಬೆಂಗಳೂರು: ನಗರದ ಪ್ರತಿಷ್ಠಿತ ಸಿಎಂಆರ್ ವಿಶ್ವವಿದ್ಯಾಲಯದಲ್ಲಿ "ಅರ್ಥಶಾಸ್ತ್ರ, ಹಣಕಾಸು, ನಿರ್ವಹಣೆ ಮತ್ತು ತಂತ್ರಜ್ಞಾನ ಕ್ಷೇತ್ರದಲ್ಲಿ ಇತ್ತೀಚಿನ ಪ್ರಗತಿಗಳು ವಿಷಯ ಕುರಿತು 2 ದಿನಗಳ ಅಂತರಾಷ್ಟ್ರೀಯ ಸಮ್ಮೇಳನ –2024 ಯಶಸ್ವಿಯಾಗಿ ನಡೆಯಿತು. ನಗರದ ಒಎಂಬಿಆರ್ ಲೇಔಟನಲ್ಲಿನ ಸಿಎಂಆರ್ ವಿಶ್ವವಿದ್ಯಾಲಯ ಸಭಾಂಗಣದಲ್ಲಿ ಸ್ಕೂಲ್ ಆಫ್ ಎಕನಾಮಿಕ್ಸ್ ಮತ್ತು ಕಾಮರ್ಸ್ ವಿಭಾಗಗಳು ಎ.5 ಮತ್ತು ಎ.6 ಆಯೋಜಿಸಿದ್ದ ಅರ್ಥಶಾಸ್ತ್ರ, ಹಣಕಾಸು,ನಿರ್ವಹಣೆ ಮತ್ತು ತಂತ್ರಜ್ಞಾನ ಕ್ಷೇತ್ರದಲ್ಲಿ ಇತ್ತೀಚಿನ ಪ್ರಗತಿಗಳು ಕುರಿತ ಅಂತರಾಷ್ಟ್ರೀಯ ಸಮ್ಮೇಳನ – 2024 ಕಾರ್ಯಕ್ರಮವನ್ನು ಮುಖ್ಯ ಅತಿಥಿಗಳಾಗಿ ಭಾಗವಹಿಸಿದ್ದ ಪ್ರೊ. ಪ್ರೇಮ್ ವ್ರತ್, ಐಐಟಿ ಧನ್ ಬಾದ್ ಆಡಳಿತ ಮಂಡಳಿ (ಬಿಒಜಿ) ಅಧ್ಯಕ್ಷರು ಮತ್ತು ಗುರುಗ್ರಾಮ್‌ನ ದಿ ನಾರ್ತ್ ಕ್ಯಾಪ್ ವಿಶ್ವವಿದ್ಯಾಲಯದ ಪ್ರೊಚಾನ್ಸಲರ್ ಉದ್ಘಾಟಿಸಿ ಸಮ್ಮೇಳನದ ಸ್ಮರಣ ಸಂಚಿಕೆ ಬಿಡುಗಡೆ ಮಾಡಿದರು.

ನಂತರ ಮಾತನಾಡಿದ ಪ್ರೊ.ಪ್ರೇಮ್ ವ್ರತ್ ಅವರು ಅರ್ಥಶಾಸ್ತ್ರ, ಹಣಕಾಸು ನಿರ್ವಹಣೆ ಮತ್ತು ತಂತ್ರಜ್ಞಾನ ವಿಷಯಾಧಾರಿತ ಅಂತರಾಷ್ಟ್ರೀಯ ಸಮ್ಮೇಳನ ದೇಶದ ಪ್ರಗತಿಯನ್ನು ಅವಲೋಕಿಸಲು ಮತ್ತು ಚರ್ಚಿಸಲು ಆರ್ಥಿಕ ತಜ್ಞರು, ಉದ್ಯಮಿಗಳು, ಸಂಶೋಧಕರು, ವಿದ್ಯಾರ್ಥಿಗಳು, ಪ್ರಾಧ್ಯಾಪಕರುಗಳಿಗೆ ಉತ್ತಮ ವೇದಿಕೆಯಾಗುತ್ತದೆ ಎಂದು ಅಭಿಪ್ರಾಯಪಟ್ಟರು.

ಅಂತರಾಷ್ಟ್ರೀಯ ಸಮ್ಮೇಳನದಲ್ಲಿ ಪ್ರೊ.ಎಂ.ಎಂ. ಗೋಯೆಲ್, ಗುರುಗ್ರಾಮ್‌ನ ಸ್ಟಾರೆಕ್ಸ್ ವಿಶ್ವವಿದ್ಯಾಲಯದ ಮಾಜಿ ಉಪಕುಲಪತಿ ಮತ್ತು ನೀಡೋನಾಮಿಕ್ಸ್ ಸ್ಕೂಲ್ ಆಫ್ ಥಾಟ್‌ನ ಸಂಸ್ಥಾಪಕರು, ಪ್ರೊ ಪ್ರಹ್ಲಾದ್ ಕುಮಾರ್, ವಾಣಿಜ್ಯ ವಿಭಾಗದ ಮಾಜಿ ಡೀನ್, ಅಲಹಾಬಾದ್ ವಿಶ್ವವಿದ್ಯಾಲಯ. ಇವರುಗಳು ಮುಖ್ಯ ಅತಿಥಿಗಳಾಗಿ ಭಾಗವಹಿಸಿದ್ದರು.

ಮುಖ್ಯ ಅತಿಥಿಗಳಿಗೆ ಡಾ.ಕೆ.ಸಿ ರಾಮಮೂರ್ತಿ, ಐಪಿಎಸ್ ನಿವೃತ್ತಿ, ಮಾಜಿ ರಾಜ್ಯಸಭಾ ಸದಸ್ಯರು, ಸಿಎಂಆರ್ ವಿಶ್ವವಿದ್ಯಾಲಯ ಮತ್ತು ಸಿಎಂಆರ್ ಸಮೂಹ ಶಿಕ್ಷಣ ಸಂಸ್ಥೆಗಳ ಅಧ್ಯಕ್ಷರು ನೆನಪಿನ ಕಾಣಿಕೆ ನೀಡಿ ಸನ್ಮಾನಿಸಿದರು.

ಸಮ್ಮೇಳನದಲ್ಲಿ ಸಿಎಂಆರ್ ವಿಶ್ವವಿದ್ಯಾಲಯದ ಕುಲಾಧಿಪತಿ ಡಾ.ಸಬಿತಾ ರಾಮಮೂರ್ತಿ, ಉಪಕುಲಪತಿ ಡಾ.ಎಚ್.ಬಿ.ರಾಘವೇಂದ್ರ, ಕುಲಸಚಿವ ಡಾ.ಪ್ರವೀಣ್ ಆರ್, ನಿರ್ದೇಶಕ ಸ್ಕೂಲ್ ಆಫ್ ಎಕನಾಮಿಕ್ಸ್ ಮತ್ತು

CMR University's ICREFMT Concludes with Grand Success

Published on April 8, 2024

Bengaluru – The School of Economics and Commerce at CMR University, Bengaluru, conducted an International Conference On Recent Advances In The Field Of Economics, Finance, Management & Technology (ICREFMT-2024). Held over two days, on April 5th and 6th, at the university's AV Hall, OMBR Campus, this pivotal event gathered renowned personalities from various sectors, enriching the discussions with profound insights and experiences.

The conference was honored by the presence of distinguished guests, including Prof. Prem Vrat, Chairman of the Board of Governors at IIT (ISM)-Dhanbad and Pro-Chancellor of North Cap University, Gurugram, who graced the occasion as the chief guest who had inaugurated the conference. Joining him were Dr. K. C. Ramamurthy, IPS (Retd), former Member of Parliament, Rajya Sabha and chairman of CMR University & CMR Group of institutions, and Prof. Prahlad Kumar, Ex-Dean, Faculty of Commerce, University in Allahabad, Uttar Pradesh, adding significant prestige to the proceedings.

Prof. M.M. Goel, the pioneering former vice-chancellor of Starex University, Gurugram, and founder of the Needonomics School of Thought, served as the conference host, guiding the event towards a platform for groundbreaking research and innovative discussions. Dr. Sabitha Ramamurthy, the Chancellor of CMR University, delivered the keynote address, offering invaluable insights and guidance to the attendees. Along with the dignitaries Dr. H.B.Raghavendra, Vice Chancellor, CMR University, Dr. Praveen.R, Registrar Presented the report of conference, Dr B.B.Tiwari, Conference General Chair and Director, SOEC,CMR University presented vote of thanks at the event.

The conference showcased the expertise of over 244 delegates from India and abroad, with more than 150 full-length research papers submitted by paper presenters from both national and international spheres, participating in the event both online and offline. Dr. Hemakshi Chokshi, Deputy Head, Guildhall School of Business and Law, London Metropolitan University, UK participated in the Conference. Dr. Chokshi chaired the Panel Discussion on Viksit Bharat 2047. Research scholars from Taylors University, Malaysia presented their papers. The conference acted as a melting pot of ideas, fostering discussions spanning the latest trends and challenges within the realms of economics, finance, management, and technology.

Prof. Prem Vrat, in his address at the conference, had emphasized the importance of nurturing academic spaces that promote creativity, innovation, sustainability, and entrepreneurship, urging students to cultivate a positive mindset conducive to achieving their envisioned dreams. He had also launched the ICREFMT-2024 souvenir.

The esteemed guests were honored with the mementos as the token of gratitude from CMR University. ICREFMT 2024 successfully fulfilled its mission as a catalyst for innovative thinking and cooperative dialogues. It not only brought together academics, researchers, business professionals, and policymakers from around the globe but also paved the way for future collaborations and advancements in these critical fields.